The Kurdish Model of
Political Community

KURDISH SOCIETIES, POLITICS, AND INTERNATIONAL RELATIONS

Series Editor: Bahar Baser, Coventry University

This series strives to produce high quality academic work on Kurdish society and politics, and the international relations of Kurdish organizations and governments (Kurdistan Region of Iraq) both regionally and globally. The books in this series explore themes of contemporary relevance as well as presenting historical trajectories of the Kurdish populations. The series contributes to the rapidly growing literature on this topic with books that are original and make substantial empirical and theoretical contribution. The series' main focus are the Kurds and the social, cultural and political environment in which Kurdish issues play out. The subjects that we are interested in include but are not limited to: the history of the Kurds, Kurdish politics and policies within Iraq, Iran, Turkey, and Syria, as well as Kurdish politics and their impact on the international relations of the Middle East. This series also publishes books on the policies of the USA, Europe, and other countries towards Kurdish movements and territories, and interdisciplinary research on Kurdish societies, religions, social movements, and the Kurdish diaspora. Lastly, our aim is to contribute to the academic literature on Kurdish culture, arts, cinema and literature. This series speaks to audiences outside academia, and is not limited to area-studies topics. All books in this series will be peer-reviewed and demonstrate academic quality and rigor.

Titles Published

Customized Forms of Kurdishness in Turkey: State Rhetoric, Locality, and Language Use, by Ceren Şengül

Methodological Approaches in Kurdish Studies: Theoretical and Practical Insights from the Field, by Bahar Baser, Yasin Duman, Mari Toivanen, and Begum Zorlu

Kurdish Alevis and the Case of Dersim: Historical and Contemporary Insights by Erdal Gezik and Ahmet Kerim Gültekin

The Geopolitics of Turkey–Kurdistan Relations: Cooperation, Security Dilemmas, and Economies by Mustafa Demir

Kurds in Turkey: Ethnographies of Heterogeneous Experiences by Lucie Drechselová and Adnan Çelik

Social Media and Democratization in Irai Kurdistan by Munir Hasan Mohammad

The Kurdish Model of Political Community: A Vision of National Liberation Defiant of the Nation-State by Hanifi Baris

The Kurdish Model of Political Community

A Vision of National Liberation Defiant of the Nation-State

Hanifi Baris

LEXINGTON BOOKS
Lanham • Boulder • New York • London

Published by Lexington Books
An imprint of The Rowman & Littlefield Publishing Group, Inc.
4501 Forbes Boulevard, Suite 200, Lanham, Maryland 20706
www.rowman.com

6 Tinworth Street, London SE11 5AL, United Kingdom

British Library Cataloguing in Publication Information Available

Library of Congress Cataloging-in-Publication Data

Names: Baris, Hanifi, 1978- author.
Title: The Kurdish model of political community : a vision of national
    liberation defiant of the nation-state / Hanifi Baris.
Other titles: Kurdish societies, politics, and international relations.
Description: Lanham, Maryland : Lexington Books, 2020. | Series: Kurdish
    societies, politics, and international relations | Includes
    bibliographical references and index. | Summary: "National sovereignty
    entails exclusive ownership of territories and natural resources, which
    often leads to uncompromising domination and subjugation of life by a
    central political authority. In a stark contrast, the Kurdish vision of
    political community invokes communal sovereignty, which is detached from
    the nation and the territorial state"—Provided by publisher.
Identifiers: LCCN 2019057155 (print) | LCCN 2019057156 (ebook) | ISBN
    9781793600004 (cloth) | ISBN 9781793600011 (epub)
Subjects: LCSH: Kurds—Turkey—Politics and government. |
    Kurds—Syria—Politics and government. | Kurds—History—Autonomy and
    independence movements.
Classification: LCC DR435.K87 B368 2020 (print) | LCC DR435.K87 (ebook) |
    DDC 320.54/09561—dc23
LC record available at https://lccn.loc.gov/2019057155
LC ebook record available at https://lccn.loc.gov/2019057156

Contents

Acknowledgments

I am thankful and eternally indebted to many people who have supported, encouraged, and inspired me along the way. Without them, this work would have never seen the light of the day. It is not possible to acknowledge them all by name, and I would not know how to thank them properly, for words are not enough to express my gratitude.

I would like to start with thanking my wife Ayşe, who has been there for me through thick and thin in our very adventurous latest years and has given me her unconditional love and support all along. She nurtured me emotionally and spiritually and opened my eyes to certain aspects of work and life when I was not able to see them for myself. More importantly, there is no limit to my gratitude for her generosity, as she paid all the bills for a long time while I was working on this book.

Special thanks go to my dear friend Dr. Bahar Başer who not only encouraged me to publish and made the publication of this book possible with her recommendations, but also inspired me to do so by her exemplary hard work and shining publications.

I am eternally indebted to my editors Ms. Alison Keefner, Ms. Bryndee Ryan, and Mr. Joseph C. Parry, for all the meticulous and hard work they put into revising my raw manuscript and transforming it into a fine literary work, worthy of publication.

I am eternally thankful and grateful to Dr. Trevor Stack, Dr. Tamas Gyorfi, and Dr. Andrea Teti for opening new horizons before my thoughts. I deeply appreciate the invaluable guidance and the relentless support they have granted me. This work owes its finest qualities, if not its existence, to their elegant input.

I would like to thank my friend and colleague Rose Luminiello for her excellent editing and proofreading work, as well as for her very valuable feedback on the entire project. Very special thanks to my friends Dr Wendy Hamelink and Dr Joost Jongerden for their support, encouragement, and very helpful feedback on chapters.

I thank and am grateful to my colleagues and friends at Centre for Citizenship, Civil Society and Rule of Law (CISRUL) at the University of Aberdeen for guiding, inspiring, encouraging, supporting and helping me along the way as professionals, friends, colleagues and mentors. Without their contributions this work would be a lot poorer in quality and insight.

Very, very special thanks to my brother Devrim Barış and my sister in law Sirayet Barış, my dear friends Güldestan Yüce, Miriam Bektaş Çankaya, and Metin İlbasmış, for their love, friendship and care, as well as for their hospitality, generosity and the contributions they made to the work that culminated in the publication of this book.

Transliteration

Kurdish pronunciation different from English

Alphabet	Sounds like	IPA
Ç/ç	*Church*	/tʃ/
C/c	*Judge*	/dʒ/
Ê/ê	M*ay*	/e/
G/g	Gamble	/g/
Î/î	M*ee*t	/i:/
I/i	B*i*t	/I/
J/j	Pleasure	/ʒ/
Ş/ş	S*h*oe	/ʃ/
Û/û	C*hoo*se	/u:/
U/u	Fig*u*re	/u/
X/x	[Scottish:] lo*ch*	/x/
Q/q	Arabic Qaf]	/q/

Turkish pronunciation different from English

Alphabet	Sounds like	IPA
Ç/ç	*Church*	/tʃ/
C/c	*Judge*	/dʒ/
Ğ/ğ	[often not pronounced]	/:/
İ/I	F*ee*t	/i/
I/ı	Op*e*n	/ɯ/
J/j	Pleasure	/ʒ/

Alphabet	Sounds like	IPA
Ö/ö	S*e*t, but rounded lips	/ø/
Ü/ü	Fl*u*te	/y/
Ş/ş	*Sh*oe	/ʃ/

(Courtesy of Dr. Wendy Hamelink)

Chapter One

Introduction

This book aims to capture a distinctive feature of Kurdish politics in Turkey: its tendency to establish and maintain self-rule through non-State political communities. The book is meant to contribute to debates on addressing Kurdish political demands in the context of constitution-making in Turkey. Existing discussions on the dominant Kurdish political movement[1] in Turkey and its politics tend to place them within classical nationalism. However, although engaged in nation-building, the dominant Kurdish political movement does not pursue state-building. In that sense, it differs from classical nationalist movements in its goals. My central thesis is that the politics of the dominant Kurdish political movement in Turkey goes beyond *integration,* multicultural *accommodation*, and *state-building*: it aspires to found co-existing transnational political communities on the basis of residence, not on cultural identity.

The question I try to answer is whether Kurdish politics in Turkey is confined within frameworks of multiculturalism and nationalism or does it go beyond state-sanctioned group rights and state-building? This main question leads to two related ones: first, what, if anything, separates the dominant Kurdish political movement in Turkey from classical nationalist movements? Second, what implications does the movement's politics have with regard to discussions on the accommodation of Kurdish political demands in particular and on political community in general? Understanding what Kurdish politics offers to those discussions is as important as applying ready-made frameworks of political integration and accommodation to Kurdish politics. Particularly, the proclamations by the Kurdish political movement that it does not pursue state-building is not only relevant, but also crucial to the debate. Hence, this work is an attempt to detect historical and contemporary expressions of Kurdish politics that can enrich the discussion.

1

This endeavour is a long overdue task. Although there is a fairly rich literature on Kurds in Turkey and elsewhere, the focus has mainly been on *Kurdology*; i.e., the historiography, sociology, and anthropology of Kurds, with a flavour of Orientalism. Literature on Kurdish politics and political mobilization, on the other hand, is scarce. Previous literature on Kurdish politics has mainly been concerned with "Kurdish rebellions" or "Kurdish ethnonationalism." Kurdish armed struggles, political parties, their interactions with and the reactions they get from nation-states, and the development of Kurdish "identity politics" are relatively well-studied aspects. Nevertheless, the motivation of the actors and the goals of their politics have mainly been taken for granted as reactionary responses to State politics, nationalism, and state-building. Thus, analytically, Kurdish politics is mainly condemned to a politics of belated and reactionary nationalism. This work is also an attempt to demonstrate that there is much more to Kurdish politics than what meets the eye at first glance.

Put simply, I try to articulate the theoretical pillars of what I call *the homegrown model of political community,* promoted by the dominant Kurdish political movement in Turkey. By so doing, I intend to highlight, on the one hand, a neglected characteristic of Kurdish politics—i.e., its apathy to statebuilding that has deep historical roots. On the other hand, I try to articulate theoretical implications of Kurdish politics with regard to four essential elements of political community: "the act of foundation" (a term coined by Arendt), autonomy/self-rule/sovereignty, citizenship/membership, and political participation/decision-making.

THE CONTEXT: THE MAKING OF A NEW CONSTITUTION IN TURKEY AND THE FRAMERS' NEGATION OF KURDISH POLITICAL DEMANDS

The main question emerged, empirically, during and out of the constitution-making process that started in Turkey in 2011. In the fall of that year, an elected parliament set out to make a constitution. This was the second undertaking of its kind since the foundation of the Republic of Turkey in 1923: an elected parliament had drafted and passed the constitution of 1924, but the constitutions of 1961 and 1982 were drafted by selected assemblies hand-picked by the military juntas of the time. Hence, drafting a civil constitution had arguably been one of the most popular items on the agenda of political parties that would promise reform since the early 2000s. Finally, a parliamentary commission started drafting a new constitution in 2011, and so began the constitution-making process that I refer to throughout this book.

The process ended in 2013 without bearing any fruit, save the consensus reached on about one hundred articles that were unrelated to any crucial issues. This was the result of the "breakdown of consensus between today's dominant parties" (Arato 2010:6). The government has not been willing to compromise. For them, realizing the current president's "passion" of establishing a system of executive presidency has become the main goal: "Mr. President, we promise that your passion will be our passion, your cause will be our cause, your path will be our path. The most important mission we have today is to legalise the de facto situation . . . by changing the constitution. The new constitution will be on an executive presidential system" (Turkish Prime Minister, cited in Hannah 2016, 1).

The constitution-making process advanced toward a destination unprecedented in previous decades. Generally, constitutional theorists observed that the constitution-making process has been at an impasse because of the conflict between "the legal claims of two powers: the government controlled legislative and the judicial branches to structure the constitution" (Arato 2010, 1). Now, however, having consolidated its power almost to the point of merging the ruling party with the State, the current government is able to push its agenda unilaterally. It suffices to say that the process ended with the government making some changes that consolidated power in the presidency and dropped the whole rhetoric of progress and reform. It would be fair to say that the current constitution is "the act of the government," not "the act of people constituting a government."[2] Therefore, the constitution-making process had provided me with the *problematique* that I am going to grapple with throughout this book.

However, the process of constitution-making or the constitution itself is not the focus here. What is relevant in the context of this book is whether the issue of addressing and/or accommodating Kurdish political demands was part of the process or not. I examine the constitution-making process through the lens of its overall coverage of Kurdish political demands, because the long awaited "civil constitution" was expected to reform the entire political system, "resolving the Kurdish Question" included (Kentel, Köker, and Genç 2012).

There were and are other major issues, such as redefining citizenship along non-nationalist lines, revoking ideological provisions in the current constitution, recognizing further rights for non-Muslim minorities, whose thin protection granted within the limits of the Treaty of Lausanne has been wearing off, and introducing political diversity through decentralization. However, the pivotal challenge was "making peace" with the Kurdish minority within and outside Turkey, and that needed to be done via some sort of constitutional recognition for Kurds. The expectation was that the new constitution would accommodate at least some Kurdish political demands through provisions reflecting certain standards and principles in *The European Framework Convention for the Protection of National Minorities*, such as the recognition of cultural rights and the introduction of decentralization.

Alas, as the Turkish saying goes, *the mountain gave birth to a mouse*. Turkish political parties chose to ignore their Kurdish counterpart(s). The status quo prevailed and Kurdish political demands did not make their way to the constitutional drafts of Turkish political parties. More importantly, even the draft of the governing party did not survive the political upheaval that followed the decommissioning of the commission in 2013, as the government changed course and became more conservative and nationalistic in its policies, due to the civil war that broke out in 2011 in Syria. Turkish foreign policy assumed a more ambitious tone and character, and domestic politics got aligned with this shift.

The ruling party tried to restore the long-gone Turkish dominance in the Middle East, and Kurdish gains in Northern Syria were deemed incompatible with "Turkish interests." According to Öcalan (2015), the Turkish government changed its course of action vis-à-vis Kurdish political demands because the Kurds rejected the Turkish prime minister's impositions regarding which direction Kurdish political actors should take in Syria. Öcalan claims that Turkish statesmen asked him to accept Turkish leadership in Syria and instruct Syrian Kurds not to try to establish a Kurdish entity there. Öcalan refused this "instruction" outright. Then the government went off its previous course of action that included dialog with Kurdish political actors within and outside Turkey. Turkey then abandoned its policy of reaching a settlement with the Kurdish political movement through *resolution processes* (terminated government initiatives aimed at "resolving the Kurdish Question"). From there, the Turkish government arrived at a stage where it declared all armed and unarmed Kurdish political opposition in Turkey and Syria as "terrorists" (*Hurriyet Daily News* 2017).

The ruling party ultimately managed to unilaterally amend the constitution of 1982. The amendments transformed the parliamentary system into an executive presidency, concentrating enormous power in the office of the presidency. This means that the much-expected political reforms are off the agenda of the ruling elite now. Along with that goes any hope for re-establishing dialog between the Turkish political establishment and its civil or armed Kurdish opposition.

Political accommodation of the Kurds, too, was discussed under the banner of *Kurdish Question* during the process. Nonetheless, although the pro-Kurdish political party was also part of the official process, the model of political community promoted by the Kurdish political movement and its theoretical implications have not been given the attention they deserve. The movement introduces a model of political community that goes beyond integration and accommodation, but falls short of statehood. This has important implications for discussions on accommodating Kurdish political demands, citizenship, political participation/diversity, and sovereignty in Turkey and other countries that incorporate a part of Kurdistan, such as Iran, Iraq, and Syria. However, these aspects of Kurdish politics were completely left out of discussions.

Conceptually, this has a general and perhaps systemic explanation. There is a tendency in Turkish politics to "solve problems" in a top-down manner. Negotiation and democratic deliberation do not have deep roots in Turkish political culture (Bacık 2016). Political diversity or Kurdish political demands thus represent "a problem to be solved" by authorities. However, denying political rights to the Kurds, Kurdish resistance to assimilation, and Kurdish political activism that involves many actors pursuing a variety of political goals is not 'a problem' that could be addressed by administrative reforms in the narrow sense of the word or by security measures. There is an armed political conflict with deep historical roots and more or less destructive precedents. The parties involved in the conflict should reach an agreement through negotiations and compromise. Alas, the dominant political elite in Turkey, as well as mainstream media and most of the literature, see and analyse Kurdish politics from the perspective of eighteenth century thinkers who thought that "if moral and political problems were genuine—as surely they were—they must in principle be soluble; that is to say, there must exist one and only one true solution to any problem" (Berlin 1969, 22). Also, as Bacik (2016) points out, the Turkish political elite prefer counselling (*meşveret*) to democratic deliberation and negotiation. This means that those in authority might listen to some community leaders, politicians, and civil society activists with similar views among the Kurds in order to "solve the problem," a method which has been used in the last decade. However, the Turkish government is not willing to directly negotiate a settlement with political and armed wings of the Kurdish movement. Politics in Turkey in general, and addressing Kurdish politics in particular, have been reduced to a zero-sum game, where the goal is seizing power, defeating the competition, and carrying out one's agenda without compromise and negotiation.

Practically, dominant political parties showed interest in Kurdish politics to the extent that it broadened their constituency. Systemic issues in electoral law that deprived Kurds from, for example, entering the parliament as a party—the highest electoral threshold in any democracy—the ban on using languages other than Turkish in election campaigns, and party closures on terrorism charges have not been addressed by political parties and governments. The best example is the policy of the current Turkish government that has been in power since 2002. Though it has been braver than any other governments in Turkish history with regard to acknowledging the Kurds as a separate group, and although it started two initiatives to address their political exclusion, the current government resumed war with Kurdish guerrilla forces in July 2015. Moreover, Kurdish deputies in the parliament, who represent five million citizens, are labelled by the president and the government alike as "terrorists" or terrorist sympathizers (Zaman 2016). Almost half of them and most Kurdish mayors were arrested and on trial now. This is many steps back from the relative ease of tension between Kurdish political actors and the Turkish establishment that existed until the end of 2013. The attempt of the Turkish army to overthrow the government in a failed *coup d'état* in July 2016 only served to exacerbate the already dire circumstances confronting democracy, political diversity, and human rights in Turkey.

Consequently, discussions on Kurdish political demands and their accommodation in the new constitution were not promising to begin with. Such discussions are now not only postponed to an indefinite future, but also buried deep in the paranoia of secession that feeds off the misunderstandings about Kurdish politics.

Problematique: Naming a Sociopolitical Issue as the *Kurdish Question* and Proposing "Solutions" based on Misunderstandings about Kurdish Politics

It is within this context that the problematique of this book originates, because, although political accommodation of Kurds was a matter of discussion during the constitution-making process, the matter was placed on a problematic ground and communicated through misunderstandings. The former—the problematic ground—is discussing Kurdish politics under the banner *Kurdish Question*. The latter—the misunderstandings—are several: that the State alone has had control over history and shaped it for the Kurds as well (state-centrism); that the statelessness of the Kurds is the outcome of their failure, but not their choice; that a polity and a political community are one and the same; and that the dominant Kurdish political movement in Turkey is a nationalist movement set to found a nation-state for Kurds. There are substantial and theoretical implications of confining the issue within the term Kurdish Question. Moreover, the misunderstandings have become genuine obstacles in several ways. They became obstacles for the Kurdish movement in Turkey to present and introduce itself or communicate its objectives and goals. They also became obstacles for Turkish statesmen and politicians to understand or try to understand Kurdish political actors. Resolution processes initiated and prescriptions suggested by Turkish statesmen and politicians are based on the term Kurdish Question and mostly have no input from Kurdish political actors. This detachment of the "question" from actors on the ground, and the misunderstandings I mentioned above, are the main factors that prevent Kurdish political demands from finding their way into Turkish constitutions because the encapsulation of the issue within the term Kurdish Question and the misunderstandings that surround the issue prevent the establishment of a genuine dialog between Turkey's political elite and the leaderships of Kurdish movements. Let me try to elaborate on the matter by expressing my substantial and theoretical concerns.

Substantially, discussing all the sociopolitical processes and interactions involved in the matter under the banner *Kurdish Question* is problematic because of a simple reason: the issue at stake is Kurdish politics and the reaction of the established political order to it, and vice-versa. Naming it the *Kurdish Question* condemns the issue to be approached in a top-down manner and leaves major misunderstandings about Kurdish politics unaddressed. The term *Kurdish Question* defines Kurdish politics as a "problem" that needs to be "solved" (see for example Barkey and Fuller 1998). If a political, social, and economic phenomenon such as the conditions of the Kurds in Turkey (or elsewhere) is considered to be and treated like a problem, involved and interested parties automatically try to diagnose what is wrong with Kurds and come up with a prescription; a "solution" as it has been called in Turkey.

However, the use of term *Question* has been notoriously problematic throughout history. Therefore, I will refrain from framing the phenomenon as the Kurdish "Question." Take for instance the function of the term *Jewish Question* in Europe in general and in Germany; or the *Armenian Question* in the Ottoman era. In both cases the ruling elite isolated cultural groups that were different from the majority or the dominant group (whether they are politically mobilized or not is another issue). The ruling elites' *final solutions* meant annihilation for each group. Or remember the famous *Eastern Question*, which referred to "maintaining the Ottoman Empire as part of an established order against the expansionist ambitions of Austria and Russia in South-eastern Europe. Change in the existing order was of vital concern to the West because it might have upset the balance of power not only in the Middle East but also in Europe" (İnalcık 1996, 22).

Likewise, ever since the term *Kurdish Question* was used to refer to the deprivation of Kurds of self-rule in Kurdistan, or to define the aggregate of complex social, economic, and political issues Kurds face, the priority has been given to diagnosing *the problem* and offering prescriptions to it. Diagnoses and prescriptions vary, but they are understandably modelled on political ideals, principles, and ambitions shared by the ruling elite. The ruling elite takes it upon themselves to "solve" the problem, mostly without involving the

Kurds, and usually with a specific *reason d'état* in mind, thus prioritizing the well-being of the State. When considered under such conditions, the ruling elite ends up treating the Kurds as an anomaly and a problem to be solved, just as the Armenians were treated in the beginning of the twentieth century. Generally, it is said that the Kurds have not developed a national consciousness early enough and hence have failed to establish their own nation-state—this is often considered as failure of the Kurds. From this failure follows the popular belief that the Kurds have to be assimilated within the majority in the countries where they live as homeland minorities. Their political mobilization for self-rule, thus, is easily labelled as "separatism," "treason," and "terrorism." Consequently, the differences in historical background, political structures, social processes, and their transformations in the region Kurds live have been completely or partially overlooked.

Theoretically, because of the aforesaid misunderstandings, Kurdish politics has been discussed only within the framework of universal/civic citizenship, constitutional identity, and minority rights. These themes fall within the frameworks of integration and accommodation in contemporary Western political theory (Galbreath and McEvoy 2012; Kymlicka and Straehle 1999; Kymlicka 2007, 2002; Patton 2008; McCulloch 2014; McGarry, O'Leary, and Simeon 2008). Both the use of the term *Kurdish Question* and the frameworks of analyses where Kurdish politics is placed within, such as nationalism and multiculturalism, regard the issue as a classic case of minority nationalism. This is a very significant misunderstanding that tends to evade scholars, observers and analysts alike. In other words, Kurdish politics has been placed within the framework of "ethno-nationalism," which limits the applicable theoretical tools available to us for contemplating and theorizing on the issue.

However, the leaderships of the Kurdish movement in Turkey and Syria have been expressing that they are not nationalists. Labelling the movement as "ethno-nationalist," nationalist, and/or "separatist," despite the movement's insistence in presenting itself otherwise, has become a comfortable description that frees the analyst from the burden of trying to understand how the Kurdish movement sees and describes itself and, more importantly, what kind of political community they want to establish. The kind of political community envisaged by the leadership(s) of a political movement accounts for most, if not all, of the difference between a political movement and others.

In the case of the Kurdish movement, the leaderships have repeatedly stressed their dislike of nationalism and nation-states. The founding leader of the movement, Abdullah Öcalan, has been trying to tailor a theoretical framework that is very different from a nationalist blueprint. For instance, his framework rejects political organization based on 'national identities' or 'national borders.' His project as well as the movement have also set democratization of Turkey and the Middle East as the ultimate goal, notwithstanding the primary objective which is "liberating Kurdistan." His project of political community envisages transnational and trans-border political organization, but sets local assemblies as the ultimate authority in local public affairs. It also replaces representative political participation with a mixture of direct democracy and delegation of power that does not include alienation of individual sovereignty to parliaments and representatives. The project, overall, identifies the nation-state as its nemesis and tries to undo it. Thus, a closer look at the movement's politics suggests, at least, that scholars should make room for a wider range of theoretical frameworks that might be applicable to the Kurdish case and not limit it to "ethno-nationalism."

Addressing State-Centrism and the Hegemony of Hobbesian Sovereignty in Scholarship on Kurdish Politics

Two problems—created by the hegemonic order of nation-states—that plague contemporary global politics are relevant in the context of this book: (I) the lack of a genuine political participation; and (II) a suspicion, even hostility, towards political diversity among the ruling elites. On the one hand, representative institutions fail to provide citizens with democratic means necessary to shape the outcome, as a result of their inadequacy to properly and fairly channel citizens' will into decision-making processes. This is one of the main issues raised by Occupy movements all around the globe (Juris 2012; Maeckelbergh 2012; Oikonomakis and Roos 2013; Abbas and Yigit 2014; Özkırımlı 2014). On the other hand, political theorists have pointed at the issue of democratic deficiency within nation-states and the international/supra-national organizations created by them (Waldron 2011; Arendt 1963; Mouffe and Holdengraber 1989; Mouffe 1992; Hardt and Negri 2004; Benhabib 2007; Somers 2008; Laclau and Mouffe 1985; Harvey 2012; Isin 2012a, b; Abizadeh 2012; Scherz 2013; Bellamy and Castiglione 2013; Näsström 2015). These authors have addressed issues such as citizen alienation, disenfranchisement, exclusion and inclusion in political communities. They draw attention to the prevailing sense among citizens that they are not able to make any change or improvement to their sociopolitical conditions via representative institutions and processes of political participation.

Despite the emergence of such movements and political commentary, political elites continue to perceive diversity as a threat and/or a destabilizing force that potentially or practically undermine cultural, political, and territorial "unity"—if such a thing exists. Ever since "the nation during the nineteenth century 'had stepped into the shoes of the absolute prince'" (Arendt

1963, 268), those excluded from the definition of "the nation" either have had to accept assimilation or build a nation and/or a nation-state of their own (A. Smith 2000, 2001; Keating 2001a, b; Kymlicka 2002, 2007; Taylor 1997; D. Smith 2013).

Thus, whether they programmatically pursue state-building or not, national liberation movements have commonly been associated with state-building and are largely assumed to make a claim to national sovereignty. This, in turn, causes suspicion and anxiety among the ruling elite who fear secession and for whom maintaining the *status quo* lies with "securitization of minority nationalisms" (Kymlicka 2007, 194), e.g., criminalizing identity politics and banning cultural and political symbols and/or activities deemed harmful to national unity. Such measures have proven to be harmful to minorities and majorities alike (Kymlicka 2007). This is one of the dynamics that perpetuate the spiral of state oppression and resistance/identity politics and fuel ethnic/ national conflicts. It is crucial, therefore, in Agamben's words, to call "into question every [. . .] attempt to ground political communities in something like a 'belonging,' whether it be founded on popular, national, religious, or any other identity" (1998, 102) rather than blindly accepting the politics of majority nationalism and condemning minority nationalism as extremism or separatism at best, terrorism at worst.

Therefore, with this book, I wish (I) to address salient misunderstandings about Kurdish politics that have mainly become the grounds for its stigmatization in Turkey; and (II) to try to understand the dominant Kurdish political movement in Turkey via studying their politics in general and zoom in on their vision of political community. This will help reassess old or imposed descriptions of Kurdish politics and the stigmatization, fear, or paranoia attached to them. It will also help take a closer look at the claim of Kurdish movement that it does not resort to "ethno-nationalist," "separatist," or even nationalist politics. How do I do this? My answer is simple: I try to focus on Kurdish politics more than I focus on how Kurdish politics has been assessed, described, labelled, and categorized so far. In other words, I try to bring Kurdish politics back into the equation.

SHIFTING THE FOCUS
FROM THE STATE TO KURDISH POLITICS

I set out to write this book with the purpose of finding the best model of multicultural accommodation for the Kurds in Turkey. I used to consider the Kurdish political movement as a case of minority nationalism myself and thought that adopting one of the constitutions in liberal Western democracies and implementing a model of multiculturalism we see there would "solve the question" once and for all. I was conditioned to think in this specific way about Kurdish politics in Turkey, because the academic and political climate there breeds this problematic mind-set.

However, as I proceeded with the work, I realized that Kurdish politics in Turkey (and by extension Syria) could hardly be categorized as a classic case of nationalism, where the goal of the dominant political actors is territorial autonomy or independence of a nation. It was unrealistic, and perhaps arrogant and ignorant, to try applying certain models of political accommodation distilled from Western political theory to the Kurdish case, without understanding Kurdish politics in its context. Therefore, I modified my objective: this book aims to understand what, if anything, distinguishes the dominant Kurdish political movements in Turkey and Syria from nationalist movements, and to articulate the aspects of their politics that might contribute to our understanding of political community. This will help highlight nuanced claims, demands, and principles put forward by Kurdish politics and to find their reference point within Western political theory.

I have mentioned that the dominant Kurdish political movements in Turley and Syria do not promote nationalism. Indeed, they claim to be anti-nationalist movements (Öcalan 2011). Unfortunately, scholarship on nationalism is mainly suspicious of minority national movements. Majority nationalisms are taken for granted as the norm and minority nationalisms are expected to justify their politics much more explicitly than the majority. This, as Keating observes, leads mainstream scholarship on minority politics to be "written from a hostile or patronizing perspective. Minority nationalisms are dismissed as archaic, narrow-minded and 'ethnic'" (2001b, xii). Likewise, mainstream literature on Kurdish politics has tended to enclose it within a spectrum that ranges from "ethnic rebellion" (Tezcur 2016; Scalbert-Yücel and Le Ray 2006) at best, to "separatism" and "terrorism" at worst, echoing descriptions of statesmen and politicians (Bruinessen 1998b, 2004, 2006; Fernandes 2015; Sentas 2015; Yavuz 2001; Bilgel and Karahasan 2017). Therefore, it is crucial to look at Kurdish politics from a nuanced perspective and highlight its distinctive features. By doing so, I hope to highlight what the dominant Kurdish movements in Turkey and Syria stand for with regard to self-rule in Kurdistan. The path for such a nuanced analysis of Kurdish politics has already been opened by recent literature. On the one hand, scholars of nationalism and multiculturalism have criticised the argument that *civic* nationalism is more accommodating to minority cultures and that it can be neutral toward citizens of varying cultural backgrounds (Taylor 1997; Kymlicka and Straehle 1999; Kymlicka 2002; Keating 2001b; T. W. Smith 2005; Özdoğan 2010; Xypolia 2016). On the other hand, political theorists have searched for models of political community that can accommodate direct democracy and transnational notions of citizenship (Isin 2007, 2012a, b; Benhabib 2007; Näsström 2015).

Why should a national liberation movement appeal to political principles other than nationalism? Does this not suggest a paradox? In what sense does this claim differ from the claim to sovereignty of a nation over *their* homeland? To what end and for what purpose is an alternative model of political community being promoted by the dominant Kurdish political movements in Turkey and Syria?

Distinguishing National Liberation from Nationalism and Polity from Political Community

The answer to the questions above could be found, most generally and superficially (I will address the specifics in the following sections), in how the idea of political freedom surfaces in the politics of the dominant Kurdish movement in Tukey. In a nutshell, this could be articulated as a civic republican formulation of political freedom; i.e., non-domination (Pettit 2003; Carter 2008; Lovett 2014; Simhony 1993). Freedom here is more than the negative liberty of Berlin (1969) as non-interference:

> Republican non-domination: political liberty might better be understood as a sort of structural relationship that exists between persons or groups, rather than as a contingent outcome of that structure. Whether a master chooses to whip his slave on any given day, we might say, is a contingent outcome; what is not contingent (or at least not in the same way) is the broader configuration of laws, institutions, and norms that effectively allows him to do so or not as he pleases. The republican conception of political liberty aims to capture this insight as directly as possible. It defines freedom as a sort of structural independence—as the condition of not being subject to the arbitrary power of a master. [A] person or group enjoys freedom to the extent that no other person or group has "the capacity to interfere in their affairs on an arbitrary basis." [W]e might equivalently say that freedom in the republican sense is the enjoyment of non-domination. Specifically, freedom must be seen as consisting in an active participation in the political process of self-determination. (Pettit 2003, 2–3)

This understanding of political freedom holds that citizens are free to the extent that they obey the laws of their own making[3] in self-ruled small communities. Nevertheless, national institutions and processes of decision-making in the Turkish parliamentary democracy do not allow that. More specifically, nationalism appears in the discourse of the Kurdish movement as an evil, dominating, and subjugating force. Therefore, a model of political community other than the nation-state, a model that enables citizens to exercise their political freedoms more directly, should be sought after if the Kurds and other peoples in Kurdistan, Turkey, and the Middle East are to taste political freedom (Öcalan 2005, 2011). This model is meant to transform sovereignty from being a relationship of domination between cultural groups—majority and minority nations—to a political structure that enables spatial communities such as villages, neighbourhoods, townships, towns, and cities to exercise and enjoy self-rule to the greatest degree possible. So, although nations do exist as an analytical and sociological category in this understanding, they are not to be construed as political subjects who are the agents and the origin of sovereignty, as it is in nationalism. The political subject as well as the source of sovereignty is *peoples:* an aggregate of citizens without cultural particularities.

This perception reflects the anti-state characteristics of Kurdish politics, which I discussed elsewhere (Baris 2016) and in chapter 2, section 3, with reference to Scott (2009). The choices made by the Kurdish political elite in crucial moments in the sixteenth and twentieth centuries, as I will discuss in detail in the first chapter, pointed in one direction: Kurdish politics has rarely been inclined toward state-building (Özoğlu 2004).

Contemporary Kurdish politics in Turkey manifests this characteristic as well. For instance, the architect of the Kurdish model of political community called *democratic confederalism,* and the leader of the dominant Kurdish movement, Abdullah Öcalan, emphasizes that his model is anti-nationalist and "aims at realizing the right of self-defence of the peoples by the advancement of democracy in all parts of Kurdistan without questioning the existing political borders." Öcalan's model ignores political borders specifically because nationalism and the dream of building nation-states for each Middle Eastern nation has plagued politics in this region for years due to interstate boundary contentions (2011, 8, 34). The idea of establishing federal structures in which *peoples* (not *nations*) can coexist within one polity is promoted by the Öcalan model.

Here, not for normative but for analytical purposes, we have to distinguish between nationality/national claims and the traditionally conceived nationalism. The former refers to the claims of a politically mobilized group, e.g., national minorities, which pursue certain political rights, privileges, and self-rule in the group's residency or in their "historical homeland" (Keating 2001b). The latter refers to the claims to statehood under the principle of national self-determination in international law (Kymlicka 2007). I will not quote definitions of nationality and nationalism in the literature, for both claims are generically of the same origin. Nationalism, in both cases, operates as "a discourse that [. . .] determines" what politically mobilized groups may claim on the basis of "produced and reproduced collective identity" (Özkırımlı

2000, 4; cited in Hamelink 2014, 31).The main difference between claims to nationality and nationalism is practical: the goals pursued by national liberation movements. Therefore, when Öcalan (2011, 34) rejects nationalism and nation-states, he does not waive the right of *the peoples of Kurdistan* to self-rule and even the claim to sovereignty of communities over their "homeland." He merely refuses to acknowledge the exclusive sovereignty of the dominant group as the only legitimate form of sovereignty, and as the only nation in unison with the State. Öcalan thus tries to open up the possibility for the coexistence of multiple political communities within the territory of nations' states. Just as several political communities existed within one polity during the Ottoman era, Öcalan envisages a form of sovereignty that allows the existence of more than one nation—not as a single political community, but as an aggregate of political communities—in one polity.

Practically, this has to do with the fact that insisting on building a nation-state in "historical Kurdistan" exclusively for the Kurds would necessitate breaking up four existing nation-states, which would entail decades of conflict, war and bloodshed — all while there is no consensus on the boundaries of Kurdistan to begin with. Kurdish national movement modified their objective of establishing a socialist Kurdistan for two main reasons: first, to pursue the dram of establishing a greater Kurdistan means the breakup of and hence endless wars with four nation-states—notwithstanding with the fact that this will most probably mean war with other Kurdish movements; second, Kurdish collective memory does not entertain the nostalgia of a golden past when an independent Kurdistan was unified under a Kurdish king. In general, a formula of self-rule with dignity is the picture of the past and the dream of the present for Kurdish nationals. Theoretically, the dominant Kurdish movement's ideology was transformed from Marxism-Leninism to *communalism* and *libertarian municipalism* of Bookchin (1995, 2015), wherein seizing state power through a revolution is replaced by building ecological and grassroots communes and autonomous towns and cities in Kurdistan, with or without authorization from centralized states.

This ideological transformation of nationalist movements is not limited to the Kurdish case. Keating argues that we live in a "post-sovereign order" where national claims take forms beyond claiming statehood in the name of a nation, "a world in which there is no longer a single principle of authority" (Keating 2002, 11). He uses the concept of "plurinationality" in order to refer to a State that is:

[A] little different from multinationality, which may just refer to the co-existence of two or more sealed national groups within a polity. In plurinationalism, the very concept of nationality is plural and takes on different meanings in different contexts. [. . .] The plurinational state is an extension of the concept of plurinationality itself, referring to the existence of multiple political communities rather than a single, unitary demos. Considering the state in this way is also consistent with historiographical approaches stressing the union rather than unitary principle. It also opens up the prospect of constitutional asymmetry. (Keating 2002, 10)

Consequently, following Keating's logic, national liberation movements may pursue founding a nation-state and obtaining independence for the mobilized group or claim/demand/proclaim self-rule without any claim to statehood. This means that the Weberian notion of nationalism that associates national claims with statehood no longer holds in the Kurdish case. In order to identify what, exactly, has replaced national claims and statehood, we will have to look for the specific demands put forward by the Kurdish movement, and the kind of political community they promote/found in lieu of statehood.

Emphasizing Choice and Agency (of the Kurdish Political Elite)

The contribution I hope to make to the literature is twofold: first, emphasising the elements of *choice* and *agency* in Kurdish politics. I draw attention to critical moments in Kurdish history where the choices made by the Kurdish political elite and the impact of their agency shaped the course of politics in Kurdistan. This is important because there are historical and contemporary aspects of Kurdish politics that are not, or cannot, be associated with state-making. Along with a strong tradition of self-rule throughout their history and a persistent pursuit of autonomy in contemporary Kurdistan, there has been a tendency in Kurdish politics *to steer away* from state-building. My interpretation is that this is a *choice*, rather than a *failure* on the part of the Kurdish political elite, nor is it a *lack* of what it takes to build a nation-state—a shared memory, national consciousness, and imagination, as famously articulated by Ernest Renan, Max Weber and Benedict Anderson—as the mainstream literature suggests. Seeing and analysing this aspect of Kurdish politics has the potential to enrich the debate on self-rule in Kurdistan and/or the accommodation of the Kurds in Turkey. For this anti-state politics has been an indispensable theme in political theory and praxis in Kurdistan, although it may have been articulated less clearly at times by political actors themselves. This tendency is well-entrenched within the contemporary Kurdish politics in Turkey and Syria as well. Despite this obvious and perhaps even salient characteristic of Kurdish political praxis, most scholarship prefers to analyse Kurdish politics within the framework of "ethno-nationalism" and nation-state building. Through this study I intend to address this gap in literature on Kurdish politics.

Second, I try to translate the choices made and the form of self-rule promoted by the Kurdish political elite into a model of political community,
although the actors themselves do not call it as such. My starting point in
history is sixteenth-century Kurdistan under the Ottoman rule, although the
practice and pursuit of self-rule in Kurdistan extends much earlier than this
period. The reason I have selected this era as my starting point is that the largest chunk of Kurdistan was incorporated into the Ottoman domain during this
century and remained as part of the Ottoman Empire until the end of World
War I. Though Kurdish nobility maintained a high level of autonomy until the
latter half of the nineteenth century, state-making and/or nation-state building
has not been the priority for Kurdish political elite for most of the first three
hundred years this work considers. Moreover, state-building appears to have
been the goal only for the minority of the Kurdish elite even after the collapse
of the Ottoman Empire (the fact that nation-building has been part and parcel
of Kurdish politics since the early twentieth century does not change this). In
other words, the kind of political community envisaged by the Kurdish political elite has only rarely been the construction of a State or the founding of a
nation-state. I hope to contribute to the discussions on political community
by analysing the model of political community developed by the Kurdish
movement in Turkey.

Contemporary Kurdish politics in Turkey is oriented toward founding a
model of political community based on principles of "democratic autonomy"
and "democratic confederalism" (Akkaya and Jongerden 2012a, 2013; Öcalan 2005, 2011). The former suggests that villages, neighbourhoods, towns,
and cities handle their public affairs on their own and make their decisions
via public forums, assemblies, and councils, without outside interference.
The latter suggests that these autonomous entities are free to form federations
and confederations that might go beyond national borders with other autonomous entities at local, national, and regional levels. The relationship between
autonomous entities is horizontal, and political participation of citizens in
these autonomous entities is based on direct democracy. Local, national, and
regional assemblies and parliaments would be established and authorized by
autonomous entities on the basis of delegation, not representative sovereignty.
Sovereignty is thus dispersed and fragmented: each autonomous entity has
sovereignty over its territory not by virtue of being authorized by a national
or regional overarching authority, but by virtue of being a full-fledged political community in its own right. Territorial sovereignty of the nation-state is
broken into territorial sovereignty of each autonomous entity in the form of a
spatial unit; i.e., a community of residents living in a settlement/a community
of space. Whereas the kind of integration and multiculturalism discussed in
Turkey suggests the existence of one State and one polity only, the Kurd-

ish model envisages plural nations in one State (Keating 2001b), as well as plural political communities within the "homeland" of one nation. At the conceptual and theoretical level, the gap between the Kurdish model on the one hand, and integration and multiculturalism as enjoying cultural rights on the other hand, is too wide. Therefore, including Kurds in the definition of citizenship in the constitution (i.e., integrating Kurds in a unified nation), or granting cultural rights to the Kurds (i.e., multiculturalism as accommodating Kurds through the recognition of their cultural rights), will not suffice to close this gap. These versions of integration and accommodation suggest that minorities should be assisted "in adapting to the dominant society" (McGarry, O'Leary, and Simeon 2008, 52). The gap between what is promoted by the Kurdish political movement and what is captured by discussions comes from a failure to distinguish nationality claims from classical nationalism as well as ignoring the specifics of Kurdish politics. Thus emerges the main thesis of this work: Kurdish politics in Turkey and Syria is not oriented toward state-building, integration, or accommodation. Simplifying the issue via stamping Kurdish politics as nationalism, naming it as the *Kurdish Question,* and offering constitutionalism and/or multiculturalism as *cures* does not help us understand Kurdish politics and address Kurdish political demands. We need to invoke, if not understand, the Kurdish model of political community, i.e., *democratic confederalism,* if we are to have a more accurate reading and a better grasp of Kurdish politics in Turkey and Syria. The model is about founding a plethora of autonomous residential political communities within or outside nation-states, not about nation-state-building, multicultural rights or autonomy, and constitutional recognition of Kurdish identity.

BETWEEN THEORIZING ABOUT KURDISH POLITICS AND EXPLORING A THEORETICAL FRAMEWORK FOR THE KURDISH MODEL OF POLITICAL COMMUNITY

I have no intention of laying a normative ground for Kurdish politics or for the model developed by the Kurdish movement; that is a task for further research. What I am interested in is shifting the focus of analysis from state-centric theoretical frameworks of accommodating diversity to the kind of political community pursued by the Kurdish political elite.

In order to do that, I have to ask the question whether national liberation movements can make claims to or demand self-rule without imitating states or a claim to national sovereignty. Put in other terms, can politics of national emancipation "escape from the system of Law-and-Sovereign which has captivated political thought for such a long time" (Foucault 1990, 97), when they have traditionally invoked territorial claims to sovereignty of a nation over a historical homeland (Keating 2001b, 4–6)? Is there a ground in contemporary political theory for developing "a political philosophy that isn't erected around the problem of sovereignty" (Foucault 1980, 23, 121)? If the answer is yes, which theoretical framework can be utilized by political movements in their pursuit of self-rule? Since the primary goal for liberal political theory and praxis is taming the *Leviathan*,[4] i.e., limiting the government by means of entrenching a set of fundamental rights in constitutions tailored for individuals and groups (Arendt 1963; Mahajan 2017), it can safely be said that there are existing mechanisms of *accommodation* and *integration* in liberal politics. These mechanisms range from assimilation to full territorial autonomy. The best-known models or theoretical frameworks of this spectrum are *integration, multiculturalism, consociationalism, centripetalism,* and the rather traditionally known *federalism.* McCulloch (2014), Patton (2008), and Kymlicka (2002, 2007) have studied these models in detail, which are the focus of chapters 2 and 3 in this book. Here, I emphasize that this work considers the models above as inherently hierarchical, homogenizing, and conflictual. Hierarchical because groups are *ranked* in a way in which the dominant group appears to be *the owner of the state* and superior to others, while minorities come secondary in their claims to self-rule. Indeed, minorities are *granted* (a term used by Kymlicka 2007, 149) certain rights and privileges by the State, and do not enjoy unconditional access to the right to self-determination equal to that held by the dominant groups. This work considers the models homogenizing because they envisage the political community as *the nation*: one and united on the grounds of a common history, a common identity, and a shared goal, etc. This eventually makes some groups, cultures, languages and histories *more equal* than others (Patton 2008; Keating 2001b; 2001a; 2002; 2003; Taylor 1997; Bourdieu et al. 1994). And finally, these models are conflictual because they tend to create, exacerbate, freeze, and "fix" both territorial and cultural boundaries, in an attempt to limit porousness of the borders, and to contain the very fluidity and flow of "social processes" (Harvey 2000, 39). Additionally, these models incite nation-building in the sense that they send the message that without independence or autonomy in the name of a nation, no cultural/ethnic group can survive nation-building policies of existing states. These dynamics put the wheels of peaceful or violent secession in motion, a process that more often than not ends in partition.

So far, we are more or less in the charted waters of liberal politics: national sovereignty, territorial integrity of the State, nation-building, cultural and territorial borders, and boundaries are considered as given (Mahajan 2016; and see for instance Rawls 2001). Representative democracy and electoral politics on a national scale remain as the norm, and those who criticise or oppose them are expected to proceed with additional justifications. Nevertheless, Abizadeh (2012) and Scherz (2013), for instance, invoke democratic principles and argue that democratic theory has not yet solved the problem of *closure*, i.e., that borders and boundaries of political communities remain arbitrary. Benhabib (2007), Isin (2012b), and Näsström (2015), speaking from cosmopolitan perspectives, observe that representative politics are not democratic enough in that they gravely limit genuine political participation. Additionally, they argue that representative politics place social diversity under great stress because of homogenizing tendencies inherent to the category of nation, and due to the encroachments of forces of globalization upon the local. In other words, taming the *Leviathan*, even within the limits of liberal democratic politics, does not seem to sufficiently address political problems created by the trio of modernity: sovereignty, nation-states, and globalization. Thus, we arrive at a point where integration and accommodation of minorities within the hegemonic global order of nation-states do not seem to answer more fundamental questions about sovereignty, boundaries, citizenship, and cultural or national bonds—belonging—as the basis of political communities. As Foucault argues that the political philosophy of Hobbes and other "jurists," the absolute, indivisible model of sovereignty aims "to discover how a multiplicity of individuals and wills can be shaped into a single will or even a single body that is supposedly animated by a soul known as sovereignty" (2003, 28–29). Hence, the task is to look for (I) a formulation of sovereignty that allows plural political communities or diverse forms of governance to coexist, rather than create any central power; (II) a definition of citizenship that is not based on national or cultural identities; and (III) the means of exercising political power that may compensate for the failure of representative institutions in channelling the will of citizens into decision-making processes in a fairer and more direct fashion.

There are theoretical approaches that try to do just that, and I will refer to those most relevant to the content of this book. Keating (1998, 2001a, 2001b, 2003) for instance, approaches the matter from a nuanced perspective and questions the consistency of the notion of sovereignty, referring to its ambiguity and interpretive nature, while introducing the model he calls "plurinational democracy." Nationality, Keating argues, "is to be distinguished from other forms of collective identity [. . .] above all by its claim to self-determination. This does not, however, necessarily entail sovereign statehood" (2001b, ix). Taking his examples from Scotland, Catalonia, and Quebec, among others, Keating questions the widely accepted Weberian formula of associating nationality claims with state-building, pointing out that "plurinational accommodation and dispersed authority" are not "a mere remnant of the past, but can provide new ways of coping with the present, post-sovereign order" (Ibid.), in which states increasingly share their sovereignty with supra/sub-state political entities. Drawing mainly on Jellinek (Petrovic 2002), Keating re-opens the discussion on forms of dispersed and fragmented sovereignty: "Sovereignty is not an absolute concept, or vested exclusively in states. Rather there can be multiple sites of sovereignty or 'normative order' below and above the state. If national communities are asymmetrical, then asymmetrical constitutions can be defended on liberal and democratic grounds" (2001b, viii).

While Keating's work is refreshing regarding discussions on sovereignty, it nevertheless does not capture the essence of the Kurdish model. The core organising idea behind Keating's *plurinationalism* is the territorial sovereignty of the nation/nations (since he argues that multiple nations may coexist and rule within one polity). More precisely, in Keating's theories, political community is based on national identity and the territorial claims of the nation. Citizenship does encompass multiple nations here, but cultural identity coupled with territorial claims remains intact. Thus, Keating's formulation, although helpful, does not capture the main principle within the Kurdish model: political community based on physical borders of towns and cities, not on national identities or a nation's claim to territorial self-rule. Citizenship, too, remains to be based on a particular identity in Keating (e.g. British), not on residence, as suggested by the Kurdish model.

Waldron (2011), on the other hand, offers a refreshing perspective on the basis of political community and citizenship. After conveying a robust criticism of nationalisms *in toto,* Waldron argues that cultural bonds and identities, i.e., relationships of *affinity*, are not suitable categories for political communities to be founded upon. Waldron introduces "the principle of proximity"; i.e., spatial closeness, as a better ground for forming political communities (2011, 7–11). He draws mainly on the Kantian idea that the goal of political communities is to regulate conflict. For Waldron, conflicts are likely to erupt between those who live close to one another, and thus proximity alone should be the basis for forming political communities.

Among others, the work of two scholars from the left is also very relevant in the context of this book. Hardt and Negri's (2004) political subject/agent, *multitude,* can be thought as an alternative to *the nation;* though their critics point out that *multitude* cannot be the constitutive subject of a political community because there is no substantial bond between the individuals who make up *multitude.* Also, their extensive critique of Hobbesian formulation of representation and sovereignty in *Empire* (2000) is very useful in looking at the matter from a critical perspective.

The dominant Kurdish political movement in Turkey has apparently been following these debates. They have modified their previous Marxist-Leninist oriented ideology with a light flavour of nationalism in order to adapt to these developments in political theory. It has been observed that the ancient Greek *polis* and the Athenian democracy, as well as a system of government developed by Bookchin (2015), are the main reference points of the Kurdish movement (TATORT 2011; Akkaya and Jongerden 2012a; Jongerden 2015). *Communalism,* the overarching ideology in Bookchin, proposes "a theory or system of government in which virtually autonomous local communities are loosely bound in a federation" (2015, 34). The political program of this system, *libertarian municipalism:*

> [S]eeks to eliminate statist municipal structures and replace them with the institutions of a libertarian polity. It seeks to radically restructure cities' governing institutions into popular democratic assemblies based on neighborhoods, towns, and villages. In these popular assemblies, citizens—including the middle classes as well as the working classes—deal with community affairs on a face-to-face basis, making policy decisions in a direct democracy and giving reality to the ideal of a humanistic, rational society. (Bookchin 2015: 36)

Thus, making use of and being inspired by a plethora of theoretical approaches, ideas, ideologies, and of course cultures as well as myths and mythologies, the Kurdish movement, with its project of *democratic confederalism,* aspires to formulate and implement a political project that is meant to radically alter the established political order with an anti-state, decentralist, confederationist agenda based on a hybrid socioeconomic program that combines the traditional, even the mythical, with the modern and the revolutionary. Since the socioeconomic face of the project is not of concern in this book, I will try to look at the project through the lens of political theory.

I argue that, rather than resembling a modern territorial state, a nation state, or a territorial sub-state entity, the kind of political community that the Kurdish movement aspires to found is a *residential political community* (and a confederation built by as many in numbers as possible of them). What the movement tries to establish or revive is not a glorious Kurdish realm, but autonomous communes, neighbourhoods, towns and cities organized at the sub-national level but in solidarity, cooperation, and confederation with transnational political entities of the same orientation. These political organizations are, ideally, designed to prevent the birth or the rise of a centralized territorial state based on one cultural identity.

I name them as *residential political communities* because such political entities, on the one hand, can be traced back from the Paris Commune all the way to antiquity and thus, are reflective of the tradition of political community (Stack 2019). On the other hand, they are based on the civic bond of *proximity* (Waldron 2011) as the ground of political community—the glue

that holds the political community together—and hence *residential.* The tradition of political community, in the context of this book, refers to political
organizations in which political power is exercised through direct participation or community representation of some kind. The notion of proximity
refers to the civic bond in political communities in which membership is
obtained through residence only. In other words, the theoretical lens through
which I view the Kurdish project is a combination of a tradition, the tradition
of political community, which refers to self-ruling communities with more
or less direct or semi-direct mechanisms of political participation; and the
notion of proximity, which refers to a civic bond based on residence as the
membership criterion in a political community. Thus, I intend to separate the
Kurdish model of political community from others by its two most important
characteristics: its anti-statist form and its communitarian spirit. To be more
precise, what distinguishes the Kurdish model of political community is its
community-based understanding of sovereignty and the voluntary membership in the community. Voluntary membership in the political community is
modern and is informed by Waldron's notion of *proximity,* whereas it is the
tradition of political community that informs us of medieval understanding
of sovereignty that finds its source in community-based customs (Ebenstein
and Ebenstein 2000, 227).

Drawing on the tradition of political community and the notion of proximity, I am aware, is not the same as drawing on a fully developed theory of
political organization in political or legal theory. The combination of the two
remains to be evolved into a sound theoretical framework. Nevertheless, the
tradition of political community helps me to reflect on the Kurdish project
in a way better than I can do by referring to forms of political organization
available in contemporary political and legal theory. The Kurdish project
necessitates a vessel of political organization other than the state and its varieties; and I am not convinced that we can find such a form in contemporary
political and legal theory. Neither sub-state political entities in Europe that
are mostly comprised of territorially autonomous nations/national minorities
nor indigenous communities of Central, South, and North America which
have a virtual autonomy but are not able to make their own laws (Kymlicka
2007) reflect the parameters of the Kurdish model of political community.

The vessel of *political community* presents itself as an appropriate form of
political association here: because, in this tradition, a political entity does not
necessarily have to function like a state and its varieties or to be recognized
by a state or supra-state institutions in order to "qualify" for self-rule. The
very notion of *qualifying for self-rule* is a modern European construct that
was utilized by colonizers to deny self-rule to the colonized. The Kurdish
model reflects a frustration with the current international order that makes

recognition of hegemonic/oppressive/repressive powers—the colonizers of today and of yesterday—a prerequisite for self-rule. In the Kurdish project, self-rule is given and is the right of all "natural communities" in the Aristotelian sense, not a privilege of some and a dream to be achieved by others.

The flexibility of the form(s) of political communities in that tradition allows even communes, villages, and neighbourhoods, along with towns, cities, and regions, to be or become political communities of their own. Besides, in this form(s), being or becoming an autonomous political entity is not conditioned on the approval and endorsement of individual nation-states or the international order installed by them, i.e., the United Nations. Both mechanisms have been harshly criticised by the Kurdish movement. Therefore, the kind of political entity they envisage will be reflected aptly only if we refer to the tradition of political community, which enables us to revisit self-ruling small-scale political communities with varying degrees of autonomy either outside or within larger polities. This tradition allows us, I argue, to illustrate more clearly the form of political community the Kurdish project envisages than any contemporary theoretical tool available to us can.

Drawing on Waldron (2011), I utilize the concept of proximity for analysing the Kurdish movements, as it is very useful in identifying the kind of civic bond they envisage as the basis of their model. However, the mere fact of living together in spatial communities such as villages, towns, and cities appear to be a strong enough bond for the Kurdish movement to replace the bond of nationality and become the basis of political community. They do not appeal to the Kantian idea of regulating conflict. Unlike in Kant and Waldron where sharing the same space seems to necessitate intervention and regulation with the purpose of managing hostilities, proximity appears to induce solidarity in the Kurdish model.

This solidarity, in turn, warrants the right to self-rule because it is what binds the members of a community of residents who are bonded through *real*, i.e., physical, everyday relationships. Proximity as such is the foundational glue that creates the civic bond between citizens in a political community. Proximity, thus construed as a civic bond, enables residents to make a claim to establish self-rule via controlling their towns and cities and defending them against the encroachments of centralized states, as it replaces or at least precedes the national bond, which is not real/physical, but imagined. Thus, the Kurdish model of self-rule rejects both the nation-state and national sovereignty.

Consequently, looking at Kurdish politics through a framework that combines the tradition of political community and proximity allows me to shift the focus from the state, the nation, the Hobbesian sovereignty to the parameters of Kurdish politics and Kurdish project of political community.

This, too, is long overdue a task and should be carried out diligently if we are to put an end to misunderstandings about Kurdish politics as I mentioned above. I am aware that adopting a perspective that is yet to be developed into a full-fledged theory, if it can be done at all, might be limiting in providing the reader with a sound theory for what I argue here. Nevertheless, it also presents me with the opportunity to speak from a fresh perspective and widen the horizon to make room for new theoretical approaches to be formed in the future.

Clarifications and Forewarnings

I should make clear that when I speak of *the Kurdish model of political community*, or *the Kurdish model*, or *the Kurdish project*, I do not mean to refer to an actual, physical, existing political entity, community, or organization of any kind on the ground. I do not refer to an established political order in any sense either. I will always be referring to a *model*, or an ideal form of political community that is still on paper, which I capture from the written works of the leaderships of the Kurdish movement in Turkey and Syria. The reason is that I was not able to do the required fieldwork in Syrian Kurdistan, Rojava. The Kurdish model of political community, in its most "original" and "true" form, has been in the process of establishment in Syrian Kurdistan. The Kurdish movement there managed to assume the administration of Kurdish majority cities and towns since 2012 and they have been, and are, trying to implement their political program to the extent the conditions allow them to do so. They established communes, village and neighborhood assemblies, town and city councils, women, youth, economic and environmental chambers, canton administrations and an overarching regional government; following the blueprint provided by the movement's leader Abdullah Öcalan's pamphlet-book, *Democratic Confederalism*. Therefore, Syrian Kurdistan provides students of political science who want to study the Kurdish model of political community with its real, actual, tangible and observable form. Since most Syrian cities and towns, Kurdish or otherwise, have been devastated by the bloody civil war that has been plaguing the country since 2011, I could not visit the region to do fieldwork due to security concerns.

In Turkish Kurdistan as well, after round-the-clock blockades and sieges that lasted for months, entire neighbourhoods, quarters or even districts in cities and towns where the Kurdish model was established were destroyed. According to a report compiled by International Crisis Group in 2016, the civil war in Turkish Kurdistan claimed 1,700 lives in 2015 alone (Mandıracı 2016). The university administration was reluctant to issue me the necessary permit because of the risks involved.

Thus, my work relies on primary and secondary sources, as well as generic material such as laws and constitutional drafts of the Kurdish administration there, although I followed very closely day-by-day developments on the ground from afar as well. I present my analyses in three steps: first, I provide an account of historical foundations and contemporary characteristics of Kurdish politics that give it its distinctive features: orientation toward self-rule and detachment from state-building.

All major Kurdish political movements, especially those in Iraq and Iran, have entertained the idea of establishing a Kurdish nation-state throughout the twentieth century. While the major movements in Turkey and Syria have changed their course and transformed their politics from a left-leaning nationalism to a form of confederalism, those in Iraq and Iran have not undergone such a substantial change. Since I limited my work on contemporary Kurdish politics with Turkey and Syria, I am not able to discuss the politics of major or minor political parties in Iraq and Iran. Nevertheless, it should suffice to note that although major political parties there embrace the idea of establishing a Kurdish nation-state, it is not with certainty that they act on that idea: i.e., that they prefer letting go of their relative autonomy for a Kurdistan dominated by their Kurdish rivals in which they might have lesser leverage over the principal political authority. The results of the independence referendum of 25 September 2017 held by the Kurdistan Regional Government in Iraq and the developments in the aftermath is a good example. The overwhelming majority voted "yes." However, internal disagreements within the Kurdistan Region prevailed and the autonomous region did not act on the result. Interventions from the central government as well as Iran-backed militia surely made it riskier for Kurdish leaderships to act on the result. However, the fact that one of the two political parties in the government coalition opted for autonomy instead of a hypothetically independent Kurdistan dominated by its rival Kurdish political party is telling. The choices made by the Kurdish political leaderships in the region after the referendum demonstrate that the tendency to remain autonomous prevailed over the idea of establishing a Kurdish nation-state. Calculations of the risks involved in pursuing statehood might have determined the course of action taken by certain political actors, but that would not explain why even coalition partners in the government did not opt for the same choice and face the risk in unity or in cooperation. The determining factor in this instance was not only the intervention from outside, but also the choices made by Kurdish political leadership. Thus, although major Kurdish political parties in Iraq, unlike those in Turkey and Syria, more openly embrace the idea of establishing a Kurdish nation-state, the referendum and subsequent developments reveal that opting for stateless self-rule remains one of the dominant characteristics of Kurdish politics.

Second, I present a discussion on whether the frameworks of integration and accommodation aptly capture those features and whether they are suitable frameworks for accommodating Kurdish political demands without invoking the Kurdish model. Finally, I proceed with an analysis of why Kurdish politics amounts to founding a full-fledged alternative model of political community, instead of operating within the frameworks of nationalism and multiculturalism. I conclude by underlining the pillars of political community promoted by the Kurdish political movements in Turkey and Syria.

This work is presented through (I) an inquiry into historical characteristics of Kurdish politics in the Ottoman and republican eras, and the developments that culminated in the birth of the phenomenon known as the *Kurdish Question* (a problematic conceptualization of the interaction between state-centrist homogenizing Turkish nationalism and autonomy-seeking Kurdish resistance); (II) a textual analysis of the constitutional drafts prepared by four major political parties in Turkey in relation to Kurdish political demands; (III) an analysis of the model of political community developed by dominant Kurdish political movements in Turkey and Syria; and finally, (IV) an attempt to place the Kurdish model within a theoretical framework.

As an author, I relate to my work through two positions that can be mutually exclusive and hence very challenging to reconcile with one another. On the one hand, I speak (I) as a scholarly investigator who examines the outright rejection of Kurdish political demands and the denial of the right to self-rule of the Kurds by the Turkish political elite. On the other hand, I am (II) a politically engaged individual, critical of actors, notions, mechanisms and institutions in Turkey and elsewhere that try to squeeze politics into statecraft, indeed try to fit it into the straitjacket of the nation-state and *state-nation*. As if it is not challenging enough, I was made aware of another risky position: the platform from where I try to criticise the overwhelming influence of certain European/Western constructs in Kurdish and Turkish politics, while, at the same time, trying to fit the home-grown Kurdish model of political community into a framework of political theory of the West. Indeed, I was haunted by the awareness that I was exploring a theoretical framework in Western political theory for the Kurdish model; while, in parallel with this endeavour, I kept criticising state-centrism as well as concepts and institutions of popular, territorial, national, and parliamentary sovereignty. These are the notions and institutions I could not reconcile with the Kurdish model, but they have been the cornerstones of Western political theory for the past half a millennium. The Kurdish model, indeed, calls upon the times of St. Thomas Aquinas, who argued that "a king is one who rules over one city or province" (Ebenstein and Ebenstein 2000, 232), speaking of a form of political community where sovereignty of persons and/or nations was not yet the rule.

Yet, one could argue that reconciling these perspectives in a scholarly work (and in a person) might be manageable if one is conscious and cautious enough in trying to accommodate them. Or maybe one should leave the two aside and focus on the work from one perspective only. In this book, it proved to be fruitful to avoid adopting a rigid or fixed perspective. Nevertheless, I can see clearly that such endeavours in the future should be carried out with more focus on local/home-grown parameters of the Kurdish model.

Likewise, I did not adopt a single theoretical framework for this book. To accommodate the perspectives above with minimal conflict and contradiction, I preferred leaving the horizon open for new theoretical frameworks to be developed, with which we might be able to study the Kurdish movement's project against a system of thought that provides us with a deeper contextual background. Therefore, the lens through which I look at the issues in this book is a tradition that vanishes and resurfaces throughout history and a conceptualization that is yet to be developed into a sound theory.

What this says about the theoretical approach of this work is this: all in all, I reached a compromise. I was not able to develop a sound theory of the Kurdish model of political community with its local—that is, *Kurdistanian* and Middle Eastern—foundations and precedents in this book, mostly because I could not do the fieldwork. But I believe I opened the way for such an endeavour and have the prospect to do so in my future work.

My Choice of Words and a Critique of Terminology and Perspectives in Kurdish Studies

Scholarship on Kurdish politics in history has mainly focused on the origins of the so-called Kurdish Question or of Kurdish ethno-nationalism. I will refrain from using both terms, because they are negative rather than neutral. These terms reflect two main approaches to Kurdish politics in Turkey. The former represents the approach that tends to focus on external factors. It implies that Kurdish politics is dominated by geographical, social, political, and economic conditions the Kurds have no control over. Hence, it gives lower profile to the agency of political actors in Kurdistan, overlooks their choices, and downplays the effects of those choices.

This leads to certain misunderstandings I dwell on in detail in chapter 2: namely state-centrism, not distinguishing political community from polity, and assuming that the Kurdish political elite tried to build a state of its own but failed to do so. I argue that the role of the State is overemphasised in Kurdish politics; highlight that the Ottoman polity consisted of multiple political communities within one polity and I distinguish between the two; and finally I point out that the dominant Kurdish political elite did not try to build a Kurdish state in the first place. Hence, the explanations that emphasise their "failure" do not seem to hold.

The second term, "Kurdish ethno-nationalism," implies that civilisation is one and has a linear course and that this dictates certain political standards that "politically mature" societies uphold. This perspective suggests that there are neutral nation-building policies and ethnically particularistic nationalisms. The former are attributed to established nation-states, and nation-states are presumed to be founded by groups who have developed a national conscious-ness. The latter are labelled as political mobilizations with an "immature" ethno-nationalism. This linear approach suggests that Kurds failed to found a state of their own because they could not develop national consciousness early enough in history. Defining the Kurds as a "traditional" and "backward" ethnic group who "lacked national consciousness" and therefore "failed" to build a state of their own (Aboona 2008; Yavuz 2001; Kirişci and Winrow 1997; Arakon 2014) amounts to saying that they have only been victims and passive subjects in history. This denies them the agency of making choices. This view indicates that all important decisions regarding their fate have been determined by their physical conditions and the actions of others.

The fairest analyses of Kurdish politics acknowledge that "The various Kurdish uprisings of the nineteenth and early twentieth century were not simply isolated incidents caused by economic decline or political dissatisfac-tion" (Bruinessen 2004, 2); and that "it must be kept in mind that national-ism, which lies at the root of the Kurdish question, is largely political and psychological in nature" (Jwaideh, cited in Bruinessen 2004, 2). Despite some accurate representations of Kurdish politics, these authors still echo the hegemonic narrative that does not capture the whole political picture. For example, Bruinessen begins his criticisms of early scholarship on the Kurdish Question by observing that "earlier authors writing on Kurdish nationalism tended to analyse it from the viewpoint of the administration or the dominant groups in the state" (2004, 4), and he sees the "Kurdish nationalism as a movement in its own right and not just a reaction to the process of modern-ization and administrative reform" (2004, 4). However, he later echoes the same progressive narrative of failure referred to above when he argues that "Aroused by the success of the surrounding nationalisms—Turkish, Persian, and Arab—and goaded into desperation by its own *failure*, Kurdish national-ism has in recent years become increasingly radical and uncompromising" (2004, 20; emphasis added).

Nation-building has become a prerequisite for state-building, as nation-building and state-making have been associated with one another since the nineteenth century (Weber 1994). It has been assumed that the Kurds do not have their own state because they failed to develop national consciousness, and that they were late in the race of founding a nation-state of their own, due to many ill conditions rooted in their social structures and their harsh geography, though their neighbours have managed to do so (Yavuz 2001; also see Burr and Price, cited in Bruinessen 2004, 4). Although the Kurdish political elite have not always sought the establishment of a Kurdish state, they claimed and pursued nationhood. However, the majority of the authors who claim that the Kurds have failed at building a Kurdish nation-state fail to ask: did they—i.e., their elites—actually pursue statehood?

An example can be seen in the historical account given by Özoğlu. He provides a relatively fair account of Kurdish history, but his thesis still ends with the argument that "after the collapse of the Ottoman Empire they [the Kurds] failed to obtain a Kurdish state of their own. The internal dynamics of Kurdish society played a large part in this failure" (Özoğlu 2004, 67). Özoğlu did not ask whether the Kurdish political elite at that time wanted to build a state of their own or not.

Likewise, the theory of Kurdish politics is understudied and underrepresented in scholarship. Although research on Kurdish political activism, peaceful and armed struggle is burgeoning, there are rather few studies that focus on the specifics of political demands promoted by political actors in Kurdistan or on the specifics of Kurdish politics. Most literature on Kurdish politics focuses on generic topics such as Kurdish nationalism or minority rights. The existing literature therefore has concentrated on human and cultural rights of the Kurds, armed groups in Kurdistan, protest, integration, or accommodation of the Kurds in Turkey. Additionally, by focusing on generic Kurdish politics, scholarship tends to overlook differences in Kurdish political activism, while in actuality there is a variety of mobilized groups and actors that have competing political interests, agendas, and worldviews. These different political projects should be studied, analysed, and understood in their own right, not under a common framework that treats any of them as an "anomaly" (Jongerden and Akkaya 2012), or as a problem to be solved.

Presentation of Arguments and Structure

The book breaks the central thesis into four correlated arguments, of which I present each in a separate chapter. The first argument is that discussions of accommodating Kurdish political demands are missing a crucial aspect of Kurdish politics in history: its detachment from state-building and its inclination toward maintaining or reviving self-rule in Kurdistan. This has led to serious misunderstandings such as associating Kurdish politics exclusively with state-building. Nevertheless, throughout the history of Kurdistan, there have been a variety of political communities that were not independent states.

Self-rule without a sovereign state has been the *modus vivendi* of Kurdish politics until the second half of the nineteenth century; and modern Kurdish politics is inspired by this fact. Consequently, I emphasise national liberation beyond or without sovereignty in the first chapter, in order to offer a nuanced perspective on Kurdish politics in Turkey.

The second argument is built on the first one and holds that since Kurdish politics is oriented toward the coexistence of multiple political communities, drafting a new constitution that maintains a single political community in Turkey does not answer Kurdish demands. Thus, the argument that the new constitution will be a "new social contract" that solves the Kurdish Question is simply another misunderstanding. Neither the old nor the new constitutions are social contracts between the Turks and Kurds, nor have Turkish political parties offered any meaningful change to their Statist nationalist views in their constitutional drafts submitted to the Grand National Assembly since 2011.

The third argument is that the model of political community promoted by the Kurdish movement is meant to be an alternative to, and is in competition and conflict with, the two dominant models of political community: the nation-state and the Islamic *Ummah*. The dominant Kurdish movement in Turkey aims to establish self-rule throughout Kurdistan and has been building local institutions for that purpose. Having control over the means of violence and natural resources, as well as setting local councils and assemblies as sovereign organs of political power in Kurdish majority cities, are part of the model. Nevertheless, building a Kurdish nation-state is explicitly dismissed by the movement. Therefore, contemporary Kurdish politics also supersedes multiculturalist accommodation and is detached from state-building.

Finally, the fourth argument is that the Kurdish model of political community offers a different approach to our understanding of citizenship, cultural/territorial boundaries, and autonomy/self-rule. The model questions the main pillars of nationalism such as national sovereignty, exclusive national identities as the basis of citizenship, and closed borders. This forces us to look beyond hegemonic doctrines of sovereignty, self-rule, citizenship, integration, and accommodation.

NOTES

1. By the *dominant Kurdish political movement* or in short, *the Kurdish political movement,* or *the Kurdish movement,* I refer to a cluster of legal and illegal organizations and institutions that emerged primarily in Turkey but spread to many countries in the Middle East and Europe. The cluster includes but is not limited to civil society organizations, political parties, and armed groups that have the outlawed Kurdistan

Workers' Party (the PKK—Partiya Karkerên Kurdîstan) at their core. These entities share a common political ideology and a common goal, which is articulated as achieving self-rule for the peoples of Kurdistan, democratizing Turkey, Syria, Iran and Iraq, and transforming the whole Middle East into a European Union–like political and economic entity. Although the Kurdish political movement as well as the model of political community I focus on in this book have originated in Northern (Turkish) Kurdistan, the dominant Kurdish movement in Western (Syrian) Kurdistan, too, has adopted the same model of political community. Therefore, when referring to the movement's model of political community, I refer not only to the model promoted by the Kurdish movement in Turkey, but I also refer to the model partly implemented and widely promoted in Syrian Kurdistan as well. Hence, I should make it clear that I do not discuss Kurdish political movements in Syria in this book. My references to Syrian Kurdish politics in general and to the dominant Kurdish political movement in Syria in particular are strictly and exclusively limited to the abstract model of political community I discuss in chapter 4 of this book, simply and only because this model was adopted by the dominant Kurdish political movement there. Otherwise, Kurdish politics in Syria and political movements there are by no means what I dwell on in this book.

2. This is in stark contrast to Thomas Paine's idea of a good constitution: "A constitution is not the act of a government, but of a people constituting a government" (cited in Arendt 1963, 145). It is noted that this is a trend in Eastern Europe; the powerful ruling party in Hungary enacted a constitution of this kind in 2011 (Majtényi 2017), and a similar tendency is observable in Poland as well.

3. The statement draws heavily on Aristotle (*Politics*, Book III, Chapter 16 and 17), Rousseau (*The Social Contract*, Book I, Chapter 6), and even lightly on Hobbes (*Leviathan*, Chapter 21).

4. The title of Thomas Hobbes' book published in 1651, in which he likens the sovereign State to the biblical monster leviathan.

Chapter Two

Autonomy Within the State

Non-State Political Communities in Kurdistan

In this chapter, I analyse Kurdish political history from a nuanced perspective. The characteristic of Kurdish politics in Turkey and Syria that is the focus of this work, i.e., detachment from state centrism, is traced in history within this chapter. The chapter demonstrates that the foundation of a separate Kurdish state was not an actively pursued goal by the majority of the Kurdish political elite throughout the Ottoman and early republican eras. In other words, Kurdish nationalism was not born out of a quest for founding a State for the Kurds, but was a medium through which the preservation of the status quo was promoted. The Kurdish elite during this period primarily sought to maintain their privileges and/or self-rule in Kurdistan, and promoted equal citizenship rights and social justice for the Kurdish population elsewhere. Hence, the history of Kurdistan demonstrates that contrary to commonly held false assumptions, dominant Kurdish political movements in general, but particularly those in Turkey, have not sought after a Kurdish nation-state.

Focusing on the interactions between the Turkish and Kurdish political elites from the sixteenth to the twentieth century, this chapter holds that there is more to Kurdish politics than what is presented in the state-centric accounts. In a nutshell, neither Orientalist approaches that see "backwardness" and a "lack" of national consciousness, nor victimising ones that deny agency to the Kurds, are suitable frameworks for explaining the statelessness of the Kurds. This book takes a different approach and asks whether the Kurdish elite pursued statehood in the first place; since, in order to fail at something over and over, one has to try it. The answer I find is no: founding a Kurdish state has not been an ambition for the decisive Kurdish political elite at least since the sixteenth century.

The chapter starts with a critique of state-centric views. The first section delineates the process of the incorporation of the greater part of Kurdistan into the Ottoman Empire and discusses political developments in Kurdistan under Ottoman rule. The contribution of this section overlaps with that of this chapter: instead of repeating a Eurocentric political narrative, it invokes a contextual perspective while analysing Kurdish politics in history. The chapter then discusses the second misunderstanding, which treats the Ottoman polity as a single political community. The existence of autonomous political entities in Kurdistan is emphasised in this section. The section argues that along with nationalism and reforms aimed at centralising the Ottoman state, sovereignty was also reconfigured on the bases of national will, which led to attempts at forming a single political community in Turkey. This, in turn, meant abolishing Kurdish political communities and revoking the privileges of the Kurdish political elite; a process that shaped the differences between Turkish and Kurdish nationalisms. The third section reveals the misunderstanding that may be the most common one: ignoring the choice and agency of the Kurdish political elite. This section argues that the fact that the Kurds have no nation-state of their own cannot be explained by sheer failure on the part of Kurdish nobility, but the element of deliberate choice to avoid and evade the state is also involved. In the last section, I try to address the most common misunderstanding: analysing Kurdish politics through European notions, constructs, and processes. This means offering prescriptions accordingly. In this section, I attempt to shift the theoretical perspective of analysing Kurdish politics from Eurocentrism to the local context.

My objective in this chapter is to emphasise that discussions on accommodating Kurdish political demands are missing a crucial aspect of Kurdish politics: that it has been inspired by the idea of the coexistence of multiple political communities (see Tas 2014; Klein 2007). The dominant Kurdish political movement pursues self-rule in Kurdistan, but independence is not the goal. The political form of this self-rule resembles "state fragments" of George Jellinek (Petrovic 2002; Keating 2001b). Jellinek categorises four political entities that are not States but show certain characteristics of them. His description fits well with political structures of the Ottoman and Austro-Hungarian empires. These empires recognised the right to self-government of certain communities and regions or the authority of petit sovereigns, for they represented a community within the empire (Reynolds 2007). Kurdistan, as a region, was home to several such political communities and Kurdish rulers enjoyed a great degree of autonomy until the centralisation reforms of the nineteenth century. In other words, if Kurdish politics is now dominated by a notion of autonomy that prioritises the coexistence of multiple and overlapping political communities dispersed throughout Kurdistan and Turkey, this is not a completely new vision. This has its roots in the fact that a variety of political communities enjoyed differing degrees of autonomy within the Ottoman polity. Kurdistan, starting from the sixteenth century, was home to a number of them. The last autonomous political community in Kurdistan was abolished during the nineteenth century. The Kurdish political elite tried to maintain the *status quo*; i.e., to keep Kurdish political communities within the Empire alive. Founding a Kurdish state was not on their agenda. Thus, for Kurdish rulers, self-rule was not associated with state-building, but it was based on their autonomy from the State. Highlighting this aspect will help us understand contemporary Kurdish politics in its historical context.

There are always exceptions to the rule, and there have been Kurdish political actors who adopt state-centric politics. However, as exceptional political actors, they are not the focus of this chapter. The question I try to answer is: why are autonomy-oriented goals and tendencies and/or evading the State, two crucial aspects of Kurdish politics, missing from discussions and literature on the subject? The main argument of the chapter is that the scarcity of specific literature on Kurdish politics and political history has led to the categorisation of Kurdish politics as ethno-cultural nationalism; to misdiagnosing political debates wrongly as the "Kurdish Question"; and to creating and apply unfitting theoretical frameworks as prescriptions created after these misconceptions. In this chapter I will highlight the crucial historical moments that have influenced the development of anti-State, self-rule tendencies found in Kurdish politics. This aspect of Kurdish politics is pivotal to understanding the goals pursued by the Kurdish political elite, and wholly necessary to reach a conceptual clarity of what and how Kurdish politicians sought to achieve. Otherwise we are left with very limited and biased knowledge on Kurdish politics, which has conditioned the Turkish political elite to approach the Kurds with caution and suspicion, and to "deal" with their political demands within the "politics of securitization" (Kymlicka 2007; Todorova 2015).

The point here is that this conditioning is based on a false assumption: that Kurdish nationalism in Turkey pursues, and has always pursued, the goal of founding a nation-state for the Kurds and that this is going to disintegrate Turkey. This perception of Kurdish politics in Turkey is indeed a misunderstanding. On the contrary, Kurdish politics has rarely harboured state-centric ambitions. By highlighting this aspect of Kurdish politics, I hope to contribute to the efforts dedicated to reaching a conceptual clarification of Kurdish political demands. My focus will be the choices made by and the agency of the Kurdish political elite.

STATE-CENTRIC APPROACHES
DENY POLITICAL AGENCY TO THE KURDS

This section departs from the idea that the role of the Ottoman and Turkish states has been overemphasised in the context of Kurdish politics. Scholarship has generally emphasized the State's central role in historical developments, thus reproducing a statist perspective and taking agency away from non-state forces, actors, and dynamics. Even balanced accounts of modern history have put the State at the centre, as Abrams (1977) points out, via constructing a linear narrative in which modern political institutions appear as the culmination of political organization (e.g., Zürcher 2004, 2010; Özoğlu 2004). The biased accounts go further, often displaying a statist discourse (e.g. Akyol 2006; Yavuz 2001). Therefore, labelling Kurdish political activism as "reactionary," "violent," "ethno-nationalist," or "terrorism" is not just a by-product of such historical narratives, but its primary outcome. For instance, Barkey and Fuller acknowledge their bias by stating that "Our first concern in preparing this study is for the future stability and well-being of Turkey as a key American ally, and for the Turkish government's ability to deal satisfactorily with the debilitating Kurdish problem. We are concerned for the preservation of the territorial integrity of Turkey" (1998, xv). Similarly, others have observed Kurdish politics through political biases, and promoted narratives that serve an agenda. Such perspectives have contributed to the assumption that the (Ottoman or Turkish) State was and is the main force driving history in the context of Kurdish politics. The effects of Kurdish political actors on the history of Kurds and Kurdistan, on the other hand, have been marginalized.

This is not surprising, as history is replete with marginalized societies and peoples that have no or little attachment to the State. Labelling them and their political structures as "traditional," "backward," or "primitive" has been a common practice (e.g., Easton 1959). This tendency is very clear in the context of Kurdish politics. Hamelink and Baris have given a few examples from the scholarship written on the Kurdish Question to underline this negative image of the Kurds in some very well-known academic works:

> McDowall (1996: 184): the Turkish state "seriously underestimated the durability of the primordial ties that bound groups of Kurds together." White (2000: 84): "In so far as they were tribesmen acting completely along traditional (that is, pre-modern) lines, they were acting as the blind instruments of political modernization. It would not seem an exaggeration to describe them as 'primitive rebels.'" Van Bruinessen (1992: 316): "Kurdish nationalism and, to some extent, radical and populist varieties of socialism had become the dominant discourse among the Kurds; many, moreover, explicitly and sincerely denounced narrow tribal loyalties. This did not mean, of course, the end of primordial loyalties. Nationalism and socialism, rather, came to be used to lend additional legitimacy to traditional authority." (Hamelink and Baris 2014, 43–44)

The problem here is that there is an evolutionary reading of history, which suggests that peoples who managed to build their own state demonstrate the ultimate contemporary political "maturity," while others are bogged down in "primordial" ties and lack qualities needed for founding their own state.[1] In evolutionary history, the state appears not only as the ultimate example of political organization that highlights differences between the "progressed" and the "primitive"; but it also occupies the central place in literature as the locomotive of sociopolitical developments. Initiative and social innovation is taken away from non-state political actors and social forces; the actions of non-state actors are seen as mere reactions to the State's deeds and their appearances as mere reflections of the State's image.

The Kurds, as a stateless nation, are depicted as latecomers in the competition for modern nation-building/state-making (Kirişci and Winrow 1997, 78–79); whose political activism is said to be plagued by "a culture of violence" and is believed to be trapped in a fruitless ethno-nationalism at worst (Yavuz 2001, 6); or a nation that is becoming "radical and uncompromising" at best (Bruinessen 2004, 20).[2] Although Kurdish political activism has been among one of the main pillars of political developments in the Middle East in general, and in Kurdistan in particular, for the last millennium, scholarship has mainly suggested that the Kurds have only reacted to policies implemented by the State (Kirişci and Winrow 1997; Özoğlu 2004; Yavuz 2001), thus downplaying their role and agency, overlooking (to the extent of condescension) what they value as a political mode of existence; any other history that suggests otherwise is ignored.

For instance, while the State's role in social, political, and economic life is in many respects generally exaggerated, it does not get its fair share from the existence and persistence of perceived problems mentioned above, the chief among them being "fragmentation." The State has benefited from dividing and ruling, and from buying loyalty of those in power. This practice is one of the main sources of political fragmentation, and an important cause of internal competition and conflict in Kurdistan. Guida (2014), for instance, offers a discussion of electoral incentives offered to local leaders in the province of Urfa in Kurdistan by the State and major Turkish political parties, which helps sustain the enmity and conflict between the pro-state tribes and the rest in that region. It would appear, based on this research and the state of the Turkish-Kurdish relationships, that ongoing local conflict and competition between Kurdish communities is sustained partly by the bribery and in the interest of Turkish officials and the State. The Turkish State, therefore, does not appear as a stabilizing influence in Kurdistan.

Another example is the description of dissidents as *rebels*, a label used for those uprising against—supposedly—legitimate authorities. Interestingly, these labels are not just used by the "enemies" of the Kurds in modern-day Turkey (e.g., Yavuz 2001), but *rebellion* and *revolt* and their derivatives are also terms used to create a negative image of Kurdish political activism in some scholarship. Considering this negative description, one should question whether those who fought the Ottoman and Turkish governments considered themselves as *rebels*. As Danforth (2013) demonstrates, naming armed resistance or battles between government forces and the Kurds as *rebellion*, and dividing the region and the people who participated in them as *tribes*, has been practiced by the Ottoman and Turkish states with the purpose of belittling the undertakings against those states. Labelling armed resistance and/or competition as *rebellion*, calling those who resist or compete in Kurdistan as *bandits* is another way of demonising resistance throughout history.

For the Kurdish rulers, elites, and organizations that have fought the Ottoman and Turkish states, however, their resistance is much more than *rebellion* or *revolt*. While both rebellion and revolt suggest disobedience to a more or less legitimate authority, it is doubtful whether one actually *still* considers her/his adversary or enemy as a rightful *authority* when one wages war against, or rejects to accept, a political power.[3] According to Arendt "authority precludes the use of external means of coercion, where force is used, authority itself has failed! If authority is to be defined at all, then, it must be in contradistinction to both coercion by force and persuasion through arguments" (1954, 2).

Also, it is obvious, from the etymology of the terms, that they have been used by states to discredit political opposition and their adversaries in wars.[4] Perhaps it is helpful to quote a passage from James Robertson's novel *Joseph Knight* in order to point out the nuance between pursuing a cause and rebellion, without invoking semantics, and through a sensitive evaluation of these concepts which allows us to see how nobility views them: "[H]e was always punctilious in describing the Forty-five as a *rising*. To call it a rebellion was to debase the cause and its motives, to make it sound like something quite different. When he thought of rebels, he thought of slaves" (108). I think it would not be a stretch to contend that a similar understanding could be attributed to the Kurdish nobility as well. Thus, I will refrain from using the terms *rebellion* and *revolt* while addressing armed conflicts, wars, and battles between the Kurds and the Ottoman and Turkish states.

That the Incorporation of Kurdistan into the Ottoman Empire Was Initiated by Kurdish Rulers

It is true that politics in Kurdistan has always been fragmented on different levels, but that does not mean it has always been politically reactionary. In fact, one can find enough evidence in history to argue that many significant events that represent turning points in the history of Kurdistan seem to be initiated by internal socio-political forces and actors in Kurdistan. I will start enumerating those cornerstones in history from the sixteenth century onwards.

The first important historical element to note when discussing Kurdish-Turkish/Ottoman relations is that the incorporation of certain parts of Kurdistan into the Ottoman Empire was *not* through conquest, but through an agreement of alliance and allegiance between Ottoman and Kurdish rulers. Aboona notes that the agreement between Sultan Selim I (who ruled 1512–1520) and the Kurdish delegation headed by Îdrîs-î Bîdlîs-î (Idris of/from Bitlis, 1452–1520),[5] the ruler of Bitlis[6] Emirate, had enabled Kurdish rulers:

> [T]o enjoy autonomy in their administration on the condition that they acted as a guardian force for the eastern border. The arrangement freed the Ottomans to pursue their design to expand in Europe—a task that kept them busy for three successive centuries, advancing and retreating, without seeking an effective role in their Asiatic non-Turkish provinces. [. . .] [A]fter Chaldiran, the Kurdish presence in the region was continuously increased and consolidated. (Aboona 2008, 163)

Özoğlu, too, notes that thirty Kurdish leaders joined together under the leadership of "Bitlisi, who assembled a large Kurdish army by forming alliances among Kurdish emirates, including Çemiskezek, Palu, Çapakçur, Bitlis, Hasankeyf, Hizan, Cezire (Cizre), and Sasun. [. . .] Sultan Selim charged Bitlisi with establishing an administrative framework for these Kurdish territories" (2004, 48). Tas emphasizes that Bîdlîs-î gathered a force of sixty thousand troops, a formidable power, to help the Ottoman army in the Battle of Çaldıran fought between the Ottoman and Safavid empires in 1514 in Kurdish lands (2014, 508). This alliance between the Ottoman and Kurdish forces was pivotal in gaining the Ottomans a decisive victory over *their* greatest rivals in the Islamic world for the upcoming centuries.

The alliance between Kurdish and Ottoman rulers, who followed the Sunni way of Islam, was directed particularly against the Shia Safavid expansion from Iran.[7] Aboona (2008) and Özoğlu (2004) note that the Safavids were getting closer to the Ottoman border through conquering, plundering, and destroying the Kurdish and Assyrian heartland, threatening to absorb Sunni Muslims. This Safavid expansion thus pushed the Sunni Kurds towards a union with their fellow Sunnis, the Ottoman Turks. In the face of the Safavid violence, the Kurds saw no alternative to forging an alliance with the Ottoman Sultan to encounter the growing menace to Sunni Islam (I will dwell on the alliance between the Ottoman and Kurdish rulers on the grounds of their faith later in this chapter). For the purpose of this section, it suffices to note that Kurdistan was not absorbed by the Ottomans via conquest, and that no

Ottoman troops were stationed there until late nineteenth century (Özoğlu 2004).

Another episode that points to a Kurdish-Ottoman alliance rather than a form of fealty on the part of the Kurds is the clear statement issued by three Ottoman sultans in their edicts known as *ferman* (see Aboona 2008; Ates 2013; Özoğlu 2004). These edicts also demonstrate the longevity of the Kurdish-Ottoman alliance, as they were first issued by sultans Selim I (1470–1520) and Suleyman (1494–1566) in the sixteenth and Murad IV (1612–1640) in the seventeenth centuries. In these edicts, the sultans rewarded the Kurdish rulers for their services to the Ottoman throne:

> As a reward for their services and in recognition of their power, Sultan Selim, as described by the sixteenth century reformer Aziz Efendi, granted that 'From that time on, apart from the requirement of doing battle and combat with the heresy-embracing "redhead" [the Safavid Iranians] they [Kurdish notables] were freed from all obligation to pay extraordinary impositions (*tekalif*) and autonomy was granted to them over their ancestral lands (*odjak*) and homes (*yurt*) on the traditional basis as "cut off from the feet [of intruders] and set aside from the pen [of surveyors] and so on" confirmed in perpetuity generation after generation in order to console and gratify their minds. (Ates 2013, 38)

It is clear from this passage that the alliance was not only fruitful for the Ottomans because it helped securing of their Eastern borders. Rather, this alliance was an exchange which was more favourable for the Kurds. These three edicts guaranteed that in the alliance, the Kurds were more than rewarded for the security they offered to the Ottomans and their contributions to the Ottoman's military strength, as they not only secured their political autonomy and ancestral lands, but were also exempted from paying the usual taxes (*tekalif*) that other nations in the Ottoman Empire were bound to pay.

To summarize: first, the Kurds forged an alliance with the Ottomans due to a threat directed at their common faith, which is Sunni Islam. This means that the political alliance between the Kurds and Ottomans was based upon a common enemy. Second, Kurdish rulers believed that serving the Ottoman Sultan's *cihad* (*jihad*) in spreading Sunni Islam as highly beneficial for themselves as well. Through serving the Ottoman *cihad* they could gain recognition and protection from one of the most powerful regional empires, while preserving their autonomy and the property they inherited from their ancestors. Common political principles, common political institutions, language, culture, common ancestry, ethnic or biological ties, and other factors had almost no or little effect on the formation of this alliance. Both sides seemed convinced that they were facing a common enemy and that acting together would be in their interest. The Ottomans gained a firm ally for the safety of their eastern borders,[8] while the Kurdish rulers secured protection from a regional patron and the preservation of their privileges.

Which common interests and political values, which shared goals and principles can we enumerate as factors that ensured an Ottoman-Kurdish alliance of the sixteenth century and incorporated the majority of Kurdistan into the Ottoman body politic? The argument of this section is that it was nothing else than having a common enemy that pushed the Kurds toward the Ottoman state, and that both sides benefited greatly from this alliance. However, this alliance did not end up creating any common bond between the two sides, nor was a common identity for the Kurds and the Turks forged in the process.

According to Ciwan, Sultan Selim I decided to wage his first campaign on the Shia Safavids of Iran, instead of marching on the Christian Europe, because the Kurdish leader Bidlis-i convinced him to do so (2014, 2–5). Otherwise, Ciwan argues, Selim would have marched on Hungary. Aboona, on the contrary, suggests that "Sultan Selim I succeeded in directing Idris al Bidlis-i to rouse the religious feeling of the Sunni Kurds against the Safavid Shi'a" (2008, 99). Based on historical sources and documents, including Bidlis-i's biography of Sultan Selim, *Selim Şahname* (Selim Shahname), the *Şerefname* of Şeref Xan (The Sharafnama of Sharaf Khan, the Emir of Bidlis Emirate, 1543–1599), and the Venetian traveller and merchant Giovanni Mario Angiolello's accounts, Ciwan's interpretation appears to be more plausible. It sits well within the historical context, as waging war on the "infidels" of the Christian Europe (instead of shedding Muslim blood) was a well-known Ottoman policy throughout centuries. This also explains their rapid expansion westward and ascendance from being a small suzerain entity (*beylik*) on the margins of a fallen empire to becoming a regional empire in less than two hundred years. Given this well-known and longstanding policy, it would have been odd for an Ottoman sultan to choose to wage war upon other Muslims, rather than Christian Europe, without some instigation or convincing argument that a danger was rising from the East. It is plausible that not only was the incorporation of Kurdistan into the Ottoman Empire the outcome of an agreement between Kurdish and Ottoman rulers, but also that this incorporation was the idea conceived by a Kurdish strategist who managed to change the course of action of the Ottoman Sultan. Incentives were provided by Kurdish princes (*mirs*) and heads of tribes and tribal confederacies (*begsbeys*—landlords, local/petit sovereigns), and the whole undertaking was initiated by the Kurds themselves, according to Ciwan's account. Ciwan notes that a Kurdish envoy visited the Sultan, who was in his court in Edirne to pass the winter and to prepare for his campaign on Hungary (2014, 5–7). After a period of lobbying, the Kurdish envoy convinced the Sultan that the real threat was coming from Iran and that the first military campaign should be waged on this eastward enemy, the Safavids (5–7). Thus, Kurdish rulers appear to have supplied the main agency behind this very important episode that is now a cornerstone of the political history of Kurdistan. The Kurds were also the main beneficiaries of this new political campaign until the second half of the nineteenth century.

The Impact of the Ambitions of Kurdish Rulers on Generating Conflict with the Ottoman Throne

The most significant Kurdish political figure of the nineteenth century and clearly the greatest source of inspiration for Kurdish nationalists is Mîr Bedirxan (1803–1868).[9] Mîr Bedirxan (Prince Bedirkhan) seems to have moved for conquest of the Christians in Kurdistan unilaterally when he carried out a series of devastating campaigns against the Assyrians of Hakkari, a province in the Botan Emirate (Bhotan) ruled by the House of Bedirxan. The involvement of the Ottoman capital in this massacre is neither firmly established nor totally dismissed by historians; however, British officials believed that

> Official Turkish participation with the Kurds in the massacres of the Assyrian tribes was attested throughout the region and also in western circles, it was reported that Bedr Khan had not initiated his massacres until he had got the green light from the Turkish authorities. According to well-informed British sources in Mosul, Bedr Khan sent to Mohammed Pasha, the Turkish Governor of the Pashalic of Mosul, and asked permission to punish the Christians. This was at once granted, for their power and reputed wealth had long aroused the jealousy and the cupidity of the Turks. (Aboona 2008, 200–203)

Nevertheless, the matter is too complicated to be settled only by the accounts given by British sources, for two reasons. First, British sources clearly served the agenda of the British Empire in the Ottoman sphere of influence, and the accounts given by these sources should be taken with a grain of salt. The sheer fact that Christian communities existed within the Ottoman polity constituted an agenda against the Ottoman sultan (see Zürcher 2004). According to Aboona, the presence of American missionaries and their activities in the region deteriorated the conditions of the Assyrians to a degree that there is reason to believe that they were involved in the process that led to the massacres (2008, 206–207). These two interconnected and ambiguous factors make the matter even more difficult to understand. Thus, the argument with regard to involvement of the Ottomans and the Americans remains unclear until further evidence clarifies their role, and cannot be referred to as a source of conflict with any certainty. As long as it was Bedirxan and his forces that carried out the campaign and the ensuing massacres, the involvement of other actors is of secondary importance.

The Ottoman state, under heavy pressure from European colonial powers (who started to influence Ottoman politics from 1830s onwards under the pretext of protecting Christian minorities), undertook a punitive campaign against Mîr Bedirxan only a year after the massacres. Mîr Bedirxan fought the Ottomans and strove to unite Kurdistan under his rule to no avail: he was defeated and taken captive.[10]

The dominant thesis that the activities of this very ambitious and visionary Kurdish leader were triggered by the Ottoman centralization would defy all the descriptions made about him by Özoğlu and Aboona, since the picture of Bedirxan they draw does not seem like a figure who would be too easily manipulated into committing massacres. On the contrary, he appears as a "visionary" leader who would not shy away from ordering massacres and resisting the capital in order to see his dream of uniting Kurdistan under his rule was realized. The fact that Bedirxan's unifying policies are widely celebrated by Kurdish historians, especially by nationalists, and the fact that they consider Bedirxan as the first Kurdish ruler who had the vision of founding a Kingdom of Kurdistan, or who attempted to unite Kurdistan under one political authority (Diken 2013) suggest that his politics were not designed by the Ottoman capital. Therefore, Özoğlu's argument that Bedirxan's actions were only reactions to Ottoman centralization does not hold—as Özoğlu himself notes that Bedirxan established a state-like administration under his rule (2004, 58–59). Establishing a state-like political entity can hardly be interpreted as a reaction to the central government, as it would require a vision in advance of acting on it, and long years to carry out the wok to realize that vision.

Moreover, the second instance in which Kurdistan is envisaged as a separate kingdom or as a political project/aspiration, emerges shortly after Bedirxan's ambitious undertakings. The uprising organized by Şeyh Ubeydullah Nehrî (*Sheikh Ubeydullah Nehrî*) in 1880–1881 shows that *Kurdistan* evolved from being the homeland of Kurds in the sixteenth century to a political ideal in the seventeenth, and finally into a political project in the nineteenth century. At this time, while Kurdistan was merely a region that was regarded by other nations as the land of the Kurds, it had evolved into an idea through Kurdish literature, and then into a political project through the efforts of Kurdish rulers to expand or preserve their autonomy. This is discernible from the fact that political figures like Bedirxan and Ubeydullah Nehrî claimed to be rulers of Kurdistan in the nineteenth century, while a few others also did so in the twentieth (see Özoğlu 2004, 101). This is not a conventional reading of

Kurdish history; however, historical developments themselves suggest such an evolution, without the need for further interpretation.

First, throughout the sixteenth and seventeenth centuries, Sultan Selim (I), Sultan Suleyman (I), and Sultan Murad (IV), each referred to a separate political geography when they mention or address *Kurdistan Beyleri* (notables or rulers of Kurdistan) in their decrees (*ferman*) and laws (*kanunname*) (Özoğlu 2004; Tas 2014). For instance, Sultan Suleyman mentions *Kurdistan* as part of his empire in his letter addressed to the King of France in 1526. Additionally, as mentioned earlier, the Ottomans did not station an army in Kurdistan and they did not interfere with the affairs of rulers and notables in Kurdistan, unless they were asked to. These facts all demonstrate that *Kurdistan* was considered and seen as a political geography of its own within the Ottoman Empire.

Within the Ottoman Empire, high-ranking Ottoman officials such as *Paşas* (General) represented the sultan in various regions of the empire. Though Kurds were not represented at the capital, the capital was represented by top high-ranking officials in Kurdistan. Here it should be stressed that the high-ranking officials representing the sultan in Kurdistan were not *Ottoman* officials, but *Kurds.* It is also noteworthy that Kurdish notables were not addressed as *Kürt Beyleri* (Kurdish rulers), but as *Kurdistan Beyleri* (rulers of Kurdistan). This is an important distinction because it means that Kurdistan, as a political geography, held far more significance as a political category than did Kurdish nobility. This makes more sense in the context of the Ottoman administration, as the empire was not governed on the basis of ethnicity, but on the basis of religion and territory. Given the various mentions of Kurdistan as a political territory in state documents, the lack of an Ottoman military presence in Kurdistan, and the existence of Kurdish representatives of the sultan, the *Kurdistan Beyleri,* it is only natural to conclude that Kurdistan was an established political geography within the Empire since its incorporation into it.

With its firm standing as its own geographical and political entity upheld by the Ottomans, the next step toward founding Kurdistan as a distinct political entity came in the form of Kurdish literature. The Kurdish intellectual and author Ehmedê Xanê (1650–1707) spoke of the need for Kurdish unity and the foundation of a kingdom of *Kurdistan* in his most celebrated work, *Mem û Zîn* (Mem and Zin, published in 1692). It is in this work that Xanê argues that if the Kurds are to free themselves from the yoke of their neighbours—the Turks, the Arabs and the Persians, they need to be united.[11] This is a clear step in the evolution of Kurdistan from a political geography into a political idea (note that nationalism starts with literary and cultural works, as Smith (2001) and Hroch (2010) argue).

The third step in the evolution of Kurdistan as a political community is the transformation of Kurdistan from a political idea into a concrete political project in the nineteenth century, when *Kurdistan* was imagined as a realm to be united and ruled, and as a throne to be claimed. The aspirations of Mîr Bedirxan led the way to the formulation of such a political project. Most of the political activities that followed this trajectory invoked this notion of Kurdistan: a realm to be united and ruled by a Kurdish king. Although in the nineteenth century there does not appear to be any forms of modern nationalism and nationalist movements amongst the Turks, the Kurds, and other Muslim groups in the Ottoman Empire, it does appear that Kurdistan had already emerged as a political project during this period. Thus, it would not be fair to contend that Bedirxan's politics were mere reactions to the Ottoman states' centralization policies. There is something historically novel in the political activities of Bedirxan: the crystallisation of the idea of Kurdistan as a separate realm.

The fact that the Ottoman administration carried out punitive campaigns against Bedirxan also supports the hypothesis that he intentionally followed strategies aimed at establishing Kurdistan as a realm. Mîr Bedirxan's political activities, including his crimes, seem to be initiated by him for a clear purpose, and they were not mere reactions to Ottoman reforms (which, back then, were mostly about reforming the army and passing some laws on the equality of Ottoman subjects). Indeed, Bedirxan's actions and those of the other Kurdish rulers were not simply in defence of something in the face of reform; rather, they were actions intended to further their political standing and political gains. As Verheij notes, the Egyptian defeat of the Ottoman army at Nizip in 1839 encouraged Bedirxan and other Kurdish leaders to "reinforce their independence from the Porte [the capital Istanbul] (2014, 2)," which is a much different political strategy than protesting reforms.

Additionally, administrative centralization and bureaucratizing taxes came after Bedirxan's defeat. Bedirxan was known as a *mutesellim*—tax collector (Aboona 2008; Özoğlu 2004), who was authorized to collect taxes in his area of rule. If the Ottoman reforms, aimed at stripping Bedirxan of his political and fiscal privileges, if the centralization policies had affected Bedirxan before 1847, the year in which he was defeated militarily, would he still be titled as *mutesellim* until that year? Bedirxan held this title when he "punished" the Assyrians, because he was "a Turkish official with the duty to subdue those who resisted the sultan's rule", as he told a British author who interviewed him about the massacres (Aboona 2008, 234). Now, if Bedirxan was indeed a government officer, it would not be necessary to seek evidence proving the involvement of the Ottoman state. Since Bedirxan was autonomous in his emirate, British sources looked for a connection that tied the Ottomans to the massacre, in order to provide London with leverage over the sultan. Otherwise, Bedirxan would have been charged and tried as an ordinary criminal, not as a politically autonomous emir who enjoyed certain privileges. It looks like the Ottoman state took this episode as an opportunity to eliminate the latest autonomous entity in Kurdistan, using Bedirxan's activities as a "legitimate" pretext. Otherwise, there would have been no legal ground for them to do this as

> In [. . .] autonomous principalities, succession to rulership remained within the family, even when for some reason the incumbent ruler was deposed by the central government. Government interference in such principalities took the form of recognizing one member of the ruling family rather than another. Kurds had total fiscal, judicial and administrative autonomy over their region and applied their customary laws over disputes between their members. In return, Kurds had a duty to provide soldiers and military supplies to the central government when the Ottomans entered any war. According to Van Bruinessen, Kurdish customary laws were in use and the authority of the Kurdish qanunname was maintained by Kurdish rulers, tribal and religious leaders until the beginning of the 19th century. (Tas 2014, 511)

Now, although an absolute monarchy, it was not in the interest of the Ottoman state to antagonize all Kurdish rulers by taking away their titles and privileges without any grounds to legitimize those actions. Additionally, the Ottomans were reforming their army and it would have been unreasonable for them to lose their closest allies in the east, who had been invaluable in restraining Iran. Zürcher notes that with the destruction of the Janissary (*Yeniçeri*) corps in 1826, the Ottoman state did not have an effective army for twenty years; that the administrative reforms were applied only in several provinces close to the capital; that the Ottomans reformed the administration system to include a modern bureaucracy only after 1860s; and that while new laws and tax regimes were introduced as early as 1840, they did not abolish the old ones (2004, 39–46). Most importantly, it was not Kurdish emirs who actually resisted the reforms introduced by the sultan, but the Ottoman intelligentsia (*ulema*), the Muslim majority, and the "reformist groups of bureaucrats" (2004, 67–69). There is no mention of reaction or resistance initiated by Kurdish notables until the 1860s, because, with the exception of the introduction of a new taxing system, the reforms did not curb their power. As mentioned earlier, the old taxation regime was restored due to the failure of the new one. Zürcher suggests that the system of "tax farming" was not replaced by a system of direct collection of taxes until the end of the nineteenth century, and that 95 percent of taxes were collected indirectly (2004, 59–60). Given this timeline, it seems that "punishing" Bedirxan for his crimes against the Nestorians just shortly before the administrative reforms of the 1860s proved to be a useful pretext for the sultans to end self-rule in Kurdistan. Bedirxan's crimes provided the Ottomans with the British support as well.[12] The Ottomans were also provided with domestic support from Bedirxan's peers and rivals in Kurdistan, who saw this time as an opportunity to escape his ambitious and dominating leadership; thus, the Ottomans were granted domestic "legitimacy" in their abolition of self-rule in Kurdistan.

In some historical accounts, it appears that something pushed Bedirxan to "deal" with a "potential source of instability," a Christian minority, which could endanger his dominance through inviting and inciting European intervention (it is not clear what "it" was, although Aboona claims that it was religious fanaticism). This attempt to wipe out the Assyrian minority shows that the Kurdish political leadership started toying with the idea of an independent Kurdistan long before the Ottoman and Turkish states persecuted Kurds. Now, whether that was a nationalist undertaking in the modern sense or not is another problem, but it is clear that the idea of a Kurdistan ruled by Kurds has been there for a longer time than suggested by historians of nationalism. In short, the idea of consolidating a realm called Kurdistan among Kurdish rulers precedes punitive Ottoman assaults on Bedirxan and the abolishment of autonomous emirate system in Kurdistan.[13] This idea was already present among the Kurdish intelligentsia, but it became manifest in certain political acts and projects only in the nineteenth century. Hakan Özoğlu already points at this dynamic in the formation of early Kurdish nationalism, and underlines the fundamental importance of the geography, the *homeland Kurdistan,* in the formation of Kurdish identity and the formulation of Kurdish political aspirations—nationalist or non-nationalist: "The role of territory in the process of identity formation has always been very crucial. This is a very significant fact in understanding the nature of early Kurdish nationalism, which demanded the self-rule for the Kurds in their historic homeland of Kurdistan" (2004, 42).

However, I would not be as certain about the "territoriality" of this geography as Özoğlu seems to be. Kurdistan as a territory would have differing borders for different actors, but as an idea, it makes sense for those who identify themselves as Kurds. That is why politics in Kurdistan has always been fragmented: borders of Kurdistan depend on who is drawing them and which Kurdistan one has in mind—e.g., a greater Kurdistan that includes four parts of larger Kurdistan, or a partial one that relates to one part of the country in each of the four nation-states of Iraq, Iran, Turkey, and Syria; a Muslim Kurdistan or a Kurdistan with Êzidis[14]/Yezidis and Christian minorities; a Kurdistan that includes some portions of former Western Armenia; or a Kurdistan without any settlement of former Armenia.[15]

Kurds seem to have been the initiators of the Armenian massacres of 1894–1896 in Kurdistan as well. We see no political figure such as Bedirxan in this case who designs and executes policies single-handedly; however, there was a systematic harassment and persecution directed at Armenians of Sassoun (*Sason,* a town in Batman province in Kurdish majority South-East Turkey-Northern Kurdistan), including land-grabbing, plundering, and massacring of tens of thousands, carried out in concert with and at the hands of their neighbours, the Kurds (Payaslian 2007, 120–21). Although Payaslian points out that those horrific deeds were not carried out only in Kurdistan, but in all Armenian settlements of the East, Southeast, and South Anatolia, we cannot blame the Ottoman administration for the deeds in Kurdistan because none of them were carried out by Ottoman military forces. The infamous Hamidiye Alaylari (*Hamidiye Regiments*)[16] carried out the whole persecution, and they were the beneficiaries of the plunders and land-grabbing. Klein (2007) notes that the head of those irregular corps were threatened and arrested by the new government formed after the proclamation of the Ottoman constitution in 1908. Thus, fearing to lose what they had "amassed" in the last two decades, they organized various activities in protest of the new government in towns and cities of Kurdistan. The corps was disbanded and many were charged with serious crimes (Klein 2007).

Consequently, it is imperative to balance the state-centric perspective we have seen working so far in the context of Kurdish politics. The relationship of Kurdish rulers with the Ottomans and the Turks has more often than not been a symbiotic relationship of utility and convenience. The historical fact at hand is that the Kurds were not passive victims and the Ottoman/Turkish State has not always been their oppressor. The Kurds took initiative when they saw fit, and they often used the State to achieve their own ends, as the State used them for its own. In the relationship between the Kurds and the Ottoman state, one has to be careful not to put the State at the centre of all developments and deny agency of the Kurds and their leaderships. Countless examples and cases like the ones I have given above can be presented, but I think these will suffice for my purpose here.

The Alliance against Another Common Enemy in the Twentieth Century

The most important period of modern Kurdish politics was the turning point during the years 1919 to 1923. In this period, the majority and most influential members of the Kurdish nobility preferred to seal their destiny with that of the Turkic population of the Ottoman Empire, represented by the Anatolian Movement led by Mustafa Kemal (1881–1938, the founder of the Republic of Turkey). Zürcher notes that "By and large, the Kurds supported the resistant movement, despite the efforts of British agents to influence them and despite the fact that they were granted autonomy under the Treaty of Sevres" (2004, 170). A choice such as this is very telling about the state of Kurdish politics in the period following the First World War. There has been no doubt about the loyalty of the Kurds during the war. However, the post-war period is a completely different story, since there emerged an opportunity for the Kurds to obtain a state of their own, or at least to gain political autonomy, and the majority opted for a union with Mustafa Kemal and his movement. For instance, Kirisci and Winrow note that 22 delegates out of 56 present at Erzurum Congress, in which Mustafa Kemal started to organize the resistance, were Kurds (1997, 79). More importantly, Şerif Paşa (Sharif Pasha, 1865–1951), a Kurdish general in the Ottoman army and a diplomat, presented a map of Kurdistan in Paris Peace Conference in 1919 and lobbied for establishing a Kurdish state. Nevertheless, conservative Kurdish leaders protested against him and sent telegrams to Paris, in which they said Şerif Paşa and his friends did not represent the Kurds (Özoğlu 2004, 112).

The main reason for such a stand taken by the conservative and rural Kurdish leaders, was that the map Şerif Paşa presented at the conference took some disputed towns and cities from the Kurds and they were "given" to Armenia (Özoğlu 2004). Apart from that, Kurds were involved in the Armenian genocide of 1915[17] and they clearly feared facing political and legal consequences: tribunals, compensation, and the return of Armenian properties looted during and after the genocide would probably be initiated if Paşa's map and plans were accepted (Ketsemanian 2013; Kurt 2015). The conservative Kurds were afraid to lose too much if they did not unite with Turkish nationalists.

As it is obvious from this and other examples, Kurds were not just passive victims of or reactionaries to state policies, but they were active and influential actors who made choices and shaped their own destiny, at least until the establishment of the four nation-states that partitioned Kurdistan. What happened after the establishment of those states is a different matter. What I established here, I believe, is the fact that it would not be fair to give so much credit to states and picture Kurds as reactionaries, radicals, and "primitive" ethno-nationalists who only respond to State policies through violent means, in an incompetent and unsuccessful way, as most of the current literature suggest. The Kurds, up until partition, were always involved as the agents of the development and evolution of Kurdistan.

DISTINGUISHING BETWEEN
POLITY AND POLITICAL COMMUNITY

If the first misunderstanding about Kurdish politics is adopting state-centric perspectives that deny agency to the Kurds, the second misunderstanding follows from the first one: that the Ottoman polity was a single political community, when, in truth, the Ottoman polity encompassed numerous political communities. Distinguishing polity from political community helps us to separate administrative units from a community that has a political identity and a political and/or legal status; i.e., one that enjoys a degree of autonomy as a political entity. Administrative units are arranged hierarchically and the ultimate authority within the polity has no need to further legitimize reforms and re-arrangements in the bureaucracy—at least so long as it observes the rule of law or does not appear to be operating arbitrarily. But when a change is made to the status of a political community, further justification is needed. Also, the legitimation of the new order will take some effort, because when the status changes, the source of authority is shifted. This determines who gets to make the important decisions about and for the community. Therefore, even with further justification and legitimation under way, it is unusual that the prerogatives of rulers in and the status of a political community is revoked by the central authority without dispute, conflict, and even war.

For example, the *Sadrazam* was the second man in the Ottoman Empire. Coming after the sultan, he was the head of the executive cabinet, the equivalent of prime minister. He was appointed by the sultan and tasked with executing imperial laws and decrees. His rank was higher than any other ruler or bureaucrat in the Empire. Nevertheless, since he was appointed by the sultan, he could be relieved of his duty and his title could be revoked by the sultan, without further justification other than the sultan's order. On the contrary, the rulers of Kurdistan were not appointed by the sultan; they inherited their title and privileges from their ancestors and the source of their authority was their leadership and prominence within the community they ruled. Certain decisions were at their exclusive discretion. Even the sultan would not interfere with how they arranged their affairs in Kurdistan. Kurdish rulers took their authority to rule not from the sultan, but from the communities they represented in Kurdistan (Reynolds 2007). Although they needed to be on good terms with the capital, the sultan's approval was not constitutive, but had the effects of recognition. Hence, Kurdistan was not only an administrative unit of the Ottoman Empire, but it had a distinct political identity with its own customs, laws, and rulers (Kuehn 2011). It is important to emphasize that although the administrative unit of Kurdistan within the Ottoman Empire overlapped, at times with Kurdistan as a political entity, Kurdish identity was never absorbed into a common Ottoman identity.

Political Communities in Ottoman Kurdistan

I will not get into a discussion of the specifics of the political structure in the overarching Ottoman Empire as my focus is Kurdistan. It is suggested that "a separate political geography has been formed in its [Turkey's] Southeast" (Akkaya and Jongerden 2015, 185). This indicates that historical dynamics laid the ground for the emergence of this "separate political geography". For instance, for most of the previous millennium, the rulers of Kurdistan maintained varying degrees of autonomy in different forms. Indeed, there has always been a distinct or "separate political geography" in the Southeast of Turkey since the twelfth century, although that geography ceased to be officially named and recognized as *Kurdistan* in Turkey since the 1920s.[18] Its borders and boundaries have shifted and changed throughout history and thus have been contested, but Kurdistan has nevertheless been a historical reality. Starting with the rule of the Great Seljuq Empire (1037–1194), continuing through the Timurid (1370–1507), Safavid (1501–1736), Ottoman (1299–1923), Afsharid (1736–1796) and Qajar (1785–1925) dynasties, Kurdistan appears either as a political geography that was home to more than several semi-independent emirates, as an autonomous administrative unit, or as a province (Barkey and Fuller 1998, 5–7; Özoğlu 2004, 48–52; Aboona 2008, 160).

Historically, Kurdistan, as a politico-geographical entity, first appeared in the twelfth century during the reign of the Great Seljuq ruler Sultan Sencer (Aboona 2008, 95: Özoğlu 2004, 26). Aboona notes that while the Kurds inhabited and controlled the mountainous region of today's north-western Iran, which they managed to establish as an administrative unit in the Great Seljuq Empire through allying themselves with the Seljuqs, they were able to stretch their control over parts of Armenia and Assyria (Upper Mesopotamia) after allying themselves with Timur, who became the dominant power in the Muslim World in the fourteenth century (2008, 96). However, this does not seem to be a plausible historical analysis, since, according to Özoğlu (2004) Kurds had enjoyed their golden age in the tenth and eleventh centuries, long before any protection or support was granted them by the Great Seljuqs and other regional powers emerging after them. Indeed, the arrival of the Seljuqs and Mongols weakened Kurdish political entities. Kurdish dynasties such as Marwanids (990–1096), Shaddadids (951–1174), and Rawadids (955–1071) were dominating the geography called Kurdistan during the eleventh century. The Ayyubid Dynasty (1171–1341) emerged in the twelfth century, indicating a noteworthy Kurdish political existence in Kurdistan long before the emergence of the Seljuq, Mongol, Safavid and Ottoman powers, whom the Kurds forged alliances with, and often shifted those alliances in order to maintain or advance their political prominence in Kurdistan (Özoğlu 2004).[19]

Kurdish dynasties did not survive the Turkic invasions of the twelfth century nor the Mongol invasions of the thirteenth century (with the exception of a fraction of the Ayyubid Dynasty in today's Syria). Nevertheless, Kurdish rulers were able to maintain autonomous emirates and principalities through their alliances with Timurid, Safavid, Afsharid, Qajar, and Ottoman powers from the fourteenth until the mid-nineteenth centuries. The most renowned of those emirates were "The emirate of Baban (region of Sulaimania), the emirate of Soran (Rawanduz), the emirate of Bahdinan (Amadia), the emirate of Botan (Jazerah)," and "the Kurdish section of the emirate of Hakkari" (Aboona 2008, 160). Thus, a persistent cycle of various forms of Kurdish political establishments appeared to be a significant dynamic in Kurdistan for the whole of the last millennium.

As previously discussed, there were autonomous, semi-independent Kurdish emirates until the second half of the nineteenth century, and the basis of Ottoman-Kurdish cooperation was an alliance against a common enemy. This brought Kurdistan under the Ottoman rule, but imperial rule is not the same as the establishment of an alliance with a single political community with its own political identity. On the contrary, Kurdistan, Egypt, Yemen, and other regions kept their distinct political identity intact while joining the Ottoman Empire. This separated them from one another as well as gave them autonomy in local matters, although the Ottomans occasionally tried to establish a unified legal system (Kuehn 2011).

The *nation* as a single political community is a European construct and there are deep and far-reaching contradictions in applying that notion to the Ottoman context. Jalki points out that in the context of pre-modern India, European concepts and political principles do not apply, and that

The practices of empire in the two worlds were as different as their principles. No imperial formation arising in the Sanskrit cosmopolis ever stationed troops to rule over conquered territories. No populations were ever enumerated. No uniform code of law was ever enforced anywhere across caste groupings, let alone everywhere in an imperial polity. No evidence indicates that transculturation was ever the route to imperial advancement in the bureaucracy or military. (Jalki 2013, 2–3)

Likewise, a uniform code of law was never enforced in the Ottoman era, apart from two short-lived constitutional experiences of 1876 and 1908, which still allowed different regimes of law (Tas 2014); and no troops were stationed in Kurdistan, because it was not a conquered realm. Kurdish political establishments of the Ottoman era are now named as *confederacies*, a socio-political category defined by Richard as "heterogeneous in terms of culture, presumed origins and perhaps class composition, yet [. . .] politically unified, usually under a central authority" (quoted in Özoğlu 2004, 45). Özoğlu notes that "The main difference between the tribes and confederacies, therefore, appears to be heterogeneity, class composition, and leadership. The confederacy is formed usually when a strong leader seeks to control a larger territory at the expense of his local competitors" (45). Therefore, Kurdish confederacies in the form of emirates and principalities were political communities in their own right. A number of Kurdish political entities enjoyed a high degree of political autonomy, including keeping an army of their own and collecting taxes, under the administrative status named *hükümet*[20] (*government* in Turkish) until the mid-nineteenth century. Thus, they qualify as distinct political communities within the larger Ottoman polity.

Did Centralization Attempts of the Nineteenth Century Ottoman Empire Create a Single Political Community?

Ottoman sultans introduced a set of modern laws and institutions, reformed the army, and modernized bureaucracy in order to increase the efficiency of taxation and administration. The objective was the optimization of the fiscal system through collecting direct taxes in order to finance increasing military expenditures, creating a bureaucracy that was directly accountable to the sultan, and tightening its control over the periphery. Some of the reforms were carried out under the pressure of European powers with regard to the legal status of non-Muslim communities. For instance, a penal code was introduced in 1843, and then a commercial code followed in 1850. These were the first steps taken towards "modernization/rationalization" of the legal system, arguably to ensure equality of all Ottoman subjects before the law (Zürcher 2004, 61). The judicial system, nevertheless, maintained its dual character in the sense that for Muslims, family law was based on Islamic law, *Sharia,* and non-Muslims retained their autonomy in terms of applying their own laws in matters pertaining to family and trade. Even specific tribunals existed for settling judicial matters of commercial cases of non-Muslim traders (Zürcher 2004). Thus, these early reforms did not end up in achieving their objectives: installing a universal legal system that would transform subjects with varying statuses and rights into citizens who were equal in status, rights, and dignity. In fact, Zürcher points out that the nineteenth century reforms in the Ottoman Empire led to the institutionalization of secular ideas among the Ottoman *millets* (non-Muslim communities) due to the effects of the French Revolution, and that each of them ended the power monopoly of churches (2004, 62). This was followed by the establishment of nationalist organizations. This widened the rift between the subjects, and between the subjects and the political authority. Kurds as well maintained their customs and procedures with

regard to settling disputes among themselves, although they did not create
any specific codification as non-Muslim communities did:

> Ottoman millet practice reflected the multi-ethnic, multi-religious and multi-
> linguistic social and economic realities of the Ottoman Empire. In modern-day
> terms, it supported both territorial and non-territorial autonomy. As Kasaba
> points out, as more and more different ethnic and religious communities came
> under Ottoman rule, the weakness and selectivity of the centralised system meant
> that each group was allowed to carry out their customs. When contemporary
> researchers like Inalcık, Demirağ and Kenanoğlu choose to focus on only a few
> of the non-Muslim groups in the Ottoman Empire—the Jews, the Armenians and
> the Greeks—they seem to see the Ottoman millet practice as one limited in the
> same way in which Turkish leaders claimed during and after the Treaty of Laus-
> anne (24 July 1923). In this way, the groups that were not accepted as worthy of
> notice by Turkish leaders in Lausanne—including Kurds, Assyrians, Alevi and
> Yezidis—are again airbrushed out of history. (Tas 2014, 502)

Ironically, the attempts to centralize administration and consolidate political
power at the capital in the nineteenth century did not bond together different
ethnic and religious elements within the Ottoman society. On the contrary, it
induced sentiments of national "emancipation" within certain groups. Thus,
multiple political communities persisted throughout and until the collapse
of the Ottoman empire. Even the two constitutional proclamations of 1878
and 1908 failed to create a shared identity among the subjects of the empire
and the multiplicity of political communities remained until the collapse of
the empire in 1919. Now, although the Kurds did not organize around such
nationalist ideas and did not establish nationalist organization as early as the
Armenians and the Balkan nations (the Greeks already gained independence
in 1824), they maintained their distinct and separate sense of being: "Yeğen
agrees that the pluralistic Ottoman solutions and flexible legal system helped
Kurds to maintain their separate identity" (Tas 2014, 511). In order to speak
of the Ottoman Empire as a single political community, multiple political
communities should have merged with one another and given rise to a single
entity; this simply did not happen.

On the one hand, although religion has always been considered to be the
glue that bonded the Kurds and the Turks together, we see that as soon as
their common enemy vanished from the scene, no sense of solidarity surfaced to hold them together as a political community. On the contrary, a
competition prevailed between the sides immediately after the collapse of the
Ottoman Empire (Zürcher 2004, 170). The last time that the two sides had
had a common enemy was the three year period from 1919 to 1922 in the
aftermath of the First World War, in which three factors made cooperation

between Muslim Turks and Kurds inevitable: (I) the ongoing occupation of European powers in Kurdistan and Turkey; (II) the fear of an Armenian state that included some cities and towns in today's Eastern Turkey, as promised in Paris Peace Conference in 1919; and (III) the fear and probability of legal proceedings and ensuing indemnifications with regard to the Armenian genocide, including the possibility that Muslims might have been forced to return the plundered Armenian properties. Those who amassed a great wealth and power during the Armenian genocide saw that a united front between all Muslims of the collapsed Ottoman state was the only way to keep what they had taken. Nevertheless, even during the War of Independence, fought under the leadership of Turkish nationalists, three Kurdish leaders opposed the Anatolian Movement and fought the forces of Mustafa Kemal. Two of them aimed for the foundation of a Kurdish state, inspired by the Treaty of Sevres, while the other was more interested in winning a local dispute (Kirişci and Winrow 1997, 79–81).

On the other hand, Kurdish political communities in the form of emirates, as mentioned in the first section, endured until the 1850s. What I mean by political community in this book is very close to what Stack formulates: "[O]ne whose members accept (in some sense) the claim of institutions (of some kind) to govern many (or even all) dimensions of their lives in their name, giving those institutions (some kind of) authority over other entities to which members belong" (2017). There is one aspect of this formulation that I do not agree with: that "members *accept*". It shall suffice to say that the acceptance or consent of members of a political community is not at all an inherent characteristic of a political community. In all political communities there are members who do not accept the claim that they belong to that political community. Hence, they resist and challenge the claims that they are part of this or that political community just because they happen to live in a certain territory under the control of a political authority. Even members that do not accept such a claim are forced to comply with rules and regulations. Also, it does not matter if members are represented in political institutions or if they are able to participate in political processes. The political authority will still govern in the name of members, or in the name of god, or in the name of some other sources of authority.[21] I would argue that just as sovereign territorial states, nations-states, kingdoms, and empires are political communities, so are self-ruling, autonomous political entities. The recognition of other actors is not constitutive to the foundation of a political community, but externally legitimizing. In sum, the Ottoman polity was an aggregate of political communities with distinct laws and customs. This is something that is still praised by historians.

The Transformation of *Millet* from Being a Religious Community within the Ottoman Empire to *The Nation* in the Republic of Turkey

How were sub-state political entities within the Ottoman Empire eliminated and the Ottoman polity came to designate a single political community? During the Ottoman rule, *millet,* now understood and translated as *the nation* in Turkey, was used to designate a community of faith (Genc 2013). This is why the *Millet System*, a term that refers to the commended "religious tolerance" within the empire, was named thusly: *millet* simply referred to Christian and Jewish populations of the Empire. Turks, Arabs and Kurds belonged to the Muslim core of the empire (Arakon 2014). The *Millet System* basically acknowledged the right of non-Muslim communities to implement their own laws with regard to civil matters, while the State was known to belong to the core, i.e., the Muslims. Non-Muslims would not be assigned to bureaucratic, military or political posts, but in principle, Muslims of all ethnic origins had equal access to public offices.

The rise of nationalism and the ascendance of Turkish nationalists to power in 1913 changed the whole dynamics: now, the State was designated as "Turk" (Bardakci 2015). The Treaty of Lausanne, signed in 1923, recognized the "Turkishness" of the new State and the non-Muslim minorities within it, but the rest of the population were designated as "Turkish citizens." Yeğen (2007) notes that after the foundation of Turkey, the Muslim population within its borders would be called Turks and expected to assimilate into Turkishness. Poulton (2001) quotes new leaders of Turkey, whose public statements revolved around the theme that the State belonged to the Turks only, and those who do not identify themselves as Turks can only hope to be servants. Consequently, the term *millet* that used to designate all Muslim subjects of the empire was now referring to Turks, Turkish, and Turkishness.

These efforts to *racialize* the State in the early years of the republican Turkey equated political community with the territorial (nation-)state. Thus, the term *millet* ceased to be a multi-ethnic composition that included all Muslims. It was transformed into a supposedly homogenous Turkish community with common linguistic, ethnic, and cultural particularities. The non-Turks who happened to be trapped within the borders of the new state, including the communities designated as minorities in the Treaty of Lausanne, ceased to be political categories altogether.

This interpretation, largely a misunderstanding, was the outcome of the ideological effects of Turkish nationalism. This formulation of political community ignores the fact that Kurdish or Greek political communities did exist during Ottoman rule. It assumes that polity is the same thing as political community. This misunderstanding is informed and influenced by early taxonomies of nation-building and nationalism, in which two categories of nationalism, namely *civic* and *ethnic* nationalism, are identified as two main trajectories of nationalist movements. As pointed out in the introduction to the book, civic nationalism has been affiliated with liberal political communities, while ethnic nationalism is affiliated with cultural communities (Smith 2000, 6–7). Likewise, Turkish nation-building has been labelled as *civic*, thus the Turkish nation is thought to refer to a civic political community. Kurdish nationalism, on the other hand, has been labelled as *ethnic*; therefore, Kurds are referred to as a cultural community. The taxonomy has contributed to the perception that the Kurds were not able to form their own state, are not a distinct people, and Kurdistan was never home to autonomous political communities.

The Nationalization of the *General Will*

Theoretically, the decisive transformation happened through the nationalization of the *general will*. Orhan (2014) notes that the founding fathers of the Republic of Turkey, and particularly Mustafa Kemal, were influenced by Rousseau's formulation of popular sovereignty, although he argues that Mustafa Kemal did not agree with Rousseau on the idea that the executive should be subordinate to the legislative. Orhan also refers to the widely accepted view in Turkey that the concept *milli irade* (national will) was coined after Rousseau's general will (2014, 216).

In Rousseau's political theory, the general will refers to the direction the State should take. For Rousseau, the State is established for the purpose of delivering the *common good*, and it is only the general will that should guide it: "the general will alone can direct the State according to the object for which it was instituted, i.e., the common good" (*The Social Contract,* Book II, Chapter I). How and when the general will emerges is the key here. The general will is not the will of all, according to Rousseau: "There is often a great deal of difference between the will of all and the general will; the latter considers only the common interest, while the former takes private interest into account, and is no more than a sum of particular wills" (Book II, Chapter III). Also, the will of a particular faction, say a political elite or a political party, no matter how legally or democratically elected or selected they are, is not the general will:

[W]hen factions arise, and partial associations are formed at the expense of the great association, the will of each of these associations becomes general in relation to its members, while it remains particular in relation to the State: it may then be said that there are no longer as many votes as there are men, but only as many as there are associations. The differences become less numerous and give a less general result. Lastly, when one of these associations is so great as to prevail over all the rest, the result is no longer a sum of small differences, but a single difference; in this case there is no longer a general will, and the opinion which prevails is purely particular. (Rousseau 1762, Book II, Chapter III)

This is because the general will cannot be represented by a faction or an individual, and the sovereign is no one other than the collective being, i.e., the whole assembly of citizens present and gathered at the agora. That is why the institution of the parliament serves the nationalization of the general will: "I hold then that Sovereignty, being nothing less than the exercise of the general will, can never be alienated, and that the Sovereign, who is no less than a collective being, cannot be represented except by himself: the power indeed may be transmitted, but not the will" (Rousseau 1762, Book II, Chapter I).

The general will "must be general in its object as well as its essence; that it must both come from all and apply to all" (Book II, Chapter IV). Here we are provided with a clue with regard to where the general will comes from. It does not come from a council of representatives or from elected members of a political party, but it comes from all. Likewise, it is not the prerogative of any council or body to make laws that are binding for all citizens, because "it can no longer be asked whose business it is to make laws, since they are acts of the general will" (Book II, Chapter VI). To be more precise then, the general will emerges when the people is assembled. What happens when the general will is nationalized is this:

As the particular will acts constantly in opposition to the general will, the government continually exerts itself against the Sovereignty. The greater this exertion becomes, the more the constitution changes; and, as there is in this case no other corporate will to create an equilibrium by resisting the will of the prince, sooner or later the prince must inevitably suppress the Sovereign and break the social treaty. This is the unavoidable and inherent defect which, from the very birth of the body politic, tends ceaselessly to destroy it, as age and death end by destroying the human body. (Rousseau 1762, Book III, Chapter X)

The implication of such a political establishment is that a representative assembly (and even the executive, when conditions are met or arranged) acts in the name of the people, thus assumes and enjoys a certain degree of political legitimacy. But what actually rules is a *particular will*. In other words, the representative assembly or the government gains and maintains an unrivalled, unchecked and uncontrolled power, and sees fit to subjugate those who resist such a rule, because the formulation of a "national will," coined after the general will, allows "that whoever refuses to obey the general will shall be compelled to do so by the whole body. This means nothing less than that he will be forced to be free" (Book I, Chapter VII). This was a problem during the Kemalist dictatorship, as it is now under the rule of the incumbent president Recep Tayyip Erdogan, who invokes the same principle. The purpose of invoking the notion of national will and succumbing to nationalism as a means to delivering *common good* or pursuing *national interest* is obvious:

> [E]very class which is struggling for mastery, even when its domination . . . postulates the abolition of the old form of society in its entirety and of mastery itself, must first conquer for itself political power in order to represent its interest in turn as the general interest, a step to which in the first moment it is forced; . . . the practical struggle . . . makes practical intervention and control necessary through the illusory "general interest" in the form of the state. (Abrams 1977, 71)

For Turkey's President Erdogan, the national assembly is the embodiment of the national will. Those who oppose the rule of the governing party and disapprove of public policies should speak only after defeating the ruling party in the polls. Therefore, when the ruling party and the president address critics who have been concerned about his authoritarian rule:

> Erdogan viewed elections as the sole instrument of democratic legitimacy, and as a result overemphasized the importance of the institutions of representation to the detriment of the institutions of constraint. This fetishism of the "national will" led to majority rule but proved inimical to democratic progress. A related and equally important challenge is the government's ability to tolerate dissent. When leaders identify themselves with the national will, almost every form of opposition, whether violent or nonviolent, tends to be viewed as an illegitimate attack on the elected government. (Ulgen 2014, 2)

The same goes for the Kemalist administration in the 1920s and 1930s, in which a long process of reforms or "revolutions" followed the foundation of the Republic of Turkey in 1923, though its effects still haunt Turkish politics. This era undermined the only common ground on which the Kurdish political elite could meet the Turkish elite: common enemies. Like every political elite, the new Turkish republican elite had to ground their rule on either territorial bases or political identities to include and exclude. As most scholars of Turkish nationalism agree, the new elite based their rule on a political identity, that is *Türk Milleti* (the Turkish Nation), and this category has ethnic Turks at its core (Cagaptay 2004; Özdoğan 2010). It also eliminated the sole medium between the state and ordinary Kurds, or Kurdish citizens of the new state, which previously tied the Kurds to the State through a weak bond comprised of intermediary actors: the nobility and the clergy. Thus, the marginalization of non-Turkic communities in Turkey, including the Kurds, has been justified on the premises of popular sovereignty that is equated with *national will*.

The Effects of Imposing a Single Political Community in Turkey

The Kemalist modernization has been labelled as a success story (Kirişci and Winrow 1997, 78–79), although it has absolutely failed to integrate the Kurds as equal citizens of the imposed political community, i.e., the Turkish nation. It is also questionable whether it is a success story or not, because the Turkish state made use of all institutional and organizational mechanisms to create a single political community since 1913, including committing a genocide and resettling non-Turkish and non-Muslim populations in order to homogenize the population (Akcam 2014). Nevertheless, it failed to integrate the Kurds into the *Turkish* political community. The Kemalist state also did not allow the Kurds to form their own political community, thus leaving them in limbo, making conflict and violence inevitable and persistent.

Charismatic religious leaders emerged stronger after the elimination of Kurdish political entities during the last decades of the Ottoman rule, and took over the role of promoting Kurdish interests (Bruinessen 1980; Aytar 2014). However, in the republican era, Kurdish political and cultural expressions were banned *in toto*. The elimination of Kurdish political leadership, the ban on Kurdish culture, language, and identity, however, did not integrate the Kurds into the Turkish political community. Instead, the Kurds have been alienated by the Turkish state, thus creating a common political identity that includes the Kurds remaining as the greatest challenge for political actors in Turkey.[22]

Hamelink and I have argued elsewhere that in the Kurdish vernacular and oral literature "the state appears as a foreign force":

> Social practices like the reluctance and even resistance to being incorporated in the spheres of state influence, the inclination to avoid being ruled, regulated, taxed, conscripted, and contained by formal state borders, could all be seen as deliberate attempts to keep the state at a distance. For instance, switching sides between imperial powers was a frequent practice for local rulers who occupied the margins of the empires and crossing state borders has been a common practice for the Kurds who live in borderlands. Many Kurds have grown up hearing stories of outlaws, bandits and ordinary peasants, who used to take shelter in the mountains of Kurdistan to escape state laws and obligations. These topics also emerged in the kilams[23]. We suggest that these social and political practices of most Kurds until the 1930s is a testimony to their determination to escape the control of the (nation-)state. (Hamelink and Baris 2014, 56–57)

Our arguments regarding the "distance" between the state and its Kurdish citizens were based on an extensive data analysis done by Hamelink on Kurdish folk poets, singers and storytellers, the *dengbêj*. In her analysis of more than a hundred songs, stories, and poems she collected in Kurdistan, Turkey, and Europe, Hamelink notes that frequently, protagonists like "outlaws" and "fugitives" appear as heroes in Kurdish collective memory (2014, 96–121). Apart from taking to the mountains or getting killed in the skirmishes with the government, many protagonists would appear to have crossed the border to pass mostly into Syria, Iraq or Iran, to be among their brethren on the other side of the border and to settle there (2014). Hamelink's research and her analyses of the extensive data show that the State mainly appears as a hostile figure, to say the least, in Kurdish collective memory and folk-art.

I must add that not much has changed since the 1930s, with regard to the distance between the Kurds and the Turkish state, although this period is not our focus. The Kurds neither have a political community of their own in Turkey, nor have they fully developed a genuine bond with the existing political community; thus, they are still in a political limbo. The idea that "the state belongs to the Turks" defies, at least in the context of democratic politics, the fundamental political principle that the State is supposed to belong to every individual living within its boundaries or it must belong to *nobody* at all. Otherwise, universal citizenship is a false promise (McGarry, O'Leary, and Simeon 2008). Additionally, focusing only on states, underestimating or dismissing other forms of political community, and overlooking the choices individuals and groups make marginalizes those without a State.

Hence, it is crucial to bring the element of *choice* to the foreground. It is important to note that evading the State and opting for the fragmentation of political power has often been the choice of Kurdish political elite. Most recent research suggest that compared to independence, a high degree of autonomy (i.e., fragmentation of sovereignty) is still a more popular choice among the Kurds in Turkish Kurdistan (Yeğen, Tol, and Çalışkan 2016). Therefore, stateless-ness has also been a choice in Kurdistan. I will dwell on this in the following section.

KURDISTAN, THE *STATELESS HOMELAND* AND THE HOMELAND OF *THOSE WHO CHOOSE STATELESSNESS*

"You should get to know these mountains. [. . .] Each of them is a shelter for a people that does not own these mountains, but have chosen to belong to them" writes Temo, a Kurdish scholar and poet (2013, 1). This is a powerful and ample capture of the imagination of *Kurdistan* which has never become a politically "recognized" homeland; and yet, a homeland it is. Temo's lines resonate with a short but powerful statement from Gellner: "Divide that ye be not ruled" (Gellner, cited in Scott 2009, 9).

I grew up listening to a story that did not strike me much at the time. My father, who was born in 1925, is a *dengbêj*, and he occasionally tells a story that explains the statelessness of the Kurds with their "failure" to unite under one leader and pursue statehood. It is a story about the famous Kurdish leader, Cemîlê Çeto,[24] who was set to fight the Kemalist movement in 1920s. It was at a moment when he sees an opportunity to call upon foreign powers and obtain their support for founding a Kurdish state. He meets the leaders of seven tribal confederacies in Kurdistan of Turkey and claims that he can bring France's air force to their help in seven days. Only he insists that a leader, either himself or someone else, who will represent the Kurdish coalition internationally and negotiate with the French, must be chosen. Emînê Ahmed,[25] one of the leaders present, stands up and says that he will never relinquish his title or give his father's legacy away to bow to anyone else. Others follow suit.

According to the story the chance to establish a Kurdish state was missed because of the lack of unity among Kurdish leaders, and never has such an opportunity presented itself again.[26]

The story did not strike me until recently. Then I read that Îdrîs-î Bîdlîs-î had advised almost the same thing to Sultan Selim (I) five centuries ago, when he asked which Kurdish nobleman he should appoint as the ruler of Kurdistan. He intended to choose one of the thirty Kurdish nobles as the ruler of Kurdistan (Özoğlu 2004, 49). But Idris advised him not to do so, as "they are all more or less equal, and none of them will bow his head before any other." The similarity between the two historical moments, despite a half millennium of time between them, is very striking. One cannot possibly assume that it is just a coincidence or a random course of events. It therefore occurred to me that what seemed to be a "failure" could have been a deliberate and conscious choice, since choices, not coincidences, have the quality to repeat themselves almost identically in history. The appealing theme in the story and the historical account is that they make room for the element of choice. We see a continual reluctance or rejection to bow before a higher political authority, a preference to remain local and small in scale, and a tendency to stay autonomous. Modernist-nationalist discourses have long suggested that it testifies to the fact that the Kurds had been the victims of their own premodern (read *backwards*) socio-political organization and primordial (read *primitive*) traditions (see Yavuz 2001).

Yet, it should come to no one's surprise that an alternative interpretation is possible:

The forms that many people identify as primitive and traditional were often creations responding to, and sometimes mirroring, more complex systems. Beck adds: "Such local systems adapted to and challenged, or distanced themselves from, the systems of those who sought to dominate them." Social structure, in other words, is, in large measure, both a state effect and a choice; and one possible choice is a social structure that is invisible and/or illegible to state-makers. (Scott 2009, 210)

Although this is not a mainstream understanding of freedom and independence in the era of nationalism, it is clearly no less valuable as a line of thought. The rationale is that once one bows to a higher authority it does not matter if this authority is foreign or familiar; it is still domination and subordination.

This section argues that the fact that the Kurds have no nation-state of their own cannot be explained by sheer failure on the part of Kurdish nobility, but the element of deliberate choice to avoid and evade the state is also involved. It does so by highlighting historical moments and socio-political phenomena which demonstrate that the Kurds did not only resist incorporation in state structures when they were pressured to do so, they also avoided state formation *per se* for most parts of their history from the sixteenth to the twentieth century; be it in the sense of escaping foreign domination or in the sense "to prevent states from springing up among them" (Scott 2009, X). Even though such an understanding of Kurdish history may seem unconventional, I think many scholars have already cleared the path toward this conclusion. Drawing on Scott's work, *The Art of Not Being Governed* (2009), I argue that the Kurds have preferred to keep the state at a distance and to remain loyal to sub-state social and political structures. Apart from the literature, this section is also based on Hamelink's research on the *kilams* (recital songs) of *dengbêjs* (folk poets). These *kilams* strengthen the view that the Kurds had a distanced relationship to the idea of the state, and that the borders of nation-states were not seen as legitimate by many Kurds.

I will start with a short discussion of Scott's thesis, and then give some historical examples to apply his thesis to Kurdish politics. I continue with main arguments that address the Kurdish history of evading and avoiding the state as a deliberate choice and a stateless conception of self-rule. This is not an attempt to prove that even the "uncivilized" are "civilized," but to challenge the entire discourse of "progress" and "civilization" that puts the state or nation-state at the core of socio-political organization and political activism.

Scott's main thesis in *The Art of Not Being Governed* is that

[H]ill peoples are best understood as runaway, fugitive, maroon communities who have, over the course of two millennia, been fleeing the oppressions of state-making projects in the valleys—slavery, conscription, taxes, corvée labor, epidemics, and warfare. Most of the areas in which they reside may be aptly called shatter zones or zones of refuge. Virtually everything about these people's livelihoods, social organization, ideologies, and (more controversially) even their largely oral cultures, can be read as strategic positionings designed to keep the state at arm's length. Their physical dispersion in rugged terrain, their mobility, their cropping practices, their kinship structure, their pliable ethnic identities, and their devotion to prophetic, millenarian leaders effectively serve to avoid incorporation into states and to prevent states from springing up among them. (Scott 2009, ix)

These "hill peoples" are inhabitants of the region called "Zomia," a vast area in South-East Asia with high altitude that used to make physical access difficult for valley states. They needed manpower to produce, maintain, and expand domination, which was difficult to accomplish in the highlands. Those who wished to "keep the state at arm's length" would therefore deliberately settle in the less accessible zones. Scott's thesis is important because "it shatters the common view that those living outside the nation state are primitive and uncivilized" (Coyne 2010, 1, 4). However, for Scott, this is not only a matter of a hierarchical dichotomy between highland *people* and lowland *civilizations*; it goes much deeper than that. The thesis is also a general criticism of associating civilization and progress with forming states and regarding sub-state political structures as uncivilized or backward. Scott argues that the old imperialistic missions of "civilizing" or "Christianizing" are carried out under the flag of "development," "progress," and "modernization" (2009, 98–102).

There are several criticisms directed at Scott's thesis. A well-known set of arguments is that he over-generalizes his insights, that he chooses his examples from areas that fit his hypothesis, and that he is too dependent on secondary literature written in English (Sadan 2010; Subrahmanyam 2011). Sadan stresses that Zomia was of central importance in Van Schendel (2002) not as a region, but as an intersection between regions or areas of study (2010, 5–7). She argues that "borderlands and process geographies" are ignored by Scott. She also adds that the peoples that Scott focuses on are those who are either "peripheral" or "invisible" in the history books of their neighbours, and thus points out the need to incorporate "oral history" or "oral tradition" of those peoples in order to account for epistemological shortcomings.

Scott's Relevance for the Kurds

Historically, a state with the name *Kurdistan* has never existed. The largest political structures that were formed in the geographical territory called Kurdistan today were several Kurdish principalities under Ottoman and Persian rule, and a province named *Kurdistan* that existed for most of the last millennium in the margins of both empires. Scholars have provided a number of geographical, social, and political reasons that prevented the Kurds from forming a state of their own. The most common one is that Kurdistan is a mountainous country, a rough geography, which makes it extremely difficult for a single political entity to gain a substantial control over the entire region. A well-known idiom suggests that "even Alexander the Great couldn't bring this region under his rule." This rugged geography, it is further argued, also prevented the formation of a collective social identity, a standard language, and the development of a shared goal among Kurds. However, Scott reverses this argument by stating that "the mountains as a refuge for state-fleeing people, including guerrillas, is an important geographical theme" (2009, xi). Likewise, Kurdistan has also functioned as a refuge for many. Due to the rugged terrain that allowed no easy access, the Kurds maintained their presence in this region despite many invasions and long centuries of foreign rule.

Another dominant theme is that the Kurds did not develop a national consciousness and a national unity among themselves, and thus could not build a state of their own. However, social practices like the reluctance and even resistance to being incorporated in the spheres of state influence, the inclination to avoid being ruled, regulated, taxed, conscripted, and contained by formal state borders, could all be seen as deliberate attempts to keep the state at a distance. For instance, switching sides between imperial powers was a frequent practice for local rulers who occupied the margins of the empires. And crossing state borders has been a common practice for the Kurds who live in borderlands. Many Kurds have grown up hearing stories of fugitives, bandits, and ordinary peasants who used to take shelter in the mountains of Kurdistan to escape state laws and obligations. Hamelink (2014) has shared her analysis of songs and stories of the *dengbêjs* in which we witness the protagonists pass borders, not like they travel from a country to another one, but like they remain within the same country. I argue that these social and political practices of most of the Kurds until the 1930s is a testimony to their determination to escape the iron clutches of the (nation-)state.

Although Scott limits the options available to the people who escaped subordination to either absorption or resistance (2009, 130), the Kurdish population under the threat of the Safavid and Ottoman empires in the sixteenth century neither resisted through military confrontation nor fled, nor were they absorbed or assimilated. The Kurdish notables adopted a third strategy: they played the two empires against each other and maintained their autonomy in the margins of political and military powers far more superior then themselves. Scott also points to such a strategy later on, when he states: "when nonstate peoples (aka tribes) face pressures for political and social incorporation into a state system, a variety of responses is possible. They, or a section of them, may be incorporated loosely or tightly as a tributary society with a designated leader (indirect rule)" (2009, 210). It must be highlighted that the indirect rule in the case of Kurdish emirates characterized a high level of autonomy. As Ateş (2013) and Özoğlu (2004) have demonstrated, the authority of the rulers in Kurdistan was not interfered with by the Ottoman sultan and they maintained hereditary privileges like ownership of the land and succession. The administrations of the least accessed territories were named *hükümet*s (governments) and behaved accordingly: "The *hükümet*s did not have the *timar, zeamet*, or *has*. They neither paid taxes to the Ottoman state nor provided regular military forces to the *sipahi* army" (Özoğlu 2004, 57). Ateş emphasizes the same phenomenon when he notes that "apart from the requirement of doing battle and combat with the heresy-embracing 'redhead' they were freed from all obligation to pay extraordinary impositions (*tekalif*) and autonomy was granted to them over their ancestral lands (*odjak*) and homes (*yurt*)" (2013, 32).

This helps us to understand two important things. First, the Kurds have played their role in shaping the course of events in Kurdistan, and are thus not mere victims of historical developments. Second, the existence of *hükümet*s that had a high level of internal political organization demonstrates that the Kurds did not lack the characteristics attributed to other social and political groups around them. This defies the argument that they are second to categorically superior groups called nations.

Additionally, when the Ottomans implemented modern reforms aimed at centralizing political power and therewith gravely diminished Kurdish autonomy, we see that Kurds followed two trajectories to resist the state. The first one was uprising against those policies. The other strategy was that they developed new structures and forms of social organization. The Ottomans had eliminated Kurdish aristocracy and destroyed political autonomy in Kurdistan by the mid-nineteenth century. The power vacuum was filled by Dervish/Sufi orders, because the Ottoman state had yet to develop a modern form of citizenship which could replace feudal political loyalties. But more importantly, the state had nothing to offer to the Kurds, because they had already re-organized themselves around religious orders, just when the power of Kurdish emirates started to fade away.

While Ateş (2013) and Özoğlu (2004) demonstrate that the autonomy of Kurdish emirates diminished substantially after the seventeenth century, Van Bruinessen (1998a) refers to the ascendance of Sufi orders and religious sects in Kurdistan almost at the same time span. When we put the pieces together, we see that the moment that Kurdish political autonomy was restricted, there appeared an increasing activity of religious orders, which is culminated in the outbreak of the Sheikh Ubeydullah Uprising in 1880. This uprising is important because it was the first Kurdish resistance that was not organized by Kurdish aristocracy or nobility against Ottoman attempts to centralize political power in Kurdistan. Sheikh Ubeydullah Nehrî was not a Kurdish aristocrat, but a well-respected cleric of a Sufi order known as the Nakşibendi. In this context, it must not be surprising to see that Scott refers to the same dynamics as a strategy of defying or evading the state:

> The Ottomans, in the same vein, found it far easier to deal with structured communities, even if they were Christians and Jews, than with heterodox sects that were acephalous and organizationally diffuse. Most feared were such forms of autonomy and dissent as, for example, the mystical Dervish orders, which deliberately, it seems, avoided any collective settlement or identifiable leadership precisely to fly, as it were, beneath the Ottoman police radar (Scott 2009, 209–10).

Here, we see a clear agency that chooses and/or creates local structures of political organization alternative to larger state-structures, even when classical political forms are not available.

Freedom as Evading the State

Kurdistan as an administrative unit existed as early as the fourteenth century. Kurdishness as an identity and Kurdistan as a country clearly appear, with boundaries and clans, in the fifteenth century (Özoğlu 2004, 26–32). Ehmedê Xanê, the famous Kurdish cleric and author, stressed the desire of those who would like to see a united Kurdish kingdom as early as the seventeenth century, in the introduction of his epic Mem and Zin (*Mem û Zîn*) (26–32). Although they were incorporated in larger state structures, their own customs, traditions, and social practices preserved the Kurds from being totally absorbed by the State. In that sense, Belge's analyses take us to the heart of the point:

> Kinship networks thus enabled a variety of resistant acts that cumulatively undermined the state-building project. First, they served as networks of information and trust accessible only to the locals, regularly disrupting law enforcement. Second, contacts in the lower-level bureaucracy enabled local society to manipulate crucial records on population, land ownership, and marriage, creating a problem of legibility and posing important challenges for the institutionalization of state law. Third, state officials who were sent from outside the region were occasionally absorbed in the local moral order and began to act according to local rules, favoring "kin" and ignoring the commands from above. On the ground, then, quotidian conspiracies rendered the boundary between state and society fuzzy, undermined the state's infrastructural power, and impeded state rationality and order from deepening its hold over the imagination of citizens. (Belge 2011, 105)

Fragmented social and political structures and the absence of a centralized political authority in a society, as Bruinessen (1992) emphasizes, may indicate
a tendency to remain out of the direct control of the state. Although Kurdish tribes have frequently formed and still form alliances with the state, this
mostly serves them to gain more power in the competition with their rivals
or to preserve their power and autonomy. It does not necessarily suggest that
they are absorbed by or incorporated into state structures.[27] Kurds are loyal,
Bruinessen (1992) argues, not to an ethnic group, a nation, or a state, but the
chief loyalty is that of local characteristics, owed to tribal chieftains (*Agha*)
and charismatic religious leaders (*Shaikh*). The (psychological) remoteness of
the Kurds to the institutional existence of the idea of the state is a dominant
theme in Bruinessen's work. One example of this is the word *binxetê*, the
word used by Kurds in southeast Turkey to refer to Syria. It means "below the
line," referring to the railway passing through the region. In Kurdish vernacular, Syria was thus not seen as a different country, but as the lands "below the
railway line." Also the continuous illegal border crossings of Kurds living in
these borderland zones show that they do not recognize the border as a legitimate structure. Crossing these artificial state borders is a daily phenomenon
for those who live near borderlines. They are preserving relationships with
their relatives across borders, they trade with each other and marry their sons
and daughters to people at the other side. Belge stresses that "The ease with
which Kurds crossed the border undermined the government's efforts to institutionalize borders as containers of discrete nations" (2011, 101).

Furthermore, those practices are not just anachronistic strategies that belong to almost a century ago. There are contemporary forms of such socio-
political activities. Anyone who grew up in a Kurdish village or city will re-
call that conflicts are mostly solved by a local "judicial" mechanism. Sheikhs
and mullahs invoked sharia law, and local notables customary law. What
they avoid to do is, for sure, to invoke the state and its courts. Additionally,
we see that legal or illegal institutions of Kurdish political movement take
upon themselves the role of arbitration and judiciary, a role that is generally
performed by a sovereign. As journalist Irfan Aktan stated (my translation),

> The Kurds, at the time being, handle their judicial conflicts on their own. The
> judicial commissions of the BDP (Barış ve Demokrasi Partisi-Peace and De-
> mocracy Party), who were labelled the "parallel state" and became the target of
> crackdowns and police operations against the KCK (Koma Civakên Kurdîstan-
> Kurdistan Communities Union), were indeed a traditional way of Kurdish
> peace-making "without invoking state institutions." Although belittled, the
> aşiret system used to provide the Kurds with principles and mechanisms of jus-
> tice that are necessary for any social organization. (*Radikal* 22 December 2013)

The aforesaid social and (a)political practices, on the other hand, also became the ground of a self-orientalist conception, especially in 1990s in Turkey, which implied that the Kurds have not yet developed a sense of nationhood, and that they are not politically mature enough to form a nation. "You cannot convince me that the Turkish nation (*Türk Ulusu*) and the Kurdish nationality (*Kürt milliyeti*) are equal" (my translation), said Birgül Ayman Güler.[28] The statement puts "Kurdish nationality" in a secondary rank as a political category, vis-à-vis the "superior" one, the "Turkish nation." What made the difference was, clearly, mastery over a territory in the ownership of a sovereign state. This self-orientalist understanding had become the grounds for some Kurdish nationalists to blame their ancestry of lacking national consciousness as well. Here, we see a clear link between the ages-old colonialist/modernist discourses that imposed dichotomies of civilized-uncivilized, modern-backward, developed-undeveloped, and the nationalist tendency to rank and hierarchize peoples on the basis of having or not having a sovereign state.

However, there surely are ways of political activism free from the dichotomy of sovereignty and statelessness; and resistance to political centralization reflected in the practices outlined above is one of those ways that conceives of political autonomy in evading the state. As Arendt suggests, "If it were true that sovereignty and freedom are the same, then indeed no man could be free, because sovereignty, the ideal of uncompromising self-sufficiency and mastership, is contradictory to the very condition of plurality. No man can be sovereign because not one man, but men, inhabit the earth" (1958, 234). Therefore, in the case of the Kurds, the tendency toward remaining autonomous could testify to a notion of freedom as the will to evade the state. In other words, not having a state of their own and not trying to found one until the early twentieth century, might, after all, just be an alternative vision of freedom.

In conclusion, the Kurds did not only resist incorporation in state structures when they were pressured to do so, they also prevented "states from springing up among them" (Scott 2009, x) for most parts of their history from the sixteenth to the twentieth century. Forming alliances with states, remaining small in scale but choosing autonomy over subordination to one another, taking refuge in the mountains to escape state domination, crossing borders with little regard to their legitimacy when needed, and forming internal judiciary mechanisms are all strategies of keeping the state at a distance in Kurdistan.

Although mainstream nationalist discourses in Turkey and academics in Kurdish studies often suggest that statelessness is an indication of the lack of national consciousness on the part of the Kurds, this section tries to provide an alternative interpretation of political fragmentation in Kurdistan. The Kurds prioritized self-rule and local autonomy; and they deliberately avoided being incorporated into larger state structures, due to a different political culture and a different understanding of freedom, not because of an inferior collective consciousness.

NATIONAL LIBERATION BEYOND NATION-STATE AND WITHOUT A CLAIM TO NATIONAL SOVEREIGNTY

The Eurocentrism Embedded in "National Consciousness"

Hegel followed Herder in saying that "human culture is evolving" (Ebenstein and Ebenstein 2000, 626), and that the Europeans, particularly the Germans, are leading this evolution. Thus, for Hegel, there appears to be a "natural division":

> World history is the progress of the consciousness of freedom—a progress whose necessity we have to investigate. The preliminary statement given above of the various grades in the consciousness of freedom—that the Orientals knew only that *one is* free, the Greeks and Romans that some are free, while we know that all men absolutely, that is, as men, are free—is at the same time the natural division of world history and the manner in which we shall treat it. (Hegel 1953, Part III)

I quoted Hegel above because his formulation of self-consciousness was later used by his fellow national, Weber, who argued that the nation is "a community of sentiment which would adequately manifest itself in a state of its own" (Weber 1994, 25). Coupled with the tendency represented in Hegelian thought that perceives history as a river flowing progressively from the past to the future, and thus ignoring multiple and diverse socio-political worlds existing simultaneously and interacting with one another, the praise for nations and nation-states created a hierarchy, in which the nation becomes the ideal political community and the nation-state is the ideal political organization. Weber's definition that nation is "a community which normally tends to produce a state of its own" (Weber 1994, 25) became a standard in politics, inspiring states to create their nations and nations to found their states. I do not mean that it so happened because Weber defined nations as such. What is meant here is that the idea that history is taking a progressive course, that some nations and/or states lead the way and the rest have to catch up with them, are represented in Hegelian thought as well as in the Weberian formulation of nation, and that these two views have set the standard for political activism. Think the opposite: not showing the tendency to have a state of its own automatically marks a society as the one that *lacks* national consciousness, and thus, a community is less than a *nation,* in its development and evolution. In Dirlik's words:

> It is the burden of the past in one form or another that marks a society as traditional, which impedes its ascent to modernity. In spite of radical challenges, including challenges from intellectuals from non-European societies, that assert that modernity and tradition, or development and underdevelopment, may be different aspects of the same historical process, the conceptual isolation of the one from the other (of a developed "inside" from an undeveloped "outside") persists not just in popular consciousness but in intellectual work as well. (Dirlik 1996, 100)

The views referred to above have become norms in political thought and activism in Turkey. The idea that the Turkish nation has developed national self-consciousness before other peoples or ethnicities is the core assumption that the political establishment in Turkey holds. Average Turkish politicians and statesmen are convinced that the Turks became nationally self-aware earlier than the Kurds and that this enabled them to found a nation-state, while the Kurds were bogged down in pre-modern socio-political structures, and failed to develop such a national consciousness early enough. This perception or view, more or less, is represented in academia as well, as I discussed in previous sections. However, the Turkish nation was created by the State, not the other way around (see Gellner [1983] for a discussion on *state-nations*). Therefore, "it is not surprising", in Zeydanlioglu's words, to see that "the state is imagined in Turkey through the familiar and familial image of the Father State (*Devlet Baba*)" (2008, 5). Ethnic, cultural and religious minorities, especially those like the Kurds who have no state of their own, have been looked down upon for these reasons.

Also, we should remember that nationalism grew out of biopolitics and racism in Europe, which are the products of governmentality and colonialism (Foucault 2008, 2009; Isin 2012). The "success" of racist/colonial European powers inspired the Ottoman and Turkish policy-makers, as well as the modernist Kurdish nationalists to follow the path of the European political elite. Ottoman and Turkish politicians and statesmen often referred to the European examples in order to justify their nationalist and racist policies. For instance, an Ottoman nationalist intellectual, Hüseyin Cahit Yalçın, and a statesman, Cemal Paşa, were certain that there was no future for the Ottoman and the Turkish state unless they succumbed to European examples of nation-building:

> We are bound, whether we like it or not, to Europeanize . . . Ibn Khaldun's philosophy of history belongs to the infantile age of the science of history. Since then, the child has grown; he became a boy in Germany; he even grew

> to old age . . . The modern science of history is to come from Europe not from
> the Arabs. . . . I am primarily an Ottoman, but I do not forget that I am a Turk,
> and nothing can shake my belief that the Turkish race is the foundation stone of
> the Ottoman Empire . . . in its origin the Ottoman Empire is a Turkish creation.
> (Tas 2014, 514–15)

This is political homogenization and reductionism, a process that ends up
with producing a sovereign nation after purging, cleansing, assimilating,
or ignoring the undesired, unruly, unfitting, or unwelcomed socio-political
groups. Thus, perceiving cultural, religious, linguistic, and ethnic plurality
as a threat to the well-being of the nation and to the stability of the state is
the end-product of this process. The Armenian genocide and the denial of the
existence of the Kurds in late Ottoman and early republican Turkish polities
are testimonies to the effect of such formulations of European nationalism on
the Ottoman and Turkish politics.

State-making and nation-building is not the work of a group of people
who have developed a national consciousness. Quite the contrary: on the
one hand, states have been built by political elites through war-making and
racketeering, as Tilly (1985) suggests. On the other, as it is suggested by
Foucault (2008), the nation is not a construct of self-conscious peoples, but
the end-product of governmentality and population management. With regard
to nation-building, the following argument has no ground: "[T]he linguistic
and cultural communities of peoples, having silently matured throughout the
centuries, emerge from the world of passive existence as peoples (*passiver
Volkheit*). They become conscious of themselves as a force with a historical
destiny. They demand control over the state, as the highest available instrument of power, and strive for their political self-determination" (Renner, cited
in Hobsbawm 1990, 101).

The emergence and development of nationalism cannot be explained
through such linear and progressive courses of history in which peoples,
one by one and one after another, obtain a kind of self-consciousness that
enable them to master their own fate. Hobsbawm and Gellner have written
extensively with regard the incorporation of language and ethnicity in nation-
building in the late stages of nationalism. Although they realize that German
and Italian nation-states made use of them earlier than other nation-states and
nationalists (Hobsbawm 1990); and despite the fact that a certain language
and culture plays role in the formulation of nationalisms, individual members
of the *folk* who speak that language and practice that culture are hardly ideal
nationalists (Gellner 1983). In an excerpt from *Nations and Nationalism,*
Gellner stresses that not the *folk*, but either the state or the elite of a "high
culture" is the agent that builds (invents) nations:

[N]ationalism is not the awakening of an old, latent, dormant force, though that is how it does indeed presents itself. It is in reality the consequence of a new form of social organization, based on deeply internalized, education-dependent high cultures, each protected by its own state. It uses some of the pre-existent cultures, generally transforming them in the process, but it cannot possibly use them all. [. . .] Nations as a natural, God-given way of classifying men, as an inherent though long-delayed political destiny, is a myth; nationalism, which sometimes takes pre-existing cultures and turns them into nations, sometimes invents them, and often obliterates pre-existing cultures: *that* is a reality, for better or for worse, and in general an inescapable one. [. . .] It is nationalism which engenders nations, and not the other way around. [. . .] The basic deception and self-deception practiced by nationalism is this: nationalism is, essentially, the general imposition of a high culture on society, where previously low cultures have taken up the lives of the majority, and in some cases of the totality, of the population. It means that generalized diffusion of a school-mediated, academy-supervised idiom, codified for the requirements of reasonably precise bureaucratic and technological communication. It is the establishment of an anonymous, impersonal society, with mutually substitutable atomized individuals, held together above all by a shared culture of this kind, in place of a previous complex structures of local groups, sustained by folk cultures reproduced locally and idiosyncratically by the micro-groups themselves. That is what *really* happens. (Gellner, cited in Hutchinson and Smith 1994, 63–65)

Tilly, Abrams, and Bourdieu also powerfully emphasize that state-making is also not the work of a people or a nation. Tilly compares protection rackets to the State, and argues that to a certain extent, governments create the threat and provide the protection against the threat they generate (1985, 185). Protection rackets are "in the same business" of offering or imposing protection against a threat of their own making. Apart from the comparison above, Tilly also traces the act of modern state-making "a few centuries" back in order to shed light to the processes after which a state is built or made. Historical evidence and convincing arguments laid down throughout the article point to a very clear and conclusive argument about the way states are made. According to Tilly, the figure of state-builder and the figure of war-maker are so close to one another that it would not make sense to look for the origin of states elsewhere. The state is the end product of war, and the small scale of such activity is organized crime:

At least for the European experience of the past few centuries, a portrait of war makers and state makers as coercive and self-seeking entrepreneurs bears a far greater resemblance to the facts than do its chief alternatives: the idea of a social contract, the idea of an open market in which operators of armies and states offer services to willing consumers, the idea of a society whose shared norms and expectations call forth a certain kind of government. The trimmed-down argument stresses the interdependence of war making and state making and the analogy between both of those processes and what, when less successful and smaller in scale, we call organized crime. War makes states, I shall claim. Banditry, piracy, gangland rivalry, policing, and war making all belong on the same continuum—that I shall claim as well. . . . (Tilly 1985, 169–70)

Tilly also emphasizes that states and governments do not rely on or derive their power from the consent of the governed, and that what distinguishes a government from the organized crime is its monopoly over the means of violence (1985, 171). Thus, he argues, although theorists like Machiavelli and Hobbes attributed legitimacy to the regimes or sovereigns who had a monopoly over means of violence, that does not mean that the monopolized force or violence is legitimate, but it could be justified at best (a similar argument is put forward by political philosopher John Simmons (1979) as well). Tilly suggests that the need for legitimizing political power arises in the later phases of monopolising power and means of violence, and that in the early stages of state-making in Europe, there was clear, close connections and relationships between bandits and state-makers (1985, 172). He also notes that in the early stages of state-making, state-makers, bandits, and pirates alike had the right to use and resort to the idea of using violence (1985, 173). The bottom line is that states, especially European nation-states so envied by all state-makers, were not made by peoples or nations, but by self-serving warlords. With the help, support and assistance of bandits and pirates; otherwise, "Why else all the legitimation work?" as Abrams (1977, 76) asks.

Abrams (1977, 67) and Bourdieu (1999, 55) argue that studies on the State end up either taking the State "for granted" or "constructing," reconstructing, and reproducing the idea of state. Abrams refers to Engels's argument that "the state is brought into being as an idea in order to present the outcome of the class struggle as the independent outcome of a classless legitimate will", and concludes that

> The state, then, is not an object akin to the human ear. Nor is it even an object akin to human marriage. It is a third-order object, an ideological project. It is first and foremost an exercise in legitimation—and what it being legitimated is, we may assume, something which if seen directly and as itself would be illegitimate, an unacceptable domination. Why else all the legitimation work? The state, in sum, is a bid to elicit support for or tolerance of the insupportable and intolerable by presenting them as something other than themselves, namely, legitimate, disinterested domination. (Abrams 1977, 76)

Herman and Chomsky (2002) argue that state propaganda, media and communications, subliminal messages delivered through entertainment, literature, and cultural codes and practices, schooling, and socialization are "manufacturing consent". This should have something to do with "the legitimation of the illegitimate" *a la* Abrams. The means and processes mentioned in Herman and Chomsky are useful means of producing compliance. Also, as Mitchell (1991) notes, mundane practices grant the State a range of spheres and processes to inscribe itself on and take a firm place in the human world as well as in the human mind.

The ways in which political authority is legitimised or justified are neither the focus of this section, nor of this book. The point of the discussion presented so far in this section is about arguing that state-making is not the work of a people or of a nation. Therefore, explaining the statelessness of the Kurds through their supposed failures or backwardness, or through their relatively late modernization, is not an accurate analysis. Modernization, developing national consciousness, and knowing or understanding freedom and liberty are irrelevant with regard to analysing and explaining the condition of statelessness in which the Kurds and many other societies are living.

Additionally, since the territorial state as well as the nation is a European construct, there are deep and far-reaching contradictions in applying a progressive and comparative logic to explain and analyse political traditions and activism in Asian, American, and African contexts in general, and in Ottoman-Kurdish context in particular. The political elite elsewhere in Asia and Africa have also aspired "to catch up with Europe," and those who did, like Japan, colonized wherever their power and ambition took them. Others such as China, Indonesia, Turkey, Syria, and Iraq suppressed minorities within their territories in order to build "homogenous" nations—as if such a thing exists. Though many Western powers returned to political decentralization after the Second World War, this mode of political thought and organization is still dominant in Turkey and many other Asian and African countries. One also has to keep in mind that no empire or colonial power, neither in Europe nor elsewhere, has ever obtained their "might and riches" through enviable means.[29] Likewise, nation-states too have left no exemplary trajectory to be emulated either by idealist visionaries in pursuit of "emancipation" or by "liberation" movements set to "deliver people(s) from domination." Therefore, the global order dominated by nation-states is not the apex of civilization in political organization. The fact that some "liberation" movements have not aimed at founding their own nation-state cannot and should not tell us anything about the level of their political "consciousness" and "maturity."

The Eurocentric idea that the origin of "the Kurdish Question" and the reasons for the statelessness of the Kurds lie with the centralization of political power in the nineteenth-century Ottoman Empire and the homogenization and assimilation attempts of the Republic of Turkey is a widely shared explanation, and wrongly so. This perception or formulation is too state-centric and renders the choices made by the Kurdish political elite and the common Kurds irrelevant. Looking at the statelessness of the Kurds from this perspective makes political communities other than the State disappear from the radar of the researcher and the policy-maker.

In conclusion, there are historical precedents, as well as novel forms of and struggle for stateless political communities in Kurdistan. And those who identified themselves as Kurds made their own history through their choices in the past, as they continue to do so today. These aspects, too, should be taken into account in discussions on the so-called "Kurdish Question" and the statelessness of the Kurds. The choices made by the Kurdish political elite might not have produced a Kurdish nation-state. But that does not mean they failed because they did not follow the path of the European nationalism early enough. It may as well mean that the Kurdish have chosen to act otherwise and preferred not to emulate European and Turkish nationalists. Therefore, it will prove useful to distinguish Kurdish nationalism from Turkish national-ism in order to see the choices of the Kurdish political elite in nuances.

Statist Turkish Nationalism versus Self-Rule-Oriented Kurdish Nationalism

There is no literary consensus as to when modern Kurdish nationalism was born. In general, Kurdish authors tend to stretch its emergence far back to the first half of the nineteenth century, but scholars seem to agree that the Sheikh Ubeydullah Uprising of 1881 was the kernel of modern Kurdish nationalism (Kirişci and Winrow 1997; Bruinessen 2004, 2006; Özoğlu 2004; Klein 2007, 2011; Zagrosi 2016). Those who adopt the official narrative of the Turkish historiography, however, insist that Kurdish uprisings were reactionary rebel-lions of local nobles who opposed modernizing reforms (Zeydanlıoğlu 2008). These approaches give way to two conflicting implications: for the Kurdish authors, Kurds form a distinct nation and have the right to self-determination. For the official narrative, produced by non-Kurds, the Kurds are not nor have they ever been a nation, not only because they have never had a state of their own, but also because they were always "lacking" national consciousness and unity. For the same reasons, the official narrative claims that the Kurds cannot make claims to a nation-state of their own and have no right to self-determination.

The disagreement over whether the Kurds have the right to self-deter-mination or not reflects what nationalism and being a nation has come to mean. The official narrative views Kurdish nationalism as non-existent or unjustified, because of their own interpretations of what a nation is. It relies on the idea that nationalism refers to the efforts of a more or less culturally homogenous community, self-aware of its national identity, set out to found (or having founded) a nation-state of its own in a territory claimed/known to be the historical homeland of the mobilized nation. This is the dominant view in Turkey, articulated as "it was the nation, *increasingly conscious of its existence*, which created, or at least helped to create, the state" (Anderson 1996, 224; emphasis added). This view suggests that the Turkish state was founded by the Turkish nation and the only nation in Turkey is the Turkish nation. Common Turks are proud of their self-image as great "state-builders", not only because school history books and state propaganda define them as such, but also because it is part of collective consciousness. The notion of "Turks the state-builders" has been displayed in prominent symbols of nationhood and statehood. For instance, the insignia of the Presidency is an emblem made of sixteen stars on a red plate with a sun in the centre. The stars symbolize the sixteen states claimed to be founded by Turks throughout history, and the sun symbolizes Turkey. Scholars have pointed out that this is historically inaccurate (Öztürk 2015). Nevertheless, this is now part of the collective knowledge and an important aspect of the "enhanced" self-image in Turkish national identity. The great value Turks place upon state-building completely colours their perception of the Kurds: they consider the Kurds neither as a nation nor as a civilization because they have no nation-state of their own. In this narrative, nationalism does not appear as a political project pursued by political elites, and the nation refers to a conscious state of being of a culturally homogenous group, a self-aware collective.

Here, the aspect of State ownership creates a rift and a hierarchy between groups within a society. The group that claims ownership to the State tends to have an elevated self-image and a sense of superiority, compared to those who have a weaker claim or no claim at all. This is as much about the notion of "national consciousness" as it is about numbers and controlling state institutions and apparatuses. Nations or ethnic groups without a state of their own can be perceived as "unconscious/unaware" of their national identity and "lack" certain qualities. This makes them weaker than or inferior to those who control a State. That is why nationalist elites refer to some of their activities as "raising the consciousness of their people" about their identity, history, or legacy. This is the case particularly in Turkey. Since the Kurds do not have a nation-state of their own, they are referred to, even in the academia, as a heterogeneous aggregate of tribes who are dispersed throughout a mountainous region. They speak a variety of dialects and this makes it difficult for them to develop a common medium of communication and form a collective identity. Hence, they "failed" to build a national identity and develop national consciousness (Yavuz 2001). This makes them less deserving to have a state of their own, and to even claim or demand self-rule, for they neither represent "a civilization," as a former deputy prime minister remarked (Derince 2013), nor do they form a nation. That is why they are not equal with the Turks, as stated in the PM Güler's comment quoted above (see endnote 28). This logic, based on the notion that the nation is prerequisite to nation-state-building, draws a vicious circle: nations have states of their own, Kurds do not; *ergo* Kurds are not a nation; *ergo* they do not deserve to have a state of their own.

Combining this logic with the emphasis on and concern for *raison d'état* in Turkish politics that I briefly dwelled upon in the previous chapter, I conclude that Turkish nationalism is *Statist* in character. This does not change the prevailing view that it demonstrates both *civic* and *ethnic,* and even racist, features (Özdoğan 2010; Xypolia 2016). Statist nationalism sees an essential interdependence between the nation and the state, and does not recognize the existence of one without the other. The suspicion toward and fear of Kurdish political mobilization is connected with this form of nationalism that not only associates the nation with the State, but also holds onto nationalism as a means to preserve the State. Considering that nationalism is "an ideology that places the nation at the centre of its concerns and seeks to promote its well-being" (Smith 2001, 9), Turkish nationalism appears as a very particular form of nationalism as it emphasizes the well-being of the State. Thus, I define it as *Statist* nationalism.

It must be one of the greatest irony of all times that Turkish, Kurdish, Jewish, and Armenian proto-nationalist elite joined together in the CUP (Committee of Union and Progress) in late nineteenth and early twentieth centuries, to prevent the collapse of the Ottoman state and establish constitutional monarchy (Özoğlu 2004; Klein 2007; Zürcher 2010). In rural Kurdistan, the political elite gained power and prestige under the rule of Sultan Abdulhamid II (1842–1918), and opted to support the regime and keep it intact as it was. The urban elite, on the other hand, cooperated with the Turkish nationalists in pursuit of modernization and political, economic and social reform; the ultimate goal was transforming the dying polity into a major European player (Rhys Bajalan 2016; Klein 2007). Nevertheless, neither of these groups desired to establish a Kurdish nation-state. They pursued certain collective and particularistic rights and privileges for Kurdish subjects of the empire but remained loyal to the sultan and the Caliph. Once the new republican Turkish elite grew hostile to non-Turks, the majority of Kurdish nobles parted ways with Turkish nationalists, led first by the urban elite. Though the urban wing of Kurdish nationalists of the early republican era mimicked Turkish nationalism, their agenda remained centred on reforming the whole political establishment in Turkey, the recognition of Kurdish identity, and self-rule in Kurdistan; despite their disinterest in establishing a Kurdish state (Ozkirimli 2013).

These differences make it imperative to distinguish between Turkish and Kurdish nationalisms. The former was transformed into a Statist ideology because its representors and proponents had managed to seize political power and control the state. While Turkish nationalism was developing into a Statist ideology, the latter maintained its orientation toward self-rule, remaining detached from state-building.

Additionally, scholars have found significant similarities in the nationalist and non-nationalist Kurds. Historically, "nationalist Kurds and non-nationalist Kurdists" were loyal to the Ottoman state while pursuing further privileges as elites or demanding certain rights for the Kurds (Klein 2007, 128–148). Most recent historical scholarship demonstrates that Kurdish nationalism during the Ottoman era was hardly about founding a nation-state for the Kurds (Klein 2007; Özoğlu 2004; Rhys Bajalan 2016). Consequently, only a minority of Kurdish political actors could accurately be defined as nationalists who openly advocated for a Kurdish state. Kurdish politics was thus self-rule oriented, not state-centric.

Where Does the Discussion Take Us?

The misunderstandings about Kurdish politics have surfaced, in the process of constitution-making, as components of two perspectives. Those who do not distinguish between polity and political community assume that constitutions can embody social contracts. Thus, they are convinced that a constitutional identity that is inclusive toward Kurds will "solve the Kurdish Question," when in fact, they entirely dismiss the historical precedent of this "problem." Kurds have lived in separate political communities throughout the majority of their history, and they aspire to found new ones in the same mode as before. This perspective could be roughly placed within constitutionalism in Western political theory. Those who do not distinguish between classical state-oriented nationalism and anti-state nationalism of the dominant Kurdish political movement assume that Kurds would settle for a multiculturalist model. They are convinced that if the Turkish state grants cultural or territorial autonomy of some sort this will "solve the Kurdish Question." The dominant Kurdish political movement, on the other hand, has developed a completely different model of political community and promotes it as the ideal prescription. I will dwell on these perspectives and the Kurdish model in the following chapters in order to place them within the contemporary Western political theory.

NOTES

1. Note that Rousseau saw only Corsicans as the ideal, politically mature people who were ready to receive laws; he did not believe that any other country had the same maturity in Europe: "There is still in Europe one country capable of being given laws—Corsica" (*The Social Contract*, Book II, Chapter X)

2. This tendency is strikingly manifest in the scholarship on the "Kurdish Question," which Tezcur also observes: "Martin Van Bruinessen also notes that the role of violence in the Kurdish question is overstated and observes that many Kurdish elites have been willing to be co-opted into the political system and to downplay their Kurdish identity (Van Bruinessen 1999b)" (Tezcur 2010, 3).

3. Arendt's answer to this question is negative: "The authoritarian relation between the one who commands and the one who obeys rests neither on common reason nor on the power of the one who commands; what they have in common is the hierarchy itself, whose rightness and legitimacy both recognize and where both have their predetermined stable place" (1954, 2).

4. "rebel (adj.) c.1300, from Old French *rebelle* "stubborn, obstinate, rebellious" (12c.) and directly from Latin *rebellis* "insurgent, rebellious," from *rebellare* "to rebel, revolt," from *re-* "opposite, against," or perhaps "again" (see re-) + *bellare* "wage war," from *bellum* "war."" Source: Online Etymology Dictionary. Retrieved from http://www.etymonline.com/index.php?term=rebelandallowed_in_frame=0; accessed on 12.05.2015.

5. The Kurdish ruler of Bitlis Emirate, who managed to join thirty odd Kurdish tribal confederacies, gathered an army of almost sixty thousand men, and allied with the Ottomans in 1514 in the battle of Caldiran in which the Ottomans won a decisive victory against the Iranians.

6. *Bitlis* is a Kurdish majority province in modern South-East Turkey (Northern Kurdistan).

7. Of course, this alliance was not between equals and on equal terms, but the main point is that there existed multiple political communities, because Kurdish nobility enjoyed a great level of autonomy in internal political affairs and property inheritance. The Kurdish nobility guaranteed Ottoman protection against the encroaching Shia Iran through this alliance, while the Ottomans stretched their rule across much of Kurdistan, and in this way obtained much more secure eastern borders (Özoğlu 2004, 48).

8. "Sultan Suleyman I (Kanuni) made the following statement: Just as God, be He praised and exalted, vouchsafed to Alexander 'the two horned' to build the wall of Gog, so God made Kurdistan act in the protection of my imperial kingdom like a strong barrier and an iron fortress against the sedition of the demon Gog of Persia . . . It is hoped that, through neglect and carelessness, our descendants will never let slip the rope of obedience [binding] the Kurdish commanders [to the Ottoman state] and never be lacking in their attentions to this group" (Tas 2014, 509).

9. The majority of Turkish sources would not use the title Mîr, meaning prince, since it has political connotations in the context of Kurdistan; thus, Beg/Bey, mean-

ing lord/landlord, is used as a title for Kurdish nobility in general, which is a lower political status and a less politically charged title.

10. Interestingly, while the Ottomans had generally dealt harshly with armed resistance and executed their leaders, they did not execute Mîr Bedirxan but sent him to exile, and continued to pay him and his family from the treasury in order to compensate for the loss of their property in Botan. More interestingly, trials on the amount of the payment continued in the courts until 1930s in Turkey as well.

11. "Ahmed-i Hani (Ehmedi Xani, b. 1651), a Kurdish man of religion and a poet, demonstrated a clear group consciousness when he distinguished the Kurds from Arabs, Turks, and Iranians. In a section titled "Derde Me" ("Our ills") in his well-known epic Mem-u Zin, which was completed in 1695, Hani writes: If only there were harmony among us, If we were to obey a single one of us, He would reduce to vassalage Turks, Arabs and Persians, all of them." (Özoğlu 2004, 31).

12. Foreign support has been a very crucial determinant in the Ottoman and Turkish politics for the last two centuries; especially reformers and revolutionaries had been seeking such a support in order to consolidate their power or to carry out certain policies.

13. This idea appeared among Kurdish intelligentsia long before Bedirxan's initiative. I will dwell on that in section three.

14. The Êzidi people are an ancient Kurdish community that hold a religion different than that of Muslims and the people of the book (*ehl-i kitap*), i.e., Christians and Jews. They have endured more than seventy pogroms and massacres throughout history due to their distinct faith, which is labelled as "devil worshipping" by their neighbors. They live predominantly in northern Iraq and south-eastern Turkey. Most of them have left Turkey though, due to persecutions and discrimination they faced. They drew much attention in the summer of 2014, after the Islamic State militants invaded their villages, towns, and cities, drove them out of their ancient lands in northern Iraq, massacred thousands, and took many others as slaves.

15. For more on this, see a variety of maps of Kurdistan in Özoğlu (2004).

16. An irregular militia corps comprised of Kurdish tribesmen, founded, equipped, paid, armed, organized and encouraged by Sultan Abdulhamit II (1842–1918), to patrol eastern borders with Iran and Russia, but also control a large portion of Kurdish population and keep Armenian nationalist organizations and activities in check in Kurdistan (Klein 2011).

17. Several prominent Kurdish political figures have repeatedly apologized for the involvement of their forbears in the Armenian genocide, the last example being Ahmet Turk, the co-mayor of the city of Mardin in Kurdistan of Turkey. See daily *Radikal*, 17.12.2014, for Ahmet Turks speech and apology: http://www.radikal.com.tr/politika/ahmet_turk_ezidi_suryani_ve_ermenilerden_ozur_diledi-1252968.

18. See Özoğlu (2004) for a lengthy discussion on the origins of the name Kurdistan and where it refers to throughout history.

19. Özoğlu notes that he does not consider the Ayyubid Empire as a Kurdish state, since it was not founded in and ruled from Kurdistan. However, this is a poorly thought argument since, if the sole criterion for naming empires, kingdoms, or states after a people would be whether it was founded in their homeland or not, the majority

of states founded by Turkic invaders would not be named after the Turks, because most of them were not founded in Turkish homeland.

20. "The second kind of administrative variation in Kurdistan, *hükümets*, enjoyed the highest degree of autonomy" (Özoğlu 2004, 57).

21. I think representation is not necessarily relevant to the formation or existence of political community, although it could mark the difference between more and less democratic political communities. It is much more secondary in its importance in this debate, and relates to the ways in which sovereignty is exercised, or the way in which binding decision-making processes work. Representation is a practical solution to the deficit of legitimacy in kingdoms, empires and nation-states. It helps to legitimize a rule, but it has no place in a political community in which all citizens insist on participating in decision-making processes. One can argue that although there might not be a relationship of representation between the ruler and the ruled, rulers still using the idea of representing god's will, representing a certain bloodline, or representing a community should also be counted as representation. In this version of representation there is no authorization granted by the represented, and the representative is not accountable to the represented through legal or political processes, which are the two fundamental properties of a genuine relationship of representation that goes beyond the claim of representation (Bellamy and Castiglione 2013). Although democratic representation has its own flaws and weaknesses, as it is evident in Schumpeter's criticism that "Leaders recruit their electors through charisma or the policy package they offer rather than being authorised by them as their representatives"; or as it is emphasized by Przeworski that "The representative's responsibilities and responsiveness to the represented is no more than a technical mechanism through which the electors express satisfaction or dissatisfaction with the way in which they have been governed or expect to be governed" (Bellamy and Castiglione 2013, 9). Nevertheless, it differs from the claims based on the divine right of the king or those based on inherited privileges like the right of the nobility, in the sense that it allows the represented to express their will through certain institutional mechanisms and political processes.

22. It seems that creating such a shared political identity or introducing common political principles that may establish a bond between the Kurds and the Turkish state depends largely on the work of the Kurdish political elite, as it was the case until the collapse of the Ottoman Empire. What kind of a political model would do that will be discussed in chapter 4.

23. Kurdish folk-songs.

24. The head of the Baxtiyaran tribe of Xerzan, a region in today's Batman, in Kurdistan (the Southeast) of Turkey.

25. He is also known as Eminê Perîxanê, and he was the head of Raman tribal confederacy in Batman.

26. Historical records show that Cemilê Ceto fights the Kemalist leadership in the summer of 1920, after Huseyin Paşa convinces him that a promise to establish a Kurdish state in Turkey was made in Paris Peace Conference, if the Kurds demonstrate the willingness to do so. It is true that Article 64 of the Treaty of Sevres, signed in August 10, 1920, prepared during that conference, makes such a promise.

27. The state has also been receptive to this strategy in Kurdistan, because alliances with tribes might buy their support or neutrality against the ones that are seen as threats. For the state, it might also mean preventing a united front or undermining national aspirations of the Kurds.

28. An MP of the People's Republican Party (*Cumhuriyet Halk Partisi*-CHP) and a former professor of politics at Ankara University. Source: *Today's Zaman*, 24.01.2013.

29. Fanon reminds us that "From all these continents, under whose eyes Europe today raises up her tower of opulence, there has flowed out for centuries toward that same Europe diamonds and oil, silk and cotton, wood and exotic products. Europe is literally the creation of the third world. The wealth which smothers her is that which was stolen from the under-developed peoples. The ports of Holland, the docks of Bordeaux and Liverpool were specialised in the Negro slave trade, and owe their renown to millions of deported slaves." (Fanon, cited in Shringarpure 2014, 9).

Chapter Three

Constitution-Making in the Shadow of the Founding Father

The Majoritarian Premise and the Legacy of Kemalism

This chapter is an analysis of how major political parties address Kurdish political demands in their draft constitutions and why. As noted in the introduction, making a new constitution has been on the agendas of political parties for the last two decades in Turkey, and concrete steps have been taken toward this goal since 2007. A constitutional reconciliation committee was formed in the parliament in 2011, but no end-product emerged after two years of meetings and deliberation. Subsequently, four political parties that have seats in the parliament prepared their partial drafts and submitted them to the parliament in 2013. I examine these drafts with regard to their approach to one of the fundamental issues expected to be addressed by the new constitution: accommodating Kurdish political demands.

The question I try to answer is twofold: do the draft constitutions accommodate Kurdish political demands or not, and what is the main rationale behind the framers' dismissive approach to Kurdish demands in the drafts? The answer will reveal the parameters of integration or accommodation the framers have offered the Kurds in their drafts, and it will elucidate what has informed the framers' choices. This is of paramount importance in the context of this book, because the answer will demonstrate whether the framers are inclined to dismiss Kurdish politics altogether or whether they are keen to accept input from Kurdish political actors. Accepting input from the Kurds depends on whether the framers acknowledge one of the salient characteristics of Kurdish politics I discussed in chapter 2, i.e., the inclination of Kurdish politics toward self-rule and its detachment from state-building. I make this assumption because the framers of previous Turkish constitutions have been reluctant to seek input from Kurdish political actors, and they have approached Kurdish politics with much suspicion. Kurdish political demands have been dismissed altogether because Kurdish politics has been associated with secessionism. In other words, Kurdish politics is still labelled as secessionist, because there has been no input from Kurdish political actors. If contemporary framers follow this logic, the new constitution will take the path of the previous four constitutions and continue the systematic exclusion of Kurds. Indeed, 2017 constitutional amendments did just that. As I argued in chapter 2, secessionism and state-building have not been on the agenda of mainstream Kurdish political movements, but assimilation into Turkishness is not a viable option for this movement either.

Thus, the thesis of this chapter follows from that of chapter 2: since Kurdish politics is inclined toward self-rule in Kurdistan through the coexistence of multiple political communities in Turkey, the new constitution must not impose a single political community nor a homogenous political identity. The fact that previous constitutions have imposed both has been the main impetus for Kurdish dissent.

My examination of the constitutional drafts reveals that none of the three largest Turkish political parties recognize Kurds as a distinct nation or as a minority, and none envisage either self-rule in Kurdistan, or the coexistence of multiple political communities in Turkey. For instance, the drafts of three largest parties define the human element of the State as "the Turkish nation." In practice, this has so far meant an ethnically defined citizenship based on Turkishness and the exclusion of non-Turkish identities, cultures, and languages. The pro-Kurdish political party's draft uses the well-known phrase of "We the People of Turkey," in order to avoid mentioning any ethnic or national identity and excluding those not mentioned. Additionally, the same draft holds that all languages can be used in private and public life, which distinguishes this draft from the others that mention the Turkish language only and define it as "the language of the State." This implies that although the pro-Kurdish party's draft is more inclusive, all of the drafts uphold that Turkey will remain as a single political community. However, the pro-Kurdish party and their draft seem to be too marginalized to make a genuine impact on the end-product of the constitution-making process. If this is the case, Turkey will not only remain as a single political community, but non-Turkish communities and their identities, cultures, and languages will remain excluded from the public sphere.

The constitutional drafts also do not include a formula of self-rule in Kurdistan, Kurdish autonomy, or a legal status for Kurds. Nevertheless, the pro-Kurdish party's draft introduces regionally potent assemblies and reinforces local administrations in a bid to decentralize the exercise of political power. This is meant to allow the Kurdish region to become a political entity and enjoy a degree of self-regulation in the Kurdish-dominated south-east region of Turkey (although there is no specific reference to any region in the draft).

As for "why," I will only provide a few rationalizations of the framers' choices that can be branded as, and gathered under, the category of *the legacy of the founding father*. The founding father set the terms of debate within the constitution of 1924. His conceptualizations and definitions of citizenship, nationhood, sovereignty, minority, nationalism, and constitution-making have played an important role in shaping the framers' approach to fundamental political issues such as the accommodation of diversity, minority rights, and decision-making in general, and Kurdish politics, language, and identity in particular. For instance, the founding father blamed diversity for the collapse of the Ottoman Empire, and thus cultural homogeneity became the cement of national solidarity which would ensure the eternal existence of the new Turkish state. This approach has been adopted by subsequent generations of framers, and the recognition of diversity in constitutions and laws has become taboo in modern Turkish politics. Political parties are not keen to formally recognize diversity because it has now become traditional political thought to consider political diversity as commensurate to divisions and partitions that would lead to the destruction of national identity, and the collapse of the Turkish State. The rhetoric and dream of creating a society that is or can be classless, unified, and homogenous has been on the agenda of Turkish statesmen and politicians ever since the foundation of the Republic. Therefore, formal recognition of political and social diversity is not an easy topic in Turkish politics, and the drafts reflect this uneasiness. It appears that the only option being offered to the Kurds by the drafts of mainstream Turkish political parties is assimilation into Turkishness. The pro-Kurdish political party's draft is much more promising in addressing Kurdish political demands. However, as the 2017 amendments demonstrate it is unlikely that the new constitution will have input from the draft constitution of the pro-Kurdish party.

Thus, the chapter argues that although the founding ideology of Kemalism has lost its tight grip on politics in Turkey, the legacy of the founding father continues to direct policies toward Kurds and Kurdistan, and Turkish framers tend to preserve the legacy of the founding father with regard to political diversity. The framers continue to exclude non-Turks in general, and Kurdish political demands in particular, from their draft constitutions, a practice reminiscent of the policies of the founding father. This means that Turkish framers have not modified their view of and approach toward Kurdish politics since the foundation of the Republic. Kurdish politics was conceived and construed as secessionism by the founders of the Turkish State, and the subsequent generations of framers have adopted this view of Kurdish politics without much modification. This is manifest in the preamble and the first four articles of not only the 1982 constitution, but of the constitutional drafts under examination here. Perceiving Kurdish politics through the lenses of the founding father demonstrates that the framers prioritize preserving the *status quo* when it comes to Kurdish politics.

I will start with a section that contains a discussion on the specifics of constitution-making in Turkey. Analysing the relevant parts of the four drafts will follow as the second section. Finally, I will engage in a discussion on the factors that direct deliberations, influence the choices of the framers, and determine why the drafts of Turkish parties negate Kurdish political demands. I argue that the early republican elite set the terms of debate about Kurdish politics and that this has led to interpretations of certain concepts and principles in political theory that are unique to the Turkish context. This, in turn, discourages contemporary framers from amending the provisions that exclude the Kurds, because these conceptualizations and interpretations are considered to be the will and the legacy of the founding father. I will point out that the eternity clauses in the current constitution are preserved in the first three drafts under examination here. Finally, I will dwell on the concept of *national will*, a modified formulation of the *general will,* which practically functions as the majoritarian premise and enables the ruling elite to suppress and/or ignore minority voices.

THE PROCESS OF DRAFTING THE
CONSTITUTION AND ITS DEMOCRATIC SHORTCOMINGS

The current Turkish constitution was made by a constituent assembly formed by the military junta that carried out the *coup d'état* of 1980. Enacted by a military junta in 1982, the current constitution has never enjoyed a high degree of legitimacy, although it was approved in a referendum. Nineteen amendments have changed more than 110 articles of the current constitution, but this has not modified its authoritarian character. Thus, since the late 1990s, there has been consensus in academia as well as in public opinion that a new constitution should be made. The common concern has been that the current constitution prioritizes the Kemalist ideology over rights and freedoms, and institutionalizes military patronage over democratic politics (Kentel, Köker, and Genç 2012, 2–3).

Admittedly, all constitutions have ideological traits. Nevertheless, even if it is not possible to produce an ideology-free constitution, "democracy demands that the means are available for heightened *popular participation*—one of the basic features of the democratic ideal—to become a reality" (Colón-Ríos 2010, 211). The current Turkish constitution prevents full political participation of citizens through limiting political activism with references to "Kemalist nationalism" and "the indivisibility of the state with its nation" (see the Preamble and Article 14 of the constitution of 1982). Therefore, after decades of military tutelage and top-down sanctioned constitutions, "Turkey has now reached the stage of social and political consensus on the creation of a new Constitution" (Kentel et al. 2012, 3).

Several factors, domestic and international, paved the way to the making of a civil constitution for the first time in the history of Turkish Republic: I) the revival of the economy in the late 1980s and the process of globalization that opened up Turkey to the world and the world to Turkey; II) the emergence of a vibrant civil society in the second half of the 1990s; III) the bid to close the gap between European human rights standards and the poor human rights records of Turkey since it became a candidate country in 1999; IV) the emergence and further development of a strong Kurdish political movement that has been pushing the limits of the current constitution; and finally, V) the consolidation of political power in the hands of a right-wing, conservative, and Islamist political party that has been in opposition to the founding Kemalist ideology.

The first concrete step to making a new constitution was taken in 2007 by the current governing party, the AKP (Adalet ve Kalkınma Partisi-Justice and Development Party). The government tasked Ergun Özbudun, a professor of constitutional law, to prepare a draft that would be the basic text to be negotiated in the national assembly. Özbudun and his team prepared a liberal constitution, but the government did not proceed with the draft. Apparently, they were minding the reaction of the military and the judiciary, traditionally known as the guardians of the *status quo*. The same government's previous attempts to amend certain provisions of the constitution to legalize headscarves in schools was struck down by the Constitutional Court, and their attempt to select a member of the ruling party as the president raised harsh criticisms and even threats from the army, one of the most powerful forces in modern Turkey that had previously overthrown four elected governments in 1960, 1971, 1980, and 1997.

The army's power was curbed after a few hundred high-ranking military officers, bureaucrats, journalists and several other influential or symbolic figures were arrested and tried on charges of attempted military coups against the elected government in 2008 and 2010. These trials, known as *Ergenekon* and *Balyoz,* tilted the balance of power in favour of the government vis-à-vis the army. This process served to weaken the military's powers:

> Following Erdoğan's diluting of the power of the 'deepstate' by what has been known as the 'Ergenekon process,' which has been under way since June 2007 and has led to the arrest of some 100 senior military officers and the subsequent weakening of the role of the military in the political life of the state, the Prime Minister's ability to challenge previous taboos has grown. (Stansfield 2013: 259)

Additionally, important amendments were made to the constitution in 2010 in order to dilute the power of the judiciary. The amendments gave the ruling party and their president the opportunity to appoint judges and prosecutors to key positions in higher courts and boards. The composition and functioning of the supreme courts of civil and administrative law, the Constitutional Court, and the higher board of judges and prosecutors underwent significant changes. For instance, the Constitutional Court consisted of eleven justices, but their number was raised to nineteen, and the number of members of the Higher Board of Judges and Prosecutors was raised from nine to twenty two (Anayasa Mahkemesi 2016; HSYK 2016). The executive, i.e., the government and the president, now have more control over the judicial system. In practice, the government managed to create a friendlier judiciary (Aralik Hareketi 2010). With the army in check and the judiciary becoming submissive, making a new constitution became more feasible. This time, the charter would be authored by four political parties in the assembly who represent mainstream political worldviews in Turkey, rather than authors handpicked solely by the military junta. Eventually, wheels were in motion:

> The Turkish Republic Constitution came into force after the military coup on September 12, 1980. In order to replace this Constitution with a more democratic one, The Constitution Reconciliation Committee which has been established with the equal participation of political parties represented in the Grand National Assembly of Turkey continues its works. The Constitution Reconciliation Committee aims maximum broad participation to make a constitution that all segments of the society participate.[1]

The entry above refers to the *Constitution Reconciliation Committee,* formed in October 2011 by the presidency of the Grand National Assembly of Turkey, comprised of twelve members of parliament—three deputies from each of four political parties that had seats in the national assembly—tasked with preparing a draft constitution.

Sessions were held for almost two years, with discussions on crucial issues such as the definition of citizenship, human rights versus security, equality versus privileges, pluralism versus the dominance of Turkish identity, and political diversity versus unity and homogeneity. No consensus was reached on most debated topics, including the accommodation of Kurdish political demands. Thus, the process ended with less than a hundred articles finalized, most of them relating to issues of secondary importance.

The political polarization between the governing party and the other two major political parties, the CHP (Cumhuriyet Halk Partisi-Republican People's Party) and the MHP (Milliyetçi Hareket Partisi-Nationalist Movement Party) rendered a consensus between the governing AKP, the CHP and the MHP very unlikely. Three Turkish-dominated parties consider the pro-Kurdish political party as the political wing of the Kurdish guerrilla forces and are not open to any alliance or negotiation with them. These parties are also distant or hostile to Kurdish political demands in general. This makes it very difficult, if not impossible, for the pro-Kurdish HDP (Halklarin Demokratik Partisi-Peoples' Democratic Party) to form a coalition with those parties. The ruling party and the pro-Kurdish HDP appeared to be "natural" allies until 2011, because both sections of the society were oppressed by the Kemalist order. Nevertheless, once the ruling party consolidated its power, it adopted the hostile approach that all other parties of the established order have adopted so far toward the pro-Kurdish party. There is no sign that a constitutive assembly will be called upon to draft the new constitution. Thus, the government is likely to proceed with its agenda and take its draft to a referendum, with the support of the nationalist MHP. As of December 2016, there is no constitutional draft in its entirety, but amendments to the existing one has been proposed by the ruling party, with the support of the MHP. The proposed amendments install a system of executive presidency—abolishing the current parliamentary system—and gives more power to the presidency against the legislative and the judiciary (Ozturk and Gözaydin 2016).[2]

In addition to these procedural and practical issues that have so far prevented the birth of a constitution that is the product of political consensus and democratic deliberation, there are conceptual, legal, and systemic limitations to address. I will dwell on them in the following two subsections.

A Conceptual Confusion: Mistaking Constitutions for the Social Contract

One of the most problematic issues of the constitution-making process has been a conceptual issue. Politicians from the ruling and the opposition parties as well as some scholars seem to agree on one thing only: that the new constitution should be a social contract or that Turkey needs a new social contract (Aktay 2014; Arınç 2014; Yamalak 2013; Yavuz 1999; Arslan and Özsoy 2016). Although they use the term *social contract*, what they mean, I believe, is *charter*. The term *social contract* refers to a hypothetical device in theories of social contractarians, not to an actual or historical contract (Boucher and Kelly 1994). So, if the advocates of this idea rely on the tradition of social contractarianism in political theory—which is a theory of legitimate political authority and has nothing to do with constitutions—naming the constitution as a social contract is a huge misunderstanding. I felt the need to address this confusion because there is a real danger in naming a constitution as a social contract, for contracts suggest that the sides to the contract are well aware of the content and their rights and responsibilities derived from the contract. More importantly, a contract suggests that the sides to the contract have gotten into a binding relationship on their own free will and that presumably they are free to terminate the contract if they want to. In that sense, no constitution bears the quality of a contract; they are documents that limit the government in their exercise of political power, and nothing more (Arendt 1963).

It is not very clear why the advocates would name the new charter a social contract. If I had to speculate, I would claim that defining the new constitution as the social contract is meant to place the undertaking on a moral high ground with this elegant but inaccurate concept, so that the defenders of the legacy of the founding father would have no higher moral ground to step on for opposing the amendment or the abolition of the eternity clauses of the current constitution—which are rendered untouchable by Article 4, and whoever has the intention to amend or abolish them in the future would need a higher moral ground to justify or legitimize their act.

Naming the new constitution a social contract claims the highest moral ground, since the name suggests that citizens, knowing completely what they do and after having deliberated and debated over the terms of the contract, have authored the constitution by their free will and entered into a relationship that benefits them all. This implies that the constitution is the product of the free will of the sovereign nation, and that the nation's will is above and over all other wills that are there. A constitution with these qualities would naturally have no trouble in replacing and out-valuing the legacy of the founding father. Alas, no constitution can have these qualities if we are to uphold the principles of Western political theory.

There is also the sense or the message of assurance that although the constitution will be amended or completely redrafted, the contract will keep the nation and the State united. In that sense, the name *social contract* functions like an offer to the spirit of the founding father in repentance for the transgressions their posterity are about to commit. Apart from releasing the psychological tension generated by the anxiety of trespassing on the sacredness of the legacy of the founding father, there is no political or practical use for naming a constitution a social contract in Turkey.[3] But I will try depicting what the advocates mean by social contract, as what they mean is slightly different than the general idea of the term.

For the Kurdish advocates, *social contract* refers to a settlement between the Turkish political establishment and the Kurdish movement (Arslan and Özsoy 2016; Yamalak 2013). Whereas for the Turkish author and politician, it refers to a new constitution that includes, at least formally, all sections of society (Arınç 2014; Yavuz 1999), in practice, this means when there is no agreement or consensus the majoritarian premise will hold sway. What the

Turkish proponents seem to suggest by social contract is, therefore, that the new constitution will carry the stamp of the majority, unlike the four constitutions posited so far that carry the stamp of the secular minority.

It is obvious that the Turkish and Kurdish advocates of the term do not agree on what the term connotes and what kind of constitution it would produce. Whether this difference of terminology or conceptualization represents a barrier to the accommodation of Kurdish demands in the constitutional drafts or not is not discernible from this discussion. Nevertheless, it is worth noting that there is serious confusion about what a constitution is and what it is not. I will dwell on this matter shortly.

That Constitutions Are Not Social Contracts

Constitutions are not social contracts of any sort. Subjectively, the arguments are based on an inaccurate conceptualization that confuses social and/or political consensus (in the case of Turkish proponents), or conflict resolution (in the case of Kurdish proponents) with the term *social contract*. Clearly, the parties act on a misunderstanding of what the social contract refers to in political theory.

Objectively, constitutions are not social contracts because they are legal documents that limit the government in the hope of preventing the abuse of power. Early contractarianism in general and Rousseau's *The Social Contract* in particular are not about constitutions *per se*. Contractarianism, as the theory of legitimate political authority, "claims that legitimate authority of government must derive from the consent of the governed, where the form and content of this consent derives from the idea of contract or mutual agreement" (Cudd 2000:1). Contractarianism mainly contends that humans are born free, and that "civil subordination without consent gives rise to an illegitimate, and ultimately despotic, form of power" (Castiglione 1994, 105). "In the traditional contract theories of Hobbes and Locke the contract was about the terms of political association. In particular, the problem was the grounds and limits of citizen's obligation to obey the state" (D'Agostino, Gaus, and Thrasher 1996, 9). Constitutions, on the other hand, install a specific regime and establish political institutions in a body politic. Neither "the terms of political association" nor a "contract or mutual agreement" are the outcome of a constitution-making process. Constitutions can only be, at best, the product of a consensus between political actors regarding fundamental principles and institutions of government in a body politic. This would still not make it a contract, because it says nothing about "the terms of political association"; since political association is given; i.e., it has *a priori* existence.

The body politic comes into being before there is even talk on what kind of constitution is going to be enacted.

Besides, in practice, constitutions are posited by kings, military juntas, a selected or elected group of technocrats or representatives, or powerful ruling parties. What we have when a constitution is enacted is a name for the body politic and a set of rules and principles/standards—mostly reflecting the ideology of the constituting power—that draw the limits of exercising political power for the governments formed in accordance with the procedures determined by that very same constitution. There is no guarantee that all or even most citizens agree with the content of the constitution. Individuals and groups within the society can—and often do—express their disenchantment with their constitution. A well-organized small group within the society can change the political order and the constitution with it, which would mean that the rules and principles that make the new constitution would in no way reflect even a consensus between political actors.

Furthermore, the element of *the initial state, the state of nature,* or *the original state* that appears in different formulations of contractarianism and is an indispensable part of the social contract theory, is merely a hypothetical device. This hypothetical device rules out the actuality or historicity, and even practicality, of a social contract. Thus, for instance, while Hume argued that no contract agreed upon by ancestors would be binding upon descendants, Dworkin objects to the idea of contract because no hypothetical contract could be binding (Cudd 2000, 2).

Contractarians themselves did not equate the social contract with constitutions. The main argument is that the legitimacy of political authority or of the government is not derived from a divine being or from the birthright of the nobility, but it is derived from the consent of the governed. That is why Hobbes envisages an absolute sovereign who rules without any limit to or constraint on his authority and power over his subjects; while Locke revises this formulation and suggests a two-fold contract: the initial contract that founds the body politic, and the second one that occurs between the government and the governed, thus formulating his famous principle *the right to rebellion* against an unjust government (Boucher and Kelly 1994).

Considering that the political thought has been primarily influenced by the French Revolution and Rousseauian principles of government in Turkey (Zürcher 2010, 2004), it is imperative to look closely at *The Social Contract* to see whether it has anything to do with constitutions. In the chapter *That It Is Always Necessary to Return to a First Convention* that comes before the chapter *On the Social Compact,* Rousseau states that "before examining the act whereby a people chooses a king, it would be well to examine the act whereby a people is a people. For since this act is necessarily prior to the other, it is the true foundation of society" (Rousseau 1762, Book I, Chapter V). Here, it is clear that Rousseau envisages the compact as a stage in social life through which society is founded via mutual agreement between atomic individuals who depend on their own strength and abilities to survive in the state of nature. Therefore, the social compact here does not yet have a political content. As Arendt sums up, "The liberties which the laws of constitutional government guarantee are all of a negative character, and this includes the right of representation for the purposes of taxation which later became the right to vote; they are indeed 'not powers of themselves, but merely an exemption from the abuses of power'; 'they claim not a share in government but a safeguard against government'" (1963, 143–44).

Thus, constitutions are fundamental laws of the State and are meant to limit the power of political authority. They should not be charged with any other role, function, or purpose. Therefore, the wishes and arguments presented by political actors regarding the new charter in Turkey as a *social contract* is problematic, to say the least.

Democratic Shortcomings of the Process and Procedures

The Constitution Reconciliation Committee was authorized to engage with civil society organizations, public institutions, and academia, to hear views and opinions of those representing different sections in the society, and to finalize provisions only after all committee members agreed on the content. According to the *Working Principles of the Constitutional Reconciliation Committee,* decisions must be made unanimously (Article 6). In other words, articles of the new constitution should be penned down with full consensus of all members of the committee. The draft, then, would be discussed in two plenary sessions and voted on in the assembly. Once it secured the votes of a qualified majority necessary for constitutional amendments, that is, 330 votes out of 550 MPs, the draft would be submitted to a referendum.

After two years, only 96 articles were agreed upon in 2013. The Constitution Reconciliation Committee was not able to reach a unanimous decision in penning all articles of the new constitution. The process was suspended in June 2014, and the ruling AKP is likely to pass their own constitution if they secure more than 330 MPs in the parliament. If they do not reach their MP quota, they will most likely abandon the whole process and settle for constitutional amendments that are beneficial to them (Yetkin 2014).

When we assess the process, we see that it was plagued by grave democratic shortcomings, and that the end-product of such a process was not likely to be a constitution that reduced the existing democratic and/or representative deficiency. I will mention several such challenges here. First, as Arato points out, the process lacks "sufficient political legitimacy" (2010, 1). Arato refers to Article 175 of the current constitution, according to which the Constitutional Court has the power to revise constitutional amendments. The classical struggle between the Kemalist elite and the elected governments used to be in the form of amending constitutional articles, and the Constitutional Court annulling the amendments on the grounds that they were against the eternity clauses in Articles 1, 2, and 3 of the current constitution. The provisions of these articles have been the ground upon which the court annulled amendments that clash with the Kemalist ideology. For example, in 2008 the court annulled the amendment allowing headscarves in public services. Although the Constitutional Court used to be pro-Kemalist, the ruling party has managed to change its composition in their favour, thus eliminating competition in the constitution-making process now. This makes the issue of legitimacy an even a bigger issue.

Second, political parties have to gather at least 10 percent of valid votes on the national scale in order to enter the parliament (The Law of Deputy Elections, Law No: 2839, Article 33). This is known as the *10 percent threshold*. Only two parties in the elections of 2002, and three in 2007 and 2011, managed to pass this threshold. Deputies of the pro-Kurdish political party circumvented this threshold by entering elections as independent candidates in 2007 and 2011. This came with a great sacrifice, however, because entering elections independently reduces their seats in the parliament by half. In 2015 they managed to pass the threshold as a party; however, this might change in the next elections and they might remain below the threshold. The 10 percent threshold has left many political parties out of legislation, causing deficiency of representation.

Third, in many provinces, especially in Kurdish towns and cities, "parties and voters actually never meet," because parties prefer "vertical mobilization" of votes "instead of horizontal solidarities based on common class or group affiliation" (Guida 2014, 178). This means that political parties may secure the votes of a large group by recruiting leaders of families, clans, unions, and other organizations rather than individual voters. For instance, what Guida observes in a predominantly Kurdish province of Urfa, in southeast Turkey, can be observed in many other provinces: "To mobilize the higher numbers of votes in Urfa, the headquarters of political parties preferred to exploit existing networks of control and select candidates from among those with the largest network, namely those that had the ability to mobilize the largest number of votes and prevent vote dispersion toward smaller parties" (Guida 2014, 178).

This pattern in party and electoral behaviour was introduced, practiced and encouraged in the 1920s by the state party, the CHF (Cumhuriyet Halk Firkasi-People's Republican Party) of the time, and picked up by other major political parties since the 1950s. It strengthens the ties between those who command large groups of people, networks, and resources, e.g., tribal and union leaders, and the State or the government. This practice is a means of control over the society. Where and when this pattern of practice applies, the delivery or withdrawal/withholding of certain public services and resources, depends on the voting preferences of the location. For instance, the tribes, organizations, neighbourhoods, villages, towns, and cities that vote for the ruling party gain certain economic goods in return, such as jobs and better public services. Those who do not vote for the ruling party are deprived of those public and private goods; this method is also used to contain opposition parties or manipulate voting behaviour. Kurdish political activism especially suffers from having their economic resources cut off by the central government, who supplies a significant amount of funding to municipalities. By cutting off or reducing municipality funding, the central government forces voters in the "disobedient municipality" to vote for the ruling party in the next elections. The networks that guarantee the vote for governing parties or other major political parties receive a variety of rewards in return, like jobs or access to public services, while those outside the networks are deprived of such benefits and are even occasionally punished for their refusal to cooperate with power holders (Guida 2014, 182).[4] Consequently, a constitution drafted by the kind of legislature that is filled with deputies elected on the premise of delivering their promise to distribute public goods to their voters will suffer from weak representative credentials.

Fourth, candidates are likely to fall short of resources necessary for presenting their case to constituencies in the absence of financial and media support for their campaigns. In general, candidates can only overcome this by joining a party that could make such resources available to them. Additionally, "Turkish electoral law does not allow voters to express candidate preferences. In fact, voters can vote only for a party, while MPs are elected in a province according to the d'Hont system, which works according to the order of candidates established by the party for its list" (Guida 2014, 179). These constraints force candidates to either remain out of electoral competition, or to join a major party in order to be elected, although they might not agree with the party platform. Although elected to the parliament, many deputies may therefore be ineffective in pushing through policies that would meet the needs of their constituency.

Furthermore, Turkish electoral law orders that political parties that pass the 10 percent national electoral threshold must be paid a certain amount of financial support from the state treasury.[5] Only three major parties have qualified for this funding since 2007. This causes inequality of resources between major and minor political parties, and a party that advocates for minorities is unlikely to ever qualify for this support. Despite the law changing in 2014, when the threshold of receiving this financial support was decreased from 10 to 3 percent, no party other than three major ones have qualified thus far. This is partially due to the necessity of having participated in elections and having spent a term in the assembly before qualification. This is a prohibitive measure intended to keep minority parties out of the parliament. It also imposes a vicious circle because certain parties cannot make it to the parliament partly because they lack material resources; and they cannot have access to those resources without making it to the parliament.

Fifth, political parties lack internal democracy. Party leaders have tight control over the mechanisms of candidate selections to party lists for the general elections: "The Turkish political system is best described as leader-based. Political continuity is sustained by leadership, not by the fragile party mechanism. The leader hence becomes a kind of living institution. Everything, from voting in parliament to the selection of new candidates in local elections, is decided by the leader of a typical Turkish party. The leader transcends the party" (Bacik 2014, 76). In addition, these leader-driven political processes bolster the authoritarian tendencies of political leaders (Ozkan 2014).

Sixth, the ruling AKP (who has won the last five legislative elections since 2002 with a majority to form a one-party government) has tried to transform the political system from a parliamentary democracy to a presidential democracy. No support has been granted for such a proposal from other political parties, and this raises concerns that the ruling AKP may not deliver the promise of drafting a constitution that is the product of a wide consensus, and that the party is likely to draft a constitution of its own if it secures the majority needed for such an enterprise (Arato 2010; Elster 1995; Chambers 2004; Özbudun 2014). Such a government-sponsored constitution would not be much different from the current "weakly legitimate" (Özbudun and Gençkaya 2009) or "suspiciously illegitimate" (Arato 2010) constitution.

Seventh, the legislation is the only actor that is expected and likely to shape the constitution, with almost no input from civil society or political opposition outside of parliament. No round-table negotiations have been held, no constituent assembly has been gathered, and no electoral process has been tailored for the election of a body that would take part in constitutional deliberations. There is no mechanism to ensure that religious or ethnic minorities are represented in the process as Jewish, Greek, Armenian, Êzîdî, Assyrian, Chaldean communities, and many other minorities have no deputies in the parliament, with the exception of a few deputies in the pro-Kurdish party and one in the CHP. In such a political setting, the constituency hardly effect governmental policies once elections are over. Turkey, then, is a good example of modern (pseudo)liberal (pseudo)democracies which Rousseau described as "free only during the election of members of parliament" (Rousseau 1762, Book III, Chapter XV). As previously demonstrated, even freedom during the elections is hardly the case in Turkey, due to financial control over political parties, the electoral threshold, and a number of other legal and structural constrains (see Kentel et al. 2012; Özbudun and Gençkaya 2009 for a detailed discussion on the legal and structural constratins).

Finally, the Turkish political process does not seem to have given any attention to the idea that "The role of experts should be kept to a minimum because solutions tend to be more stable if dictated by political rather than technical considerations" (Elster 1995, 396). The experts who dominate the process in the Turkish case are lawyers, and therefore discussions are rarely centred on major political issues such as the accommodation of Kurdish political demands or democratic reforms. Rather, discussions on the technicalities of presidential system versus parliamentary system prevail. The legacy of Kemalism, statist reflexes, and technical judicial matters occupy the central stage, as I will demonstrate in the upcoming discussion on Kurdish demands.

ASSESSING THE EXTENT TO WHICH THE CONSTITUTIONAL DRAFTS ACCOMMODATE KURDISH DEMANDS

Numerous political parties outside the parliament and civil society organizations have been working on and proposing new constitutional drafts or provisions in Turkey; however I will limit my examination to those of four political parties that have groups in the parliament, for two practical reasons. First, it would be impossible to give justice to so many texts in such a short discussion. Second, the main and actual proposals that were debated by the Constitution Reconciliation Committee were those of the four political parties that had deputies in the committee.[6] Therefore I will focus on the latter group as the most relevant set of documents, and my examination moves from less to more liberal drafts.[7]

The Criteria on which I Evaluate the Drafts

I have noted in chapter 2 that Kurdish politics is driven by the principle of the coexistence of multiple political communities within and beyond one polity. In that sense, the drafts that envisage only one political community, formulated in the Turkish constitution as "the unity of the nation with its state," are in negation of Kurdish political demands. Likewise, those that impose one official language, one flag, one nation, one language for education, and a centralized government, ignore Kurdish political demands. By Kurdish political demands, I specifically mean the nine that are articulated in the pro-Kurdish parties' election manifestos and constitutional drafts, and that are common to all Kurdish or pro-Kurdish political parties:

1. Self-rule in Kurdistan
2. Education and public services in the Kurdish language
3. Recognizing Kurdish as the second official language in Turkey or in Kurdistan
4. Modifying the definition of citizenship in the constitution to include non-Turks
5. Reducing the 10 percent electoral threshold
6. Establishing truth and reconciliation commissions in order to compensate victims of human rights violations and hold the perpetrators accountable
7. Amnesty for Kurdish political prisoners, including the leader of the PKK, and the negotiation of peace and settlement with Kurdish armed groups
8. Abolishing the village-guard system[8]
9. Reparations for the damages inflicted by security forces[9]

Of these nine demands, only the first, the third, and the fourth would typically have to be addressed in the constitution. The first demand relates to the form of the State. Whether the State is a unitary or a federal nation-state, or whether it is a confederation of federal states, or a union of federal states is a matter typically regulated in constitutions. The third demand relates to the language of communication used by State institutions, and hence, is typically regulated in constitutions as well. The fourth demand relates to how citizenship is won and lost, and if it is defined on the basis of an exclusive cultural or ethnic identity. This is typically addressed in constitutions. The current constitution imposes Turkishness as the only cultural, national, and ethnic identity. Therefore, Kurdish political actors demand its modification so that it does not exclude Kurdish cultural and political identity.

The rest of the Kurdish demands are policy issues that could be addressed by specific laws and subject to ordinary law-making. In the Turkish case, however, the second demand is also regulated by the current constitution. Providing education in Kurdish as a mother tongue will necessitate the amendment of Article 42 of the current constitution, or, the new constitution does not have to specify languages through which education and public services are provided. This will leave the matter to the discretion of the legislator or to that of regional, provincial, and municipal authorities. The abolition or reduction of the 10 percent threshold is a matter that could be addressed in the constitution, although it is currently regulated by the electoral laws. Therefore, I will evaluate the drafts in relation to the first five demands, and leave the others out of the evaluation as they are matters of ordinary law-making.

The specifics of the demands might differ from party to party, but generally, these are common demands that have been articulated by ordinary Kurds as well as by Kurdish political actors in Turkey (Yeğen, Tol, and Çalışkan 2016; Yegen 2016). It is worthwhile to note that the consensus among the Kurds and Kurdish political actors is strongest when it comes to the first demand, and weakest with regard to the fifth demand (see also Yeğen et al. 2016). Only the HDP satisfies all of these criteria as a political party in its draft and policy recommendations. Other Kurdish parties may appear hostile to the PKK and not be so adamant in their quest for the release of the PKK leader from prison. Nevertheless, it is important to note that the HDP is the largest party in Kurdistan and the third largest party in Turkey. Thus, they represent the overwhelming majority of votes in Kurdistan. This makes the HDP's demands somewhat representative of Kurdish demands in general. Therefore, I assume that the HDP's draft is the embodiment of Kurdish political demands—with the exception of self-rule in Kurdistan, as I noted earlier.[10]

The *Status Quo* Is Maintained: Kurds and Their Political Demands Are Excluded from the Drafts of Turkish Political Parties

The constitution drafts proposed by the MHP and the CHP, the third and second largest political parties respectively, are not substantially different. Both parties embrace the provisions of the current constitution designed to establish the dominance of ethnic Turks as the ruling element within an otherwise diverse society. These provisions are both remnants as well as continuations of the institutionalization of the nineteenth-century notion of *millet-i hakime*, which meant that initially Muslims (but later only Turks) are the supreme group/element within the multi-ethnic and multi-religious Ottoman polity, that is, the true holder of political power and the possessor of the State (Lewis 2002, 453–60). Thus, their drafts are homogenizing in every sense and leave no room for social, ethnic, cultural, or religious diversity. The MHP's draft is more hostile toward individual freedoms and human rights while the CHP's acknowledges the value of individual freedoms as long as they do not clash with common categories such as State security, the indivisibility of nation with its State, or the common good. The CHP also recognizes social diversity as a trait of 'Turkish society,' referred to as 'a mosaic of cultures,' thereby reducing non-Turkish or non-Muslim groups to *folkloric riches of Turkey*. Their approaches to Kurdish political demands are almost the same: both are in favour of the *status quo*. Therefore, their drafts will be examined together, in order to avoid repetition.

The two parties represent different streams in Turkish politics, and they rely on different social and economic forces or classes, although the boundary between their constituencies is permeable. For instance, the CHP is known to have inherited the legacy of Kemalism and Ataturk nationalism, both referred to in the current constitution and known for their aspiration to make a place for Turkey within Western civilization (Zeydanlıoğlu 2008; Matossian 1994). The MHP has a more conservative creed: they have an unfriendly attitude toward the West and care more about Turkey's role within Turkic and Islamic civilizations. Establishing Turkish supremacy in the region and in the world is their main goal. Moreover, they differ in their views regarding the identity of the nation: while the MHP sees Islam as a component of the Turkish identity, the CHP promotes a secular definition. These differences are reflected in the words they use to define the nation. The MHP uses the word *millet* (the Arabic word for *nation*), which highlights the Islamic, "traditional," and conservative traits in Turkishness. The CHP, on the other hand, uses *ulus* (the Turkish word for *nation*), which refers to modern and secular traits. Also, the CHP sees itself as the modernizing political force in Turkey, as it is the founding party of the Republic of Turkey. The CHP is very keen to embrace Western modernism and social, economic, political, and philosophical values that are associated with it. The MHP, however, is sceptical, even hostile, toward Western values and modernity in general. The party suggests that the political authority should use laws to minimize the negative influences of Western modernism. The CHP is the architect and the guardian of the Kemalist ideology, which has marked the contemporary West as the peak of civilization, and commissioned itself with modernizing the Turkish nation. The MHP positions itself against Western modernism and promotes the pre-modern, conservative, and traditional cultural traits of Turks and Turkic communities. Nevertheless, there is not much difference between what the two parties offer regarding the nine criteria I examine here. Additionally, the constitution of 1982 bears the trademark of these two political streams and therefore, they oppose any fundamental changes to the imposition of unity and homogeneity as provided in the current constitution.

More importantly, although the ruling AKP and the pro-Kurdish HDP previously posed the greatest challenge to the *status quo* that was backed by the military and civil bureaucratic elite, the former has now merged with the regime and no longer pushes for democratic reforms. The HDP is now alone in its bid to open up the political sphere to non-state actors and entities. Thus, promoting political diversity is a task shouldered by relatively marginalized and isolated actors such as the HDP and civil society organizations who are not welcome by the established order. Indeed, especially the HDP is labelled as the political wing of Kurdish guerrillas and the gravest threat to national unity and state security:

> Ethnic plurality within Turkey is not just denied, but indeed feared, and viewed as a serious threat to the integrity of the nation. In an attempt to protect the

dominant myth of an ethnically homogeneous nation, any articulation of ethnic or even cultural difference is prohibited. Any such articulation which even suggests a desire for autonomy, is immediately portrayed as a threat to the very existence of the nation-state. (Mckeever 2005, 10)

Thus, despite all social and ideological differences that separate the CHP and the MHP, they share common grounds in opposing the constitutional draft proposed by the HDP, with almost the same arguments: those pertaining to Atatürk nationalism, the unity of the Turkish nation, the integrity of the Turkish state, the indivisibility of the state with its nation and territory, and the dominance of Turkish culture and language.

The Drafts of the MHP and the CHP

Weighing the drafts of the two parties against the nine criteria shows that they offer no substantial change to the provisions in the current constitution. Especially the first three provisions in the current constitution that give the regime its fundamentally authoritarian characteristics vis-à-vis political diversity remain the same.

1. Self-rule in Kurdistan: Both drafts hold that sovereignty belongs to the Turkish nation. Kurds are not recognized as a nation, and often they are not recognized at all. A single and unified political community is envisaged and therefore self-rule of any kind is not regulated in the drafts. The drafts do not recognize ethnic or religious minorities in Turkey, with the exception of Christian minorities that were granted that status in the Treaty of Lausanne.
2. Education and public services in Kurdish language: Both drafts hold that education and public services should be delivered only in the Turkish language.
3. Recognizing Kurdish as the second official language in Turkey or in Kurdistan: The drafts hold that Turkish language is "the language of the State" (Current constitution, Article 3). Other languages are not recognized as regional or national official languages.
4. Modifying the definition of citizenship: Both drafts preserve the current definition of citizenship in Article 66 of the constitution. The Article says that "Everyone bound to the Turkish State through the bond of citizenship is a Turk."
5. Reducing the 10 percent electoral threshold: This matter can be addressed by the electoral law, although it can be addressed in the constitution as well. The MHP is against reducing the threshold, but the CHP leadership has declared that they are open to discussion on the reduction of the

threshold. This is the most important step the CHP has ever taken to accommodate Kurdish political demands.

One might ask why the two parties agree on drafting a new constitution in the first place, if they oppose undermining the *status quo.* The constitution was enacted by a military junta, which is increasingly indefensible even by those who defend the *status quo.* Therefore, political parties in general agree on drafting a civil constitution. The two parties are simply keeping up with the *zeitgeist* of the 2000s.

The Ruling AKP's Constitutional Draft: 'One Step forward, Two Steps backwards'[11]

What distinguishes the governing party AKP's draft from those of the two parties above is that it bears the stamp of a political movement that was once oppressed by the regime. The party's constituency is comprised of the nationalist, conservative, and Islamic middle and lower classes of mostly Sunni-Muslim-Turkish background, who suffered greatly under the Kemalist rule. They compete with the Kurdish party for the votes of conservative Sunni-Muslim Kurds. Moreover, as Tuğal (2016) notes, Turkey under the AKP rule used to be presented and perceived as a role model for countries with Muslim majorities. Their bid to democratize Turkey through political reforms during the 2000s earned them much credibility and appreciation in Turkey and abroad. Pushing the military back, opening membership negotiations with the European Union, and attempting to negotiate the terms of peace with Kurdish guerrillas twice has contributed greatly to their reputation as a democratic party. As Robins observes:

> The political conversion of Erdoğan and those around him from Europhobia to Europhilia is best explained in instrumental terms. Turkey's Islamists had suffered at the hands of the country's secular establishment in the second half of the 1990s, with the WP and its successor party both being closed down as a result of a thinly veiled constitutional authoritarianism. It was in such a context that a younger generation of rising figures cut free from their more traditionalist superiors and established the JDP in 2001. The JDP set aside the identity politics of the past and quickly embraced the goal of EU membership. Its hope was that the Union would anchor Turkey for democracy and pluralism, thereby deterring any future military interventions. (Robins 2007, 292)

However, the party's march toward establishing a stronger democracy in Turkey stopped following the Arab Spring and its repercussions in the region. The AKP's progressive politics is now replaced by a Sunni-Islam oriented neo-Ottomanism that is driven by the dream of establishing Turkish dominance in the Middle-East once more (Ozkan 2014; Bellaigue 2016). The dream of reviving the golden days of the Ottoman Empire has cost Turkey dearly in domestic and international politics, and the government is becoming increasingly authoritarian. The ruling party now seeks to consolidate its power by merging State institutions and apparatuses with the party, and there is now no doubt that the party will not contribute any further to promoting democratic freedoms (see Tuğal 2016). The most disappointing setbacks came in the reforms and policies with regard to the Kurds. The government resumed the war with Kurds in 2015 and large chunks of a dozen towns and cities in the Kurdish region have been razed to the ground since then, and half a million people have been internally displaced. Ultimately, the politics of the ruling party promises nothing more with regard to Kurdish political demands than what the current constitution stipulates.

1. Self-rule in Kurdistan: The AKP's draft offers nothing more than the formulation of national sovereignty in the current constitution. This draft also does not recognize Kurds as a distinct nation and denies them the rights and privileges that would come with such recognition. The ruling party denies the Kurds self-rule in Kurdistan.
2. Education and public services in Kurdish language: The AKP's draft is not as hostile as traditional statist parties toward other languages, and "allows" citizens to learn and teach their languages privately. There are elective classes in Kurdish and Arabic in secondary schools. However, this is insufficient for the Kurdish political movements.
3. Recognizing Kurdish as the second official language in Turkey or in Kurdistan: The draft holds that Turkish language is "the language of the State" (current constitution Article 3). Other languages are not recognized as regional or national official languages.
4. The definition of citizenship: Although it is uncertain if the AKP is going to define citizenship on the bases of Turkishness, it is obvious that the definition will not be in the form of "citizens of Turkey" either, which is what Kurdish movements suggest. The draft is settling with "the citizenship of the Republic of Turkey," and this raises no objections from the Kurds. Because in this instance, citizenship is not based on Turkishness or Turkish cultural or national identity. It refers to a bond between the political community and its members, but does not suggest that the members of the political community belong to an ethnic or national group.
5. Reducing the 10 percent electoral threshold: The ruling party rejects the reduction of the threshold. Indeed, its main objective now is to push the pro-Kurdish HDP down below the threshold, because once the HDP does

not make it to the parliament due to the high threshold, the ruling party will have at least fifty-odd more deputies.

The Pro-Kurdish HDP's Draft

The HDP, as the deputy Sırrı Süreyya Önder states,[12] is a coalition of the most oppressed, persecuted, and discriminated against sections of society, which includes but is not limited to the conservative, progressive, religious, and secular Kurds, the radical left, non-Muslim minorities, and anti-capitalist Muslim and LGBT activists and organizations. This diversity is part of what makes the HDP appealing to both Kurdish and non-Kurdish voters. But it also proves to be shaky ground for the party from time to time, and renders the party vulnerable to internal tensions and crisis. For instance, deputies of the party may adopt diverging positions with regard to certain issues such as LGBT rights, and this creates inconsistencies in the messages they deliver to the public.[13] Diversity may be or become a liability during election campaigns, because political culture in Turkey is known to favour disciplined, hierarchical and leader-centred parties and strong leaders (Bacik 2014; Guida 2014). Nevertheless, the party has the potential to become a permanent actor in Turkish politics, although its marginalization and criminalization by the regime, the media, and the judiciary makes their undertaking a highly challenging one.

It should be noted, however, that despite its diversity, the HDP is a fruit of the Kurdish political movement in Turkey. In fact, it was founded after the PKK leader Abdullah Öcalan's suggestions. As such, it follows a path that is partly determined by the forces that direct Kurdish politics. However, the fact that the cadres of this party share many commonalities with the left in Turkey, that the HDP and its predecessors have participated in national elections in Turkey since 2002 with candidates of a coalition that includes parties from the left whose cadres and constituencies are generally Turkish, and that there are those who identify themselves as religious Muslims, liberals, socialists and social democrats in the category of "the Kurds," should be taken as evidence to support the claim that the HDP is not a party of Kurdish nationalists. It surely is nothing like the Turkish nationalists' parties: the MHP, the CHP, and the AKP. Therefore, it is no surprise that the HDP would be the party that offers the most revolutionary alternative to the current constitution.

In an interview in April 2013, the co-chair of the HDP, Selahattin Demirtaş, told Neşe Düzel of the daily *Taraf* that HDP's draft is the most progressive and the most democratically written one. Demirtaş stressed that this was due to the fact that all the sections of the draft were penned down by the involvement of interest groups and civil society organizations that have a stake in those sections. For example, labour unions participated in authoring the articles pertaining to economic life, while school teachers' unions participated in penning down the articles related to education. It is also no surprise that the priority for the HDP, by every means, is the realization of Kurdish political demands. Hence, it would not make sense to apply the nine-plus criteria I enumerated above in order to evaluate the Turkish parties' approaches to Kurdish political demands. Indeed, the criteria are partly derived from the HDP's election manifesto of 2015 and their constitutional draft of 2013. However, the HDP's approach differs somewhat from that of other Kurdish political parties. For instance, some Kurdish political parties promote independence, while some others advocate for the foundation of a federal State in Kurdistan. For that reason, I will consider the specifics of precisely how these demands are formulated in the HDP's draft.

Self-rule in Kurdistan

In the HDP's draft, sovereignty belongs to "the people of Turkey," not to "the Turkish nation." This is an attempt to detach sovereignty from a particular identity, and to put an end, at least in the constitution, to the prevailing mentality in Turkey, which assumes that since sovereignty belongs to "the Turkish nation," the Turks are "the true owners of the State" and "the true rulers of the country." The HDP's draft holds that regional assemblies should be established and that the exercise of political power must be shared between the national assembly and regional assemblies. Sırrı Süreyya Önder expresses their proposal as "democratic autonomy"[14]: "We want autonomy for twenty-five regions in Turkey, we are not asking for autonomy only for Kurds. Autonomy for local administrations means weakening authoritarianism. Authoritarianism is the centralization of power, whereas autonomy is the spreading of power to the grass roots" (Yinanç 2013, n.p.).

In this clause, the HDP seeks to open the way for regional Kurdish administrations in predominantly Kurdish areas. A good deal of the Kurdish population lives in Turkish metropolitan cities as well. Regional assemblies will not secure their access to political power. Thus, along with regional arrangements, localizing the exercise of political power is also a priority for the HDP, but their formulation of 25 autonomous regions will not guarantee that. What they actually stand for is not decentralization, but the project of *democratic autonomy* (see chapter 4). However, their draft does not contain their political stance.

It is obvious that the HDP is inspired by the Spanish constitution, in the sense that its draft creates several moderately autonomous regions within a unitary nation-state and does not push for a federal structure. Rather than granting regional autonomy to a nation within a nation, the HDP's draft creates new administrative units and grants additional political power to them. These powers are additional in the sense that their elected assemblies will not be supervised by the governors appointed from Ankara, as is the case in the current system; although mayors are elected in Turkey, the governor appointed from Ankara is the ultimate authority in the province, the city, and the town. Thus, the newly created regions enjoy a degree of autonomy and are governed in many areas by their elected representatives in regional legislators. This nevertheless is a giant step forward toward introducing new state structures in the context of Turkey, because preserving the current centralized unitary system of government is a priority for other political parties and their drafts.

The HDP's proposal of founding regional assemblies and granting them autonomy, however, does not go beyond classical multiculturalism because it does not propose that the Kurds be recognized as a distinct nation in the constitution. Instead, the mother State grants autonomy to sub-state cultural or territorial minorities. This emulates the pattern where a typical liberal nation-state imposes a nation-wide cultural, linguistic and ideological "unity," while accommodating minorities through establishing sub-state political entities in order to avoid partition (e.g., Spain). Administrative decentralization will not guarantee self-rule in Kurdistan. Certain administrative powers are transferred to regional assemblies and authorities, but this does not address the quest for *self-rule in Kurdistan* as much as it assimilates Kurdistan into Turkey.

As Bozkurt partly stresses, "The real target is to write a new Constitution embracing the Kurds" (2003, 1). In subsequent lines, Bozkurt outlines the HDP's (the BDP was the previous pro-Kurdish party in the parliament, which is now HDP) "revolutionary" proposals as such:

> "Equal citizenship, equal representation." While the BDP wants "We, the people of Turkey" written openly in the Constitution preamble, it says: "We believe all individuals and people have universal human rights and freedoms. We regard everybody equal regardless of their race, language, sect, gender, sexual orientation, ethnic background and any similar discrimination. All different identities, cultures, languages and beliefs existing in Turkey are under the assurance of this constitution . . ." BDP sees this definition as "the charter of the intention of cohabitation . . ." (Bozkurt 2013, 1)

The crucial feature of HDP's draft is its emphasis on the term "cohabitation." The party clearly stresses that it has no intention to separate Kurds from other elements or sections of the society, nor does it pursue any right (privilege) that will not be recognized for all "citizens of Turkey."[15]

Language

The draft offers revolutionary change in the matter of official language and the language of education, compared with the current constitution, which forbids education in other languages (translated in Bozkurt 2013): "The state's official language is Turkish. Other main languages people of Turkey speak may be used as second official languages upon the decision of local governments. Everyone has the right to use their own mother tongue alongside the official language in their private life and in their relations with public authorities."

Citizenship

The definition of citizenship is essential to all the matters at hand, and they are typically addressed in constitutions. The HDP proposes not to define citizenship on the basis of national or cultural identity, but to regulate how citizenship is earned in the constitution. They are for *jus sanguinis* and *jus soli* together in determining citizenship. Unlike the current constitution that formulates "Turkish citizenship" on the basis of Turkish identity, the HDP uses the phrase "citizenship of Turkey," in order to detach citizenship from ethnic or national identities and redefine it on the ground of civic bond between members of the political community (I modified the translation in italics): "In obtaining, maintaining and losing citizenship of Turkey, no *discrimination can be* made regarding language, religion, race, ethnic background, culture, gender, sexual orientation and similar differences" (Bozkurt 2013, 2). The phrase "sexual orientation" is crucial here, as other parties' drafts do not accommodate the LGBT.

WHY WERE KURDISH POLITICAL DEMANDS OMITTED IN DRAFT CONSTITUTIONS?

If political community were a civic union, this would imply that the State is neutral, and that it does not promote a particular culture, identity, language, or religion. In such a scenario, citizenship/nationality would merely be a legal status. However, citizenship also gives both the political community and its citizens an identity (Leydet 2006; Taylor 1997; Peters et al. 2012; Castles 2005). Determining this identity is never a neutral undertaking. As Brubaker highlights, "Complete neutrality, to be sure, is now widely recognised as a myth" (2013, 10; also see Gordon and Stack 2007; Kymlicka and Straehle 1999; Stack 2013). Indeed, the Turkish constitution does not shy away from imposing the *Statist* Turkish nationalism as the ideology of the State: promoting Turkish language while banning the Kurdish language, and defining citizenship on the basis of "cultural Turkishness" formulated by the theorist of Turkish nationalism Ziya Gökalp (Zürcher 2004, 2010; Lewis 2002). This cultural Turkishness then evolved into racial Turkishness in the early 1930s (Poulton 2001; Zeydanlıoğlu 2008; Xypolia 2016; Uzer 2013; Özdoğan 2010).

Almost a century later, this is still the trademark of the contemporary Turkish constitution in particular, and Turkish politics in general. The argument that the State belonged to ethnic Turks only and that Turkish identity, culture, and language must erase others was popular among cabinet members such as Ismet Inonu and Mahmut Esat Bozkurt in the early 1930s (Baran 2010, 5). The argument found its way into the constitutions of 1961 and 1982, and is now reflected in the draft constitutions of the three largest Turkish political parties.

Here, the matters I want to draw attention to are the legacy of the founding father and the political culture it has created through setting the terms of debate in the context of Kurdish politics. For instance, the preamble and the first three articles of the current constitution determine the ideology of the regime as "Ataturk nationalism," i.e., the statist Turkish nationalism. The form of the State is specified as a unitary nation-state and the nation as the Turkish nation, "unified and indivisible with its State." The official language, in the case of Turkey *the language of the State,* is Turkish. Article 66 defines citizenship on the basis of Turkishness. This is the legacy of Kemalism: the aggregate of principles and practices put together by the founding father of the Republic of Turkey.

Thus, the argument of this section is that the exclusion or negation of Kurdish political demands in the constitutional drafts of Turkish majority political parties has to do with the legacy of the founding father. The founding father misunderstood, misinterpreted, or manipulated certain political concepts in order to implement and institutionalize the majoritarian premise with regard to Kurdish politics in Turkey. The maintenance of this legacy comes through the "originalist" reading of constitutional provisions by politicians, academics, and justices. The pro-Kurdish HDP's multicultural constitutional draft, thus, faces marginalization just as self-rule of any kind in Kurdistan was excluded from constitutions during the foundation of modern Turkey. Therefore, it is important to look beyond the drafts and revisit the legacy of the founding father in order to shed light on the question of why Kurdish political demands are banished from the drafts.

The *Constitution* of the Majoritarian Premise: The Founding Father's Fear of Diversity and Constitutions as Instruments of Nation-Building in Turkey

"Theory is always *for* someone and *for* some purpose" (Cox and Sinclair 1996, 87). So are constitutions. If a constitution is the product of a national vision that envisages the constitution as an instrument of nation-building, conflict is almost inevitable between the constitutional order and those left out. As Hughes points out, "Competing national visions can paralyse the constitutional process and the choice to embed one vision into the constitution risks marginalising those outside of that ideal" (2012, 1). The framers of the constitution of 1924 were of the idea that the Ottoman Empire collapsed due to its multi-ethnic and multi-religious composition (Zürcher 2010), and saw the survival and the strength of the new state in the homogeneity of its citizenry. Lerner observed that

> The Western constitutional imagination consists of two principal paradigms regarding the relationship between constitutions and the identity of "the people." In the nation-state constitution, "we the people" represents the national or cultural commonalities of a presumably homogeneous population. By contrast, the liberal constitution expresses the shared commitment of "we the citizenry" to the underlying principles of political liberalism. (Lerner 2011, 11)

The framers in Turkey have been adopting the first paradigm. Since homogeneity has never been the case in Turkey, the political establishment has been engaged in an aggressive nation-building project to change the reality on the ground. For instance, Article 3 of the current constitution states that "The Turkish state, with its territory and nation, is an indivisible entity." This "indivisible unity" of the State with its nation and territory is referred to, ten times, in Articles 14, 26, 28, 58, 68, 81, 103, and 143. The framers did not acknowledge the fact that citizens of the Republic of Turkey were the remnants of the Ottoman society, and thus comprised of many ethnic, cultural and religious elements. Instead, the three constitutions named the state as the "Turkish State," and called all citizens "Turks" (e.g., Section Five, Public Law of the Turks; Articles 69, 70, 82, 87, 88 of the constitution of 1924). This, of course, meant exclusion for non-Turkic elements of the citizenry.

Those who defend the wording of the constitution often argue that the name *Turk* in the constitution refers to all Turkish citizens, not to ethnic Turks only. It is argued that Article 88 of the constitution of 1924, which held that "The name Turk, as a political term, shall be understood to include all citizens of the Turkish Republic, without distinction of, or reference to, race or religion," was an insurance against such ethnic or racial interpretations. However, the statements of the founding father prove otherwise: "The country, eventually, has remained with its real owners again. Armenians and others have no rights whatsoever in here. These prosperous lands are essential and absolute Turkish homeland" (Atatürk 1923, my translation). Mahmut Esat Bozkurt, the Minister of Justice at the time, stated on September 16, 1930 that he believed "that the Turk must be the only lord, the only master of this country. Those who are not of pure Turkish stock can have only one right in this country, the right to be servants and slaves" (Poulton 2001: 120). Additionally, the relatively ambiguous definition of citizenship in the constitution of 1924 was revised in the constitutions of 1961 and 1982. These revisions leave no doubt that the framers of those constitutions opted for ethnic definitions of citizenship:

Citizenship

Article 54—Every individual who is bound to the Turkish State by ties of citizenship is a Turk. (The constitution of 1961)

Turkish citizenship

Article 66—Everyone bound to the Turkish State through the bond of citizenship is a Turk. (The constitution of 1982)

Moreover, while the name *Turk* (excluding and apart from Turkish) is mentioned nine times in the constitution of 1924 (the heading of section five, Articles 69, 70, 82, 87, 88), six times in the constitution of 1961 (the preamble and Articles 3, 11, 22, 57, 124), and 13 times in the constitution of 1982 (the preamble and Articles 3, 14, 26, 28, 58, 68, 81, 103, 143), no other culture or particular identity is referred to. Furthermore, the constitutions of 1924 and 1982 state that "The language of the state is Turkish" (note that it is not only the official language, but it is the State's language), and article 42 of the constitution of 1982 states that "No language other than Turkish shall be taught as a mother tongue to Turkish citizens at any institutions of training or education" (the constitution 1982).

More importantly, until they were amended in 2001, Articles 26 and 28 of the current constitution used to have the clauses on the restriction that "no language *prohibited by the law* can be used in expressing and disseminating thoughts and opinions, and in broadcasting and publishing," which put firm constraints on the use of Kurdish. Furthermore, scholarship on Turkish nationalism has established that the Turkish political elite pursued aggressive assimilationist policies against Muslim and non-Muslim minorities (Aktar

2014; Beşikçi 1990; Özdoğan 2010; Poulton 2001; Ünlü 2012; Xypolia 2016; Yeğen 1996; 2007; Zürcher 2004; 2010). Constitutions thus functioned as instruments of nation-building and assimilating diversity into the Turkish identity.

Chambers identifies the source of inspiration for this tendency in Turkey:

> The French constitution of 1789 tried to replace a fragmented feudal order with a unified and coherent state. The constitution, to quote Preuss again, "becomes a call to alter reality to correspond to [ethical principles], to make society as coherent and rational as the document." The constitution does not so much reflect reality (shaped by irrational forces of superstition and ignorance, according to the Enlightenment mind) as set out moral and institutional guidelines to organize reality into a civilized whole. (Chambers 2004:159)

Following the French example (Atakan 2007; Orhan 2014), the republican elite set out to eliminate the socio-political structures they associated with the *ancient regime*. "Civilizing" the "backward" peasants and masses of Anatolia was also a dominant theme during the Turkish revolution and modernization of the 1920s and 1930s (Deringil 2003; Dirlik 1996; Zeydanlıoğlu 2008; Hamelink and Baris 2014).

The kind of aggressive nation-building project envisaged by the founding father was also an instrument for the consolidation of their political power (Mango 1999). As Smith observes, "ethnic leaders and elites used their cultural groups as sites of mass mobilization and as constituencies in their competition for power and resources, because they found them more effective than social classes" (Smith 2001, 55). Nation-building, in Smith's words, became an instrument through which the new elite could "mobilize people, coordinate the diverse interests of social groups and legitimate their actions, in order to seize and retain power in the modern state" (2001, 56). This ethno-symbolic interpretation of nationalism, represented best in Breuilly, explains the role of nationalism in early modern Turkey very well. In Smith's words, "nationalism is not about identity, unity, authenticity, dignity, the homeland or anything else, save political power, that is, political goals in the modern state. Nationalism is simply an instrument for achieving political goals, and as such it can only emerge under the modern conditions" (Smith 2001, 56).

The interpretation above captures the instrumentality of nationalism and emphasizes its functionality in competition for obtaining political power. The framers of the Turkish constitutions have exploited this functionality. Thus, Arendt's argument that "the nation during the nineteenth century 'had stepped into the shoes of the absolute prince'" and that "it became, in the course of the twentieth century, the turn of the party to step into the shoes of the nation" (Arendt 1963, 268) puts things in perspective in the case of Turkey. Although the sultanate and the caliphate were abolished in 1922 and 1924, the outcome was not the banishment of "sacredness" and "omnipotence" from politics, but the appropriation of them by the new elite. The new regime was built in the form of party dictatorship that based its legitimacy on the sacred Supreme Being, the nation, and gave birth to an omnipotent absolute, the State. Just like the caliphate and the sultanate were merged in the person of the monarch, the nation and the State were merged in the "indivisible entity of the State with its nation" (the constitution of 1982, *Preamble*).

Constitutions in Turkey have never played "an important role in expressing the common aspirations and norms of the nation" (Lerner 2011, 24), but they have been instrumental in legitimising the agenda of the ruling elite. Turkish constitutions, yes, do "play a foundational role in representing the ultimate goals of the state" (24), but they hardly have anything to do with common good and shared goals in society in general. In this context, it is not surprising that the framers have never used the phrase "we, the people"; as the equivalent of *people* in Turkish, *halk*, does not strictly refer to a unified or homogenous body of individuals that make up a community, or to a political subject. *Halk* is not a political collective or a corporate body either. It refers to masses, or to an aggregate of individuals, communities, and groups of all kinds, who share a given space or territory at a given time (Kapani 1975). But it has no political significance. Thus, *the people* is not suitable to be named as the source, origin, and agent of sovereignty, or as the fabric of political community in Turkey. Instead, *the nation* has been the prime political category, because it signifies unity and it is claimed that it acts as a political subject (Ipek 2008; Ağaoğulları 1986). In that sense, "the nation" refers to "a unified, presumably homogenous, collectivity, resting on a shared cultural, ethnic or religious background" (Lerner 2011, 19).

The framers of the constitution of 1924 thus refrained from referring to citizenry as "a plurality of 'voluntaristic' individuals, who do not form a particular collective identity but define their shared identity in political or civic terms" (Lerner 2011, 19). On the contrary, Article 3 of the 1982 constitution states that "The Turkish state, with its territory and nation, is an indivisible entity," merging the nation, the Supreme Being, with the State and ultimately transforming the State into the Supreme Being. This leads to the establishment of the dominance of the majority, because whichever party forms majority in the parliament claims not only to be the ordinary law-maker, but they can claim that they embody the national will and that their will is the will of the nation. This was exactly what the framers of the constitution of 1924 claimed:

> This was a "majoritarian" or "Rousseauist" [sic] conception of democracy, rather than a liberal or pluralistic democracy based on an intricate system of checks

and balances. The majoritarian concept of democracy holds that sovereignty is the "general will" of the nation (which, in practice, has to be interpreted as the majority's will), and it is, as such, absolute, indivisible and infallible. Within a representative system, this means that the legislature represents the true will of the nation. (Özbudun and Gençkaya 2009, 12–13)

The irony is that although the majoritarian premise was *constituted* by the Kemalist ruling elite, and although they were the first oligarchic elite who justified their rule on the basis of forming the majority in the parliament, they started opposing the majoritarian premise once religious/conservative parties started to form the majority in the legislature in the 1950s. This pattern continued through the following fifty years, and when the ruling AKP came to power in 2002, constitutional scholars were mainly of the idea that the fact that they form majority in the parliament does not give them the right to undo what the founding father had done (see Atakan 2007 for some counterarguments against the majoritarian premise presented by Kemalist scholars).

According to this interpretation, the constituent will/power rests with the founding father, although sovereignty rests with the people. This created an impasse that could be surpassed only by military coups; *coup d'états* restored the will of the founding father and the people *regained* their sovereignty after new constitutions were posited by military juntas. Neither the majoritarian premise, which implies that people are the sovereign and they can change the constitution if they want, nor the liberal principle of constitutionalism, which implies that individuals have rights and this should limit the government, have no hold against the specific interpretation we see in Turkey. This interpretation implies that the founding father kept diversity, and the Kurds, away from the constitution, and none shall undo his will.

Eternity Clauses as the Vessel of Carrying the Initial Exclusion of the Kurds into the Future Generations

The *constituent power* is commonly referred to as the *constituent will* in Turkey. The purpose is to imply that the *national will* (more precisely, *the nationalized general will*), embodied by the Grand National Assembly, founded the Republic of Turkey. The nationalization of the general will transfers the qualities of the *general will*—that it does not err, that the citizens can be forced to obey the general will and that this means they are forced to be free (Rousseau 1762, Book II, Chapter III and Book I, Chapter VII)—to the political body/institution that claims to execute the national will, by representing the will of the majority within the body politic.

Like Rousseau's *general will*, in the Turkish case the national will directs the law-maker and dictates the common good. I do not mean that Rousseau's *general will* is theoretically applicable here. But those who invented the device of *national will* in Turkey designed it so that it has the capabilities of the *general will*. The qualities of the *general will* are ascribed to the *national will* (Atakan 2007, 62–80).

This is not too far-fetched an ascription, because there is precedence: the French revolutionaries' application of the notion of the national will, especially Sieyes's interpretation (Arendt 1963; Atakan 2007; Orhan 2014). It also serves a purpose: legitimation of the rule of the nationalist elite against the claims of the sultan and the traditional aristocracy in the case of Turkey (Atakan 2007). Indeed, whether it is a misunderstanding or a deliberate distortion of Rousseau's *general will*, it was meant to transform the general will into the national will, and the national into the will of the majority in the national assembly. This is the sovereignty of a "particular will" *par excellence*. Rousseau warned his reader against the danger of conflating the two or replacing one with the other.

The general will turns into a particular will when those who claim to represent the whole nation actually only represent a section within the nation. For, if the general will is the exercise of sovereignty by all members of the State, then the exercise of sovereignty without all citizens being present is the exercise of sovereignty by a particular will. The device of national will thus helps to legitimize the exercise of sovereignty in the absence of the sovereign, i.e., all members of the political community.

In Rousseau, "The constant will of all the members of the State is the general will," and it emerges when all citizens are present "in the popular assembly" (Rousseau 1762, Book IV, Chapter III). Since, as Rousseau argues, sovereignty is "nothing less than the exercise of the general will" (Book II, Chapter I), replacing the general will with the national will enables the nation, and by the same token, enables those who claim to represent the nation, to become the sovereign.

This formulation of sovereignty and its exercise was initiated by Sieyes after the French Revolution in 1789, and the Turkish political elite who founded modern Turkey were apparently inspired by the formulation (Atakan 2007; Orhan 2014). In Sieyes, the nation becomes the sovereign, i.e., the Supreme Being, and the parliament that represents the nation embodies the Supreme Being (Arendt 1963; Colón-Ríos 2010). Consequently, *the general will* in Rousseau is translated into *the national will*. In the Turkish political conceptualization, then, the nation has a will and it is embodied in the national assembly. But this is only half of the story. There is the constituent power and the constituted power in constitutional theory. Which one is equivalent to the national will then? According to Agamben, "Constituted powers exist only in the State: inseparable from a preestablished constitutional order, they need the State frame, whose reality they manifest. Constituting power, on the other hand, is situated outside the State; it owes nothing to the State, it exists without it, it is the spring whose current no use can ever exhaust" (1998, 29). This has been the case in Turkey. It has been argued, for instance, that the regime cannot be completely changed by elected politicians, because that would mean destroying the legacy of the founding father of the Republic of Turkey. This would mean destroying the Turkish State as we know it. The constituted power is formed through elections. It has a limited life, and it is secondary to the constituent power. Hence, it cannot modify the will of the founders where they willed clearly on a matter. An example of this dominant view among academics and justices was presented by Mumcu, who argued that (my translation):

> With the constitution of 1924, the Grand National Assembly of Turkey ceased to be the constituent power. The Grand National Assembly of Turkey that had to function as the constituent assembly under extraordinary circumstances had become an ordinary parliament. This parliament can amend a number of articles in the constitution, but it cannot make a new constitution. (Mumcu 2013, 10)[16]

This could be considered an "originalist" reading of the constitution or a personification of the constituent power in the person of the founding father. Indeed, that has been the grounds and justification for military tutelage and *coup d'états*: each time a political party, i.e., the constituted power, came close to transforming the regime into something else or was perceived as a threat to the established order, the Turkish army intervened on the basis of performing its duty as the guardian of the regime/the State. By the same token, the national assembly, although embodying the national will, is not the constituent will anymore. The parliament *acted* just once as the constituent will in 1924. This is the will that founds the State, establishes basic political institutions, and posits the fundamental law; i.e., the constitution. The constituent will, unlike ordinary political power, is not exhausted in the constituted power (Agamben 1998). Thus, the limits within which the constituted power, i.e., the government functions are those set by the constituent will, i.e. the power that posits the constitution.

Although two constitutions were enacted by two other "constituent powers" since the constitution of 1924, the military juntas that posited them defined their acts as the restoration of the legacy of the founding father. They did not present themselves as new constituent wills. In other words, the makers of the constitutions of 1961 and 1982 did not claim to be constituent powers. They justified their intervention on the grounds of merely restoring the order that was established by the will of the "true constituent power": the founding father. By the same token, no parliament/legislator/law-maker established by those constitutions, i.e., the constituted power, can claim to have the power to modify the will of the founding father. More specifically, according to this interpretation, no group or individual in the current political community can claim to possess or be the constituent power. Whoever claims so would also have destroyed the whole State with its army and institutions, and have built a new one.

The constituent will, therefore, must and ought to be preserved throughout time and direct new generations, since it is the will that established the political community *ex nihilo*—the whole myth of defeating seven great powers in the war of independence and destroying the *ancient regime* at the same time helps with this claim. Nevertheless, it should be noted that the new republic was built on the same existing and intact political institutions of the Ottoman State and its highly organized bureaucracy. A more moderate acknowledgement should be that the constituent power constituted the new State and set the goals that should be pursued by future generations. Although strong governments, i.e., potent constituted powers, have ruled in Turkey from time to time, none of them has gone beyond what the constituent will tailored for Kurds and other minorities. Despite the fact that the old strength of the Kemalist regime is fading, due to the "excesses" of the ruling party, what the constituent power willed for the Kurds remains unchallenged. If one reason is the ruling parties' nationalist creeds, the other is that the legacy of the founding father presents a formidable barrier to the accommodation of Kurdish political demands in the draft constitutions.

Article 4 of the current constitution—which follows the example of Article 102 of the constitution of 1924[17]— makes this point clear when it states that "The provision of Article 1 regarding the form of the State being a Republic, the characteristics of the Republic in Article 2, and the provisions of Article 3 shall not be amended, nor shall their amendment be proposed" (the constitution of 1982). In that sense, initiations or proposals to amend what the constituent "willed" regarding the exclusion of Kurds have failed, as this would mean destroying the legacy of the founding father.

This is a practical as well as theoretical/conceptual consequence of the dominance of the "originalist" interpretation of constitutions in jurisprudence and constitutional law in Turkey. The mechanics of this phenomenon is simple: the republican/nationalist elite founded the new "Turkish state," but their worldview and lifestyle were shared only by a minority. The trouble was that Turkey became a republic and maintaining political power would necessitate being voted for by the majority. In other words, free and fair elections would mean the replacement of the ruling party with the opposition. Therefore, authoritarian tendencies emerged as early as 1924 (Zürcher 2004, 176). Writing in 1925, Earle pointed out that "An interesting section of the constitution is that which deals with the powers and privileges of the President of the Republic. Fear has been expressed that the great personal prestige of Mustapha Kemal Pasha, combined with his leadership of the Popular Party and his constitutional prerogatives, might lead to the gradual transformation of the republic into a virtual military dictatorship" (1925, 87).

With the passing of the Law on the Maintenance of Order in 1925, Zürcher notes that the regime was turned into a one-party dictatorship where "all opposition" was silenced (2004, 176). Furthermore, a personality cult was built around the image of Mustafa Kemal, "the supreme leader and the founder of the republic" as the current constitution defines in the preamble. Mustafa Kemal soon became "the father of the nation and the eternal head of the State." The republican elite concentrated all powers in the national assembly, and indirectly in the person of the president of the assembly who was also the head of the State and the chairperson of the political party that ruled Turkey until 1950. Understandably, under their rule not only politics, but jurisprudence and constitutional interpretation, were shaped by their needs and deeds. Opposition parties did, finally, start to come to power by the majority vote, after the introduction of multiparty system in 1946 and the first multiparty elections in 1950. However, the army made a habit of intervening in favor of the established order, justifying their actions on the grounds of protecting the legacy of Mustafa Kemal (see the statement read on television by General Kenan Evren after the 1980 *coup d'état*).

Conceptual or theoretical legitimation of the Kemalist political order was, therefore, given the utmost importance, as sustaining the regime via hard power only put too much stress on the constitutional order. The hard power of the Turkish army was accompanied and supported by the soft power of scholars of jurisprudence and lawyers. Elite institutions such as universities, the Constitutional Court, and the supreme courts adopted the originalist reading of the constitution, resulting in the dominance of the interpretation that the original intention of the founders of the political order must be preserved:

> The moral reading insists that the Constitution means what the framers intended to say. Originalism insists that it means what they expected their language to do [. . .]. According to originalism, the great clauses of the Bill of Rights should be interpreted not as laying down the abstract moral principles they actually describe, but instead as referring, in a kind of code or disguise, to the framers' own assumptions and expectations about the correct application of those principles. (Dworkin 1996, 13)

The dominance of the originalist reading kept the regime under a tight military tutelage until the 2000s, but the ruling party managed to surpass it after consequent victories in the elections of 2002 and 2007. The ruling AKP made important amendments to the constitution in 2010, and modified the composition of higher courts in favour of the new political elite. Although the military tutelage has been over effectively since 2010, the originalist reading of the constitution is maintained in the draft constitutions of Turkish parties. This indicates that framers of Turkish constitutions give priority to the preservation of what the constituent "willed" for the Kurds, regardless of their ideological orientation and their own worldviews. The Turkish political elite's reaction to Kurdish demands is shaped by the shadow of the framers of the constitution of 1924, and it serves as a thick barrier that keeps the Kurds out of constitutions.

This barrier is basically the legacy of "the founding father" of the republic of Turkey, Mustafa Kemal Ataturk. Ataturk nationalism and his principles are the main political guidelines in Turkey because they have been in all constitutions. More importantly, Ataturk's legacy is deeply rooted in the minds and hearts of the Turkish political elite as well as the common folk (Bellaigue 2016). For instance, "We are still adolescents" cries a prominent actor in an interview; "Why? Because our father has not died yet, that is why! He [Ataturk] is still alive"[18] (Bilginer 2014). Bilginer points out that the founding father of the Republic of Turkey, Ataturk, has been "worshipped" and "idolized" for the last ninety years in Turkey. Unless he is understood as a plain man or as an ordinary human being, Turkish society in general and intellectuals in particular will not be able to break away from the authoritarian past associated with the founding father. Alam refers to the same phenomenon when he argues that "Turkey's historical political tradition, in which the state is looked upon as a benevolent father or guardian, personified in a strong individual, also lends its support to and legitimizes authoritarianism and the exclusion of the Kurds" (2014, 2).

Another example is the notion or belief known as *Ataturk's gift to the nation* (*Atatürk'ün ulusa armağanı*). According to this notion, Mustafa Kemal is "the immortal leader and the unrivalled hero" (the constitution of 1982, Preamble). First, independence was *his gift* to *his* nation: *he* initiated the nationalist movement, *he* won the War of Independence as the supreme leader of the nation and the heroic commander of the army. Civil and political liberties were also *his gifts* to *his* nation, for he abolished the sultanate and proclaimed popular sovereignty. Last but not least, the Republic, too, along with *a civilized and modern society*, was *his gift* to *his* nation and *the generations to come*, for he was the "supreme reformer and revolutionary leader who ensured that Turkey would remain a republic." That is why the phrase "we the people . . . do ordain and establish this Constitution" is missing in the preambles of the constitutions of 1961 and 1982. Instead, both Turkish constitutions were "entrusted to the guardianship of the *Turkish Nation's sons and daughters"* (the constitution of 1982, Preamble). This reveals the spirit of the constitutions as well as the mind-set of their framers: not the people, but Ataturk, *the father of Turks*, authored the constitution and bestowed it upon the generations to come.

No doubt that the image of a father figure bestowing public goods such as laws, constitutions, freedom, and the universal vote upon his subjects/people/fellow citizens did not emerge during the one-man rule in Turkey between 1923 and 1938. For instance, the Ottoman Sultan Abdülaziz (1830–1876) is said to have *gifted* the first constitution to his subjects in 1876. The sultans before him had also *gifted* this or that to their subjects. The point is that while this father figure might sit well with monarchy—since the monarch was considered as the embodiment of the body politic (Kantorowicz 1957)—the elevation of an office holder in a republic to this rank displays the establishment of autocracy. As Münkler (2016) emphasizes, in modern republics and democracies, too, the autocrat generally poses as a benevolent figure who assumes the title of "the father of the nation." The main problem is not that a strongman assumes this or that title or takes credit for something he has achieved, but that such an elevation of a person negates the long struggle of individuals and collectives and the sacrifices they make for the public goods considered as a gift from autocrats.

CONCLUSION

It is common for constitutional amendments to require the vote of a qualified majority in the legislator. Nevertheless, legal and political theorists agree that perpetuating the inflexibility of constitutional provisions through eternity clauses is not democratic. For instance, Agamben stresses that "it is time to stop regarding declarations of rights as proclamations of eternal, *metajuridical values binding the legislator* (in fact, without much success) to respect eternal ethical principles, and to begin to consider them according to their real historical function in the modern nation-state" (Agamben 1998, 75). We see a parallel thought in Arendt as well, as she notes that "the whole problem of an absolute which would bestow validity upon positive, man-made laws was partly an inheritance from absolutism" (Arendt 1963, 189). Arendt quotes framers of the American constitution of the eighteenth century, those of the opinion that constraining the will of legislation via eternity clauses in the constitution does not stem from the need to safeguard democracy, since democratic principles allow each generation to make and/or amend fundamental laws according to their own understanding of liberty and governance (Arendt 1963). Rousseau, too, emphasizes at least three times in *The Social Contract*

that "The inflexibility of the laws, which prevents them from adapting themselves to circumstances, may, in certain cases, render them disastrous, and
make them bring about, at a time of crisis, the ruin of the State" (1762, Book
IV, Chapter VI; for other instances in which Rousseau argues against eternity
clauses, see Book III, Chapters XI and XVIII).

   Turkish framers operated under the pretext of "protecting the legacy of the
founding father" when they excluded "domestic enemies"—the Kurds and
political Islam—from the constitutions of 1961 and 1982. That is to say, certain principles such as Ataturk nationalism, Ataturk principles and the unity
of the State with its nation had dominated the two constitutions, in order to
keep the spirit of the 1924 Constitution alive. This makes a good case for the
inflexibility of fundamental laws. The purpose was keeping political Islam
and the Kurds at bay. This seems to have changed vis-à-vis political Islam,
after the conservative-Islamic party, the AKP, came to power in 2002. Kurdish political demands, too, have been snowballing since the republican elite
declared that they "buried the dream of Kurdistan" in the Mount of Ararat
in 1930 (Beşikçi 1998, 2). Nevertheless, the legacy of the founding father
continues to impose great constraints on the representation of the Kurds or
their interests in draft constitutions. Consequently, protecting the age-old ra-
tionalization above remains the salient characteristic of Turkish constitution-
making vis-à-vis Kurdish political demands.

NOTES

   1. An entry on the official website of the Grand National Assembly of Turkey, under the section "Constitution Reconciliation Committee," available on http://global.
tbmm.gov.tr/, accessed on 6 May 2013.
   2. The aforementioned draft amendments were approved in a referendum in 2017
and Turkey abolished its parliamentary system of government for a presidential system with a strong executive.
   3. Interestingly, the constitution of Rojava (Syrian Kurdistan) was also named
Charter of the Social Contract. The choice of concepts displays the influence of the
Kurdish political discourse in Turkey over its counterpart in Syria. There, the political
authority wants to assure themselves and the world that they do not impose their will,
and that the constitution of Rojava reflects the voice of all sections and communities
within the society.
   4. A caveat with regard to Guida's approach is that he identifies one of the reasons
as "the lack of individualistic culture" (2014, 188). Apart from being a Western-
centric and an Orientalist argument, it misses the point. This pattern is by no means
peculiar to Kurdish provinces. Even in Western Turkey, a city like Izmir which, according to the standards Guida would apply, has a population that would adhere to
"individualistic culture" (whatever that is), we see a similar electoral behavior. Here

too, municipalities and central governments do not hesitate to reward their voters and "punish" those who have not voted for them (see the websites of *Milliyet*, 29.11.2009; and *Sonkale*, 11.12.2013, for two examples). Clearly, Guida assumes that there are communal/communitarian and individualistic cultures, and societies could be divided between these two lines. However, as Bauer reminds us, "Sweeping characterizations of regions or civilizations have been widely discredited since Samuel Huntington's publication of *The Clash of Civilizations*. The analysis has been accompanied by an "us" versus "them" rhetoric that reflects an unconscious but persistent failure to acknowledge that regions consist of diverse cultures and that all societies bear multiple and conflicting ethical perspectives. Careful observers know that any reference to an "Asian" perspective, for example, signals an ideological purpose: namely cultural nationalism, and likely a defensive reaction to Western pressure" (2003, 239).

5. For example, the amount granted to three major parties in 2014 was 315,707,521 Turkish Lira (equivalent to more than $137 million USD).

6. Non-Muslim minorities are not represented by a political party in the parliament, although there are a few deputies from those communities. The pro-Kurdish HDP urges the government, from time to time, to apologize to the Armenians, Assyrian-Syriacs, Greeks, and Jews and return the property of the persecuted and perished to their descendants, including extending citizenship to the descendants living abroad, because of the hostility they faced since the beginning of the twentieth century. This advocacy has its reflection in the draft constitution prepared by the HDP, which will be examined below.

7. I shall make it clear that no political party has posted a full draft on their websites. Therefore, my examination is limited to the texts released by political parties in April 2013, and the statements of their politicians on the media.

8. Village-guards are a militia group in Kurdistan, comprised of Kurdish villagers armed by the Turkish state to fight Kurdish guerrillas. Some are volunteers, while others were forced to take up arms or else they would face persecution or evacuation from their villages. For further information on the system, see Bruinessen (1999); Gökalp (2007); Gunes (2012a); Paker and Akca (2013); Scalbert-Yücel and Le Ray (2006); Watts (2009); Yarkin (2015).

9. The long years of civil war have devastated rural and urban settlements and the environment in Kurdistan. Therefore, another common demand in Kurdistan is the rebuilding of villages and cities, compensating those who migrated or those who have suffered economic losses. This is particularly important because the Kurdish region in Turkey suffers from the poorest conditions in living standards and human development. Without reparations for the damages inflicted by the state's security apparatuses and also the implementation of affirmative action policies in social and economic life, the welfare and income gap between Kurdish and Turkish citizens will keep widening. However, nothing substantial is offered in the two existing drafts. Such accommodations are also crucial in winning the hearts and minds of those affected by the disproportionate use of force by Turkish security forces. A provisional article in the drafts would address this demand.

10. Self-rule in Kurdistan does not appear in the HDP's draft. But this is not because the HDP does not demand it; it is because the HDP tends to be subtler about it

in order to attract Turkish voters as well. The HDP is subtle about demanding self-rule in Kurdistan also because their draft necessitates devolution of power to local and regional authorities. Although this practically means self-rule in all regions and provinces in Turkey, the main purpose of strengthening local administrations against the central government is promoting self-rule in Kurdistan. As a matter of fact, none of the other regions or provinces or political parties in Turkey demand devolution of power to local and regional administrations. The main rationale behind the HDP's proposal that Turkey be divided into 25 administrative regions and these regions be as autonomous as possible is conveying the message that the HDP is not only advocating for Kurdish rights and that what the party demands it demands for all of Turkey, although the rest of the political parties indeed display no interest in decentralization or devolution of power to local and regional administrations. This will become clear below where I evaluate the drafts one by one.

11. The title to a work by Lenin published in 1904.

12. "The HDP is a coalition and I represent maybe not everyone in it, but the socialists. When [the Kurdistan Workers' Party's jailed leader] Abdullah Öcalan called me, he took this representation into consideration" (source: "Unusual political figure now plays key role in PKK talks" [Yinanç 2013]).

13. See *Daily Sabah*, 30 June 2016; and *Radikal,* 25 April 2015; for two of such instances where HDP deputies stated views clashing with their parties' official stance. Kadri Yildirim criticized the party's support for LGBT marches during the month of Ramadan; Altan Tan was criticized by the LGBT organizations for alienating LGBT individuals in a party rally.

14. Actually, democratic autonomy is not the appropriate name to be used for the kind of political decentralization proposed in the HDP's draft. It is a system of creating sovereign local governments through fragmenting state sovereignty and is not reflected in its entirety in the HDP's draft. Hence I will discuss that project in detail in chapter 4.

15. Nevertheless, the Roma and Christian minorities are mentioned in the draft.

16. "1924 Anayasası ile Türkiye Büyük Millet Meclisi kurucu güç olma niteliğini bitirmiştir. Olağanüstü koşullar gereği kurucu meclis olarak çalışmak zorunda kalan Türkiye Büyük Millet Meclisi, artık normal bir parlamento durumunu almıştır. Bu parlamento, Anayasa'yı çeşitli hükümleri açısından değiştirebilir, ama yeni bir Anayasa yapamaz."

17. Article 102 of the constitution of 1924 states that "The provisions of the first article of this law that determine the state as a republic shall not be amended and its amendment shall not be proposed."

18. "Hâlâ ergeniz biz. Çünkü neden? Bizim babamız ölmedi hâlâ da ondan. Hâlâ yaşıyor. İçimizde!"

Chapter Four

Autonomy Against and Across Nation-States

Transnational Political Communities in the Making in Kurdistan

In the introduction to this book I stated that I set out to answer one question: do dominant Kurdish political movements in Turkey and Syria operate within the confines of nationalism, or do they introduce a political community other than the nation-state and its variations, as they claim? As it is a national liberation movement it would be sensible to assume, as scholarship in general does, that Kurdish movements either demand territorial autonomy for Kurds in Kurdistan or that they seek to establish a Kurdish nation-state. However, my main argument is that the movements' discourse and praxis go beyond multiculturalist/group-differentiated rights for Kurds in Kurdistan, yet they steer away from state-oriented nationalism and do not pursue the goal of building a nation-state for the Kurds. In other words, I imply that they indeed introduce a model of political community that is not confined within nationalist politics.

In this chapter, I try to understand and articulate how the Kurdish movements' model of political community differs from the nation-state and its variations such as territorial autonomy. I think this is discernible from the trajectory that the Kurdish movement in Turkey has followed so far, as well from the content of the project of *Democratic Confederalism* promoted and pursued by the movement as the goal. Thus, the chapter provides a short depiction of the movement's trajectory that separates it from a typical nationalist movement, and it will identify the pillars of the model of political community the Kurds wish to establish. To be more precise, I try to answer this question: why do the politics of the Kurdish movement in Turkey (and by extension in Syria) go beyond minority rights and falls short of building a nation-state for the Kurds? The answer will help us understand why the draft constitutions I discussed in chapter 3 do not answer Kurdish political demands, and why the movement objects to the labels of separatism and nation-state building. I also hope to place the project of Democratic Confederalism within a framework of political community in Western political thought.

The previous two chapters laid the groundwork for answering this chapter's question. In chapter 2 I argued that exercising self-rule within larger political entities, rather than building a sovereign state, surfaces as the *modus operandi* of the Kurdish political elite in Turkey. I highlighted that Kurdish politics has oriented itself around demands for self-rule, and that building a Kurdish state has not been promoted by the dominant political elite. But since the Turkish political elite have been too state-centric in their discourse and praxis, they perceive the Kurdish quest for self-rule as a threat to the integrity of the State. Hence, they label Kurdish politics as separatism and ethnic nationalism, and mainstream scholarship uses the same label. I pointed out that this was a grave misunderstanding, and I emphasized that if the Kurdish conflict in Turkey is to be addressed, the self-rule-oriented characteristic of Kurdish politics should be acknowledged. Hence, I concluded, although founding a nation-state is not on the agenda of the dominant Kurdish national movement, self-rule in Kurdistan is the priority. However, I did not specify what kind of self-rule in Kurdistan I refer to. In chapter 3 I argued that these common characteristics of Kurdish and Turkish politics were reflected in the constitutional drafts of major political parties from both sides. I highlighted that constitutional drafts of Turkish political parties do not accommodate Kurdish political demands, because they impose a single political community and do not recognize self-rule of any kind in Kurdistan. I also highlighted that the pro-Kurdish political party's constitutional draft did not promote national rights for Kurds in any sense, although it was the most promising draft with regard to Kurdish demands. What the pro-Kurdish political party envisaged was, therefore, within the limits of multiculturalism. However, it should be kept in mind that the pro-Kurdish party's constitutional draft does not reflect what the Kurdish national movement designed for self-rule in Kurdistan. Therefore, it could not answer the question of whether the Kurdish movement envisages a political community other than the nation-state or not. In this chapter I intend to answer this question.

The chapter focuses on the project of Democratic Confederalism, because the project sets out to establish a model of political community that challenges and undermines the existing hegemonic models in the Middle East: the nation-state and the Islamic *Ummah*. The crucial aspect of the model is that it is tailored not solely for liberating Kurdistan from foreign or "colonial" domination, although this is the core objective. The ultimate goal is ending the ongoing wars in the Middle East and establishing a political structure that will lead to peaceful cohabitation of a myriad of communities and their autonomous yet interdependent political entities in the region. Thus, the project is designed to establish self-rule in Kurdistan via installing a model of political community that will radically transform the political order beyond Kurdistan.

My objective here is addressing the misunderstanding that the Kurdish political movement in Turkey seeks secession or territorial autonomy in Kurdistan. This movement, represented in the person of the PKK (Partiya Karkerên Kurdîstan-Kurdistan Workers' Party), is considered a typical nationalist movement.[1] However, the movement's politics differ from a classical nationalist agenda. First, the movement has transformed the nationalist element in its discourse, i.e., the claim to national sovereignty in Kurdistan in the name of the Kurdish nation is transformed into the claim to a form of self-rule in the name of *peoples and communities of Kurdistan*. This suggests a form of communal/communitarian control (Leezenberg 2016) over the lands and resources of Kurdistan, through a form of direct democracy as collective decision-making. Second, the movement abandoned the goal of founding a Kurdish nation-state. Indeed, this was not priority in their agenda from the onset, because "ending Turkish colonialism in Kurdistan" (PKK Congress 1995) did not mean the same thing as founding a Kurdish nation-state (see section 2). Third, their politics go beyond obtaining cultural and territorial autonomy granted by nation-states, which is common to minority nationalisms. On the structural and organizational level, the movement attempts to build self-governing towns and cities in Kurdistan, and to connect them through a transnational confederation.

Thus, the movement's politics, as reflected in the project of *Democratic Confederalism*, are critical of (I) the nation-state as the hegemonic form of political community; (II) representative institutions of political decision-making; (III) absolute and indivisible sovereignty of a political authority that claims to represent a people or a nation; and (IV) citizenship based on cultural or civic identity. In these ways, the project is a challenge to the existing models of political community in the Middle East. Therefore, I aim to articulate the components of the movements' politics in relation to discussions on political community, to support my argument that the project founds a model of political community that differs from the dominant ones in the Middle East.

The methodology I follow in this chapter provides a contextual, conceptual, and theoretical analysis of the Kurdish model of self-rule through a reading of primary and secondary sources. First, I depict a historical context for the project, through a reading of secondary sources. Then I will do content analysis, relying on the writings of the architect of the project and the works of researchers who have studied the project with or without conducting fieldwork. Here, I will try to depict the pillars of the model through analysing the content and the implementation of the project. The last section is based on theoretical analyses of the project as a model of political community, in which I try to compare the model with other political communities.

The chapter has three sections. In the first section, I will try to contextualise the model of Democratic Confederalism. I will mainly draw on Akçura's *Üç Tarz-ı Siyaset* (Three Models of Politics, 1904), an essay in which he lays down the framework for three clashing visions of political community in the Middle East, in order to identify the three dominant models of political community there. In this seminal essay, Akçura identified three political currents/ thoughts and their models of political community in the early twentieth-century Ottoman Empire: Ottomanism (as the political current) and *Empire* (as political community moulded out of the communities subject to the imperial rule, in order to create an Ottoman Nation), Pan-Islamism and the *Islamic Ummah*, and Pan-Turkism/Turkish Nationalism and *the Turkish nation-state*. I will argue that Akçura focused on the dominant political currents and omitted the fourth one that should not be categorized within any of the three above: self-rule-oriented currents within the empire. Kurdish politics was one of these self-rule-oriented modes of politics that did not catch Akçura's attention. The argument in this section is that self-rule in Kurdistan without a Kurdish nation-state is a fourth model of political community in the making. As I argued in chapter 2, Kurdish principalities that lived until the nineteenth century could be considered as political communities. Akçura omitted this historical model and the quest for it by his contemporaries in Kurdistan; partly because he focused on the dominant models of political community and partly because the model was not crystallized as clearly as it is now, as a political community that differs and challenges the existing ones. Now that it is presented more assertively and as it is also partly implemented as a political project by the contemporary Kurdish political movement under the name of Democratic Confederalism, I think it is time to name *self-rule in Kurdistan without a Kurdish State* as the fourth model of political community.

The second section will be an examination of the content of the project of Democratic Confederalism and its implementation. The section was meant to be a conceptual and empirical inquiry of the project. However, I was not able to conduct fieldwork in Syrian Kurdistan where the project is being most effectively implemented, due to security concerns. Therefore, my analysis of the content will be limited to a study of primary and secondary sources. My main primary sources are two texts from the architect of the project, Abdullah Öcalan (2005, 2011), and decisions taken during PKK party congresses and the Rojava constitution. Also, I rely on many secondary sources that contain either abstract analyses of the project or empirical observations regarding its implementation in Turkish and Syrian Kurdistan. I prioritized studying the secondary sources that are based on fieldwork conducted in, or travels made to, Turkish and Syrian Kurdistan. The main argument in this section is that both conceptual and empirical examinations of the project of Democratic Confederalism demonstrate that the Kurdish movement makes claim to sovereignty through fragmenting it. Founding self-ruling towns and cities in Kurdistan through violent means, and defending them by violent means through the concept of self-defence, amounts to a reconfiguration of sovereignty. In that sense, the Kurdish movement acts like a constituent power, not like a minority movement that demands certain rights from the State. I will contend that the theory and practice of the movement demonstrates a reliance on the ideas of *radical democracy* (Laclau and Mouffe 1985; Mouffe 1992; Mouffe and Holdengraber 1989), Hardt and Negri's critical approach to representation and sovereignty and their notion of *multitude* as the political subject (2000, 2004), and Bookchin's *libertarian municipalism* (1994, 1995, 2015) to shape and implement the project.

Finally, I try to build a link between the model and the contemporary frameworks of political community in Western political theory in the last section. The section is a discussion of the parameters of *Democratic Confederalism* as a model of political community. Here, I draw mainly on Arendt (1963, 1954, 1958), Waldron (2011), and Isin (2007; 2012a, 2012b; 2013) to place the model in a framework of contemporary political theory. I will try to articulate how the project differs from the existing models of political community. Although the model is based in the tradition of self-rule in Kurdistan, it is a more ambitious project with cosmopolitan and radical democratic approaches to political participation and membership in political community.

To sum up, the answer to my question in the introduction to this chapter is "yes": the project of Democratic Confederalism is the revival of self-rule-oriented Kurdish politics with elements of cosmopolitan citizenship and radical democracy. Thus, it introduces an alternative/new model of political community. This chapter is therefore where I discuss how the Kurdish political movement goes beyond multiculturalism whilst steering away from state-oriented nationalism. However, I do not provide an analysis of the history of, nor the organization of, the Kurdish movement. Rather, I discuss the project of Democratic Confederalism that the movement promotes. The project goes well beyond multiculturalism in its formulations but falls short of founding a nation-state or promoting the right to self-determination in that sense. Therefore, this chapter is where I also emphasize that it is not accurate to label the movement's politics as ethnic nationalism (I will highlight the implications and problems of, and criticisms about the project, in the concluding chapter).

THREE HEGEMONIC VISIONS OF
POLITICAL COMMUNITY ARE CHALLENGED:
THE REVIVAL OF THE MARGINALIZED TRADITION
OF POLITICAL COMMUNITY IN THE MIDDLE EAST

Some analysts have argued that what we witness in the Middle East since 2011 is the equivalent of the Thirty Years' War in the seventeenth-century Europe (Haass 2014; Lawson 2014; MacMillan 2015). Yet others contended that the developments amount to the collapse of the Sykes-Picot Agreement of 1916, after which the post–World War I borders in the Middle East were drawn by France and Britain (Gaub and Pawlak 2013; Rabinovich 2014). Both views have valid points: the Sunni-Shia division is one of the deepest and most perpetuated rifts that breeds conflict within and across borders; and admittedly, the notoriously artificial borders are the legacy of the post-war colonial design. Subsequently, borders crumble under the pressure of defiant movements and forces, because they lacked legitimacy in the eyes of those who fared worse within and outside them since the moment they were drawn (Hamelink and Baris 2014). Nevertheless, religious tensions and artificial borders have always existed in the Middle East and in the rest of the world. These two factors hardly explain the centuries-old political crises and the catastrophes generated by it.

MERIP has pointed out that "the frustration of participatory politics, the fixation upon state security at the expense of freedoms, the stubborn growth of inequality amidst great wealth, the lack of investment in education and other public goods, all in the shadow of outside interference" inevitably led to "imminent destruction" (2015, 6). However, the problem is much more systemic. As Hardt and Negri put it, civil war is a global problem: "The theory and practices of modern sovereignty were born by confronting this same problem, the problem of civil war—and here we are thrown back primarily to the seventeenth rather than the eighteenth century" (2004, 238).

The crisis is systemic in its scope, and it is not only because of the claim that the "Third World War" is being fought via proxies.[2] It is systemic because the erosion of shared values and the death of a "common Middle Eastern spirit" (*pace* Nietzsche) have unleashed a phase of nihilism and civil wars that pit everyone against everyone. That is because none of the century-old visions of political community, i.e., the Ottomanism, the Pan Islamism, nationalism, and stateless self-rule, have been able to generate shared values for the region after the demise of the old one.

The crisis is, thus, that of sovereignty and of clashing visions of political community. The nation-state, political Islam or the Islamic *Ummah*, neo-Ottomanism, and the Kurdish vision of self-rule, *Democratic Confederalism*, are the main contenders. Europe has, in Foucault's words, settled "some of its violences" and managed to move from one "domination to [another kind of] domination" (Newman 2005, 42), via the establishment of the European Union. However, post-Ottoman societies are yet to resolve the crisis generated by the collapse of the empire. A quick look at the Nietzschean analysis of what Europe was going through will be useful in understanding the crisis in the Middle East.[3] Endowing the region with a shared vision and a common spirit is yet to be achieved by the "good" Middle Easterners, to use a Nietzschean category.

The rise of nationalism and the ensuing discord in Europe during the nineteenth century was defined by Nietzsche as "the loss of a European voice" (Elbe 2009, 75). It deprived Europeans of the tools for cultivating "a common European spirit"; and then, "the Christian ice was beginning to thaw, permitting the European continent to decompose into a set of rivalling and hostile nationalisms" (75). Nietzsche contended that this was triggered by the advance of secularism, or the "death of God," which he thought unleashed a culture of "nihilism" that was about to take Europe captive. Nihilism meant "that the highest values devalue themselves," and that "the aim was lacking" (75). The replacement of that aim, that spirit, he argues, would not be possible in the short run because "the rise of modern science cast irrevocable doubt on the Christian idea of Europe without offering a new European vision of its own" (75). In the absence of a shared vision and after the erosion of common values, Europe disintegrated into clashing and competing visions of political community, both at country and regional levels. Mishra depicts this era with a Nietzschean dark picture, pointing out that Nietzsche, Freud, and Max Weber "mounted a full-blown intellectual revolt against the oppressive certainties of rationalist ideologies" that bequeathed "an era when the disaffected masses [. . .] had begun to fall for radical alternatives, in the form of blood-and-soil nationalism and anarchist terrorism" (2016, 5). Nietzsche's predictions turned into reality after the turn of the century, as if he had stated a self-fulfilling prophecy. Secular ideologies such as nationalism, socialism, and fascism transformed the colonial contest into a competition for redesigning Europe and the world. The rest is well-known: two world wars. The emergence of a set of values; more importantly, of a cluster of institutions that made peace, stability, cooperation and integration possible was only possible after the 1950s—and it took a good deal of pressure and material contribution from the other side of the Atlantic. A European community was crystallized only after 1989, through a series of agreements that gradually turned economic cooperation between core countries into the current political integration known as the European Union.[4]

The Middle East, "as a set of peoples and societies articulated not only by [. . .] state structures but also by other ties, old and new, that cross or challenge borders" (Albo 1993, 19), was undergoing a process of discord at the turn of the twentieth century, akin to what Nietzsche described in the context of Europe. The advent of nationalism and the quest for self-rule among peoples subject to the Ottoman rule incited wars of independence within the empire. These developments did not only shrink the multinational Ottoman Empire; additionally, the ensuing appropriation of political authority and state institutions by nationalist elites, and the foundation of oppressive nation-states backed by Western imperialism and colonialism, ushered in an era of "nihilism" that has ravaged the region ever since. The Middle East has been suffering a crisis of values, identity, and purpose, triggered by the fading sense of sharing a common history and the loss of a shared vision among Muslim-majority societies. This has surfaced in discussions on how to prevent the collapse of the Ottoman Empire. Akçura depicts this picture in his well-known essay *Uc Tarz-ı Siyaset* (1904—literally the "three models of politics," but it can be translated as *Three Political Doctrines/Projects*), and then became the ideologue of Turkish nationalism.[5] He accurately and vividly captured three dominant currents of political thought within the Ottoman body politic of the time:

> [S]ince the rise of the desires for progress and rehabilitation spread from the West, three principal political doctrines have been conceived and followed in the Ottoman dominions. The first is the one which seeks to create an Ottoman Nation through assimilating and unifying the various nations subject to Ottoman rule. The second seeks to unify politically all Muslims living under the governance of the Ottoman State because of the fact that the prerogative of the Caliphate has been a part of the power of the Ottoman State (this is what the Europeans call Pan-Islamism). The third seeks to organize a policy of Turkish nationalism (Turk Milliyet-i siyasiyesi) based on ethnicity. [N]on-Turkish Muslim groups who have been already Turkified to a certain extent would be further assimilated. Those who have never been assimilated but at the same time have no national feelings would be entirely assimilated under such a program. (Akçura 1904, 6, 12)

After providing a detailed discussion on the "usefulness" and the probable success or failure of these political doctrines, Akçura suggested, just as Nietzsche did in the case of "Christian Europe," that "in recent times, under the impact of Western ideas ethnic and national feelings which previously had been subsumed by Islam began to show their force" (1904, 11–12). He was convinced that neither creating an Ottoman nation nor uniting all Muslims under the Caliph were viable projects. The project of founding an Ottoman nation was doomed because non-Turkic peoples "believed they had experienced injustice and not justice, contempt and not equality, misery and not happiness. The Nineteenth century had taught them their past, their rights and their nationality on the one hand, and had weakened the Ottomans, their masters on the other" (1904, 8). The project of an Islamic political community would also fail because "The dominant current in our contemporary history is that of the nations. Religions as such are increasingly losing their political importance and force" (1904, 12). Thus, he concludes, the establishment of a political community based on Turkish ethnic nationalism (known as *Turanism* or *Pan-Turkism)* was the best way to prevent the collapse of the Ottoman state.

Ideally, the elites that adopted these competing political projects would settle the internal discord and deal with the crisis of vision and identity through a confrontation. This would result in the foundation of one or multiple political communities, depending on whom the winner would be. This was, more or less, what happened in Europe in the course of the twentieth century. Alas, political actors in the Middle East have not been able to settle their disputes without interference from global and regional actors since the beginning of the nineteenth century.

This does not mean that they neither had nor have agency or that they have only been victims in the process. On the contrary, their agency and choices are among the main and most important factors (Baris 2016). However, their agency and choices have not been the prevailing element in the equation. The intervention of European colonial powers and the First World War disrupted the process of reshaping old political communities, founding new ones, and forming collective identities for the region. As Ulrichsen (2014) notes, major Western powers put a lid upon socio-political dynamics within the region through invasions, agreements, military interventions, and alliances before and after the First World War. This prolonged the enmities and conflicts in a way that best serves the interests of Western domination. External powers still design politics in the region:

[T]he First World War was pivotal to the creation of the modern Middle East. It hastened the demise of the Ottoman Empire and paved the way for the emergence of a state-system (albeit under mandatory rule) that remains largely in place today. The entire political landscape of the region was reshaped as the legacy of the war sapped the ability of imperial "outsiders" to dominate and influence events, and nationalist groups succeeded in mobilizing mass movements around distinctly national identities. [. . .] it is harder to establish historical distance from events whose legacy continues to resonate throughout the region. (Ulrichsen 2014, 203–4)

Moreover, as Thomas Piketty points out, the causes of the ongoing "state of war" are also rooted in the economic and social inequalities "and Western nations have themselves largely to blame for that inequality"; because "These are the regimes that are militarily and politically supported by Western powers" (Piketty, cited in Tankersley 2015, 2–5).

Not being able to resolve the crisis of vision and identity and tackle the socio-political discord on their own, Middle Eastern societies are yet to end the nihilistic phase of their history in the Nietzschean sense. Secular ideologies such as nationalism and socialism have been suppressing or clashing with political Islam, albeit none of them have been able to declare victory upon others, and the crisis is likely to be sustained until one of the century-old visions of or a new model of political community manages to establish its domination in the region. In Gramsci's words, "The crisis consists precisely in the fact that the old is dying and the new cannot be born; in this interregnum a great variety of morbid symptoms appear. The old world is dying away, and the new world struggles to come forth: Now is the time of monsters" (MERIP 2015, 6).

That "the old is dying" has to do, to a great degree, with the fact that Islamic political community, the *Ummah*, as Cündioğlu pointed out in an interview, has lost its universal voice (Oskay 2015, 4). Islam has long ceased to be the glue that used to hold a variety of communities and societies together. The partition of the Ottoman Empire between a number of nation-states has eroded the already weak solidarity between Muslims of different ethnic and cultural backgrounds. That is why the self-declared Caliph of the Islamic State proclaimed the end of the Sykes-Picot Agreement in his inauguration speech in 2014 (Çandar 2016). The agreement has been the symbol of the partition of the Ottoman Empire by colonial European powers, and thus, the moment that marks the destruction of the last Islamic *Ummah* and the Caliphate by "Christian powers" as some would put it, although the agreement was never implemented. Neo-Pan-Islamic movements or actors, e.g., the Islamic State and the Turkish ruling elite who have been in power since 2002, are known or perceived as as extremists, sectarian, or self-serving. Ozkan notes:

Davutoglu[6] is a pan-Islamist. He is deeply influenced by Islam, yet he also uses Islam to achieve his foreign policy goals. He believes in a Sunni Muslim hegemonic order led by Turkey that would encompass the Middle East, the Caucasus and Central Asia, and include Albania and Bosnia as well. And I say Sunni because Iran is not part of this envisaged world. He argues that Turkey cannot be confined to its present-day borders. Should it continue to cling to its post-Cold War policy of preserving the status quo, Turkey will be destroyed. He believes that the nation-states that were formed in 1918 were artificial. But he does not idealize post-nation-state systems such as the European Union. To the contrary, he wants to go back in time to an order based on Islamic unity. (Ozkan 2014, 2)

Therefore, Islam is no longer the grounds for a common identity or a shared vision in the Middle East. The very factors that deposed the Islamic *Ummah* and destroyed the traditional ground of solidarity between Muslim majority societies, i.e., nationalism and the establishment of numerous nation-states, can hardly offer a way out of the crisis in the region. In other words Islam, at least in the present context, has lost its hegemony as the provider of trans-ethnic/national political values, principles, and common goals, and as the overarching political identity for trans-border cooperation.

The other form of political community, i.e., the nation-state, at least for the time being, can hardly be commissioned or trusted with forging a shared vision and a transnational political identity for all in the region, because of obvious reasons such as aggressive nation-building policies, irredentism, and the oppression of minorities. In the absence of regionally potent institutions or a hegemon that could impose a sort of regime or an order (Evans 1996), it does not seem likely that nationalist ideologies and principles are going to fill the void any time soon.

Indeed, nationalism has been the problem itself since the very beginning of this crisis. It is responsible for genocides, ethnic cleansings, and massacres in almost every country with more than one ethnic community. Moreover, nation-states in the region have mostly relied on their hard power and op-pressive, repressive, and assimilationist policies to preserve their territorial integrity. They marginalized and persecuted minorities and majorities alike under their rule. National ideologies in the region have no moral or ethical force left in their articulations, even rhetorically, to create shared values and common goals. That is why it offers no viable solution to the ongoing crisis in the Middle East.

Multiculturalism comes to mind as a catalysing factor that could contribute to the stability in the region that is now dominated by nation-states. It could provide nation-states, on the one hand, with means and mechanisms to accommodate minorities without compromising their territorial integrity. Minorities, on the other hand, would be assured that they do not have to build their own state order to preserve their cultures and customs. With the imple-mentation of multiculturalist policies, as Kymlicka (2007) has pointed out, nation-states could overcome the fear of disintegration, and minorities could enjoy certain rights that allow them to flourish. However, the political elite, in general, see multicultural discourse as the Trojan horse of the West, designed to destabilise and ultimately divide countries. For that reason, Turkey offi-cially does not recognize the existence of minorities other than the Christian and Jewish communities mentioned in the Treaty of Lausanne. Turkey has not signed even the minimalist convention on minority rights, the European *Framework Convention for the Protection of National Minorities*, in order to avoid recognizing new minorities or new rights for existing minorities.

Therefore, an equilibrium of nation-state hegemony accompanied by a regime of multiculturalism that could solve most of the problems in Kurdistan and in the Middle East is not likely to be realized. The political elite in the Middle East, at least in the context of Kurds, have not been enthusiastic to recognize or implement multiculturalist policies on their own. Kurds have so far had to fight to get what they demand.

As I emphasized in the introduction, nation-states in the region perceive any manifestation of identity politics as a threat to national security. The moment political demands are articulated, propaganda of separatism and/or terrorism is put to work against politically active actors. Even advocating or demanding multicultural rights is criminalized and pushed underground by security-centred policies of nation-states. Once pushed underground, political movements then become more radical and their agenda tends to go beyond multicultural rights as well (Kymlicka 2007). The development of the Kurdish political movement and its transformation into what it is today, is a textbook example of this. In the 1960s and 70s, Kurdish politics revolved around the abolishment of the ban on Kurdish language and culture. But even those who spoke or sang Kurdish were prosecuted and imprisoned. This forced Kurdish political activists to mobilize around clandestine organizations and pushed them to adopt more radical agendas (Gunes 2012a). Therefore, multiculturalism does not seem to play the role of a stabilizing political element in the Middle East of nation-states, although it has played a great role in Europe and Latin America.

Lastly, Turkey's current government has been associated with pursuing a dream of neo-Ottomanism, which did not have currency even in the nineteenth and twentieth centuries, as Akçura pointed out a century ago (1904). Although glorifying the Ottoman past and the neo-Ottomanist discourse played positive roles in the electoral success of the ruling party in 2015, and although organizations, from associations to football clubs, that adopt the name "Ottoman" have been mushrooming lately in Turkey, creating a neo-Ottoman polity is not yet on the agenda of any major political actor. The ruling party does not openly advocate for reviving Ottoman institutions in any way, even though deputies from time to time hint at it (*Hurriyet Daily News* 2015).[7] Nationalism is the major currency in Turkey now and neo-Ottomanism cannot be built on Turkish nationalism. Indeed, nationalism, bearing a Turkish or non-Turkish stamp, was the main corrosive that had destroyed the Ottoman polity from within in the first place. Thus, the third grand vision of political community does not hold either.

Here is where the project of Democratic Confederalism assumes relevance. A careful examination of primary and secondary sources on the ideology and practice of the Kurdish political movements in Turkey and Syria will reveal that liberating Kurdistan has been only part of a larger goal for them. A more ambitious program has been pursued by the movements. They claim that the model of Democratic Confederalism is the answer to most critical questions in the Middle East. For instance, Öcalan emphasizes that "The PKK never regarded the Kurdish question as a mere problem of ethnicity or nationhood. Rather, we believed, it was the project of liberating the [whole Turkish] society and democratizing it" (2011, 7). The movement's human composition and its ideology as well, testify to this claim (Akkaya and Jongerden 2013; Casier and Jongerden 2012; Gunes 2012b; Jongerden and Akkaya 2012). Also, the movement's goals, aspirations, and actions serve a much more radical and transformative agenda than that of a typical nationalist movement (Akkaya and Jongerden 2015; Matin 2015; TATORT Kurdistan 2011).

The Blind Spot in Akçura's Essay: Stateless Models of Political Community

Akçura omitted two traditions of political community that were in opposition to the other three: stateless self-rule in the form of tribalism—tribal federations and confederations—and principalities. All three visions put the State at the core of political organization. In other words, the three visions studied by Akçura subscribe to the idea of the absolute and indivisible sovereignty of this or that political authority as the *sine qua non* of their models of political community, while the other two traditions of political community are not organized around such a supremacy or superiority of a person or an office. Both traditions existed in Kurdistan in particular, and in the Middle East in general. I will dwell on the Kurdish model of Democratic Confederalism as the revival of this stateless self-rule in Kurdistan, as "early Mesopotamian forms of democratic communal organization and the communitarian concept of freedom (*amargi*) they involved" plays a central role in Abdullah Öcalan's overall doctrine and the model he developed (Leezenberg 2016, 6).[8] As Leezenberg points out, Öcalan rejects European/Western capitalist visions of society and is drawn to the Middle Eastern and specifically Mesopotamian models of freedom and political organization. He sets out to develop a "'distinct antithesis to European civilization,' which should be developed on the 'historical foundations specific to the Middle East'" (2016, 6).

By focusing on the Kurdish model, I try to add it to the picture described by Akçura more than a century ago. I contend that Kurdish political movements in Turkey and Syria present their model of Democratic Confederalism as the way out of the crisis in Middle East. And as Ahmedi (2016), Matin (2014a, 2014b, 2015), Graeber (2014a, 2014b), and Taussig (2015) have pointed out, the Democratic Confederalist project has the potential to bring progressive movements, communities, and individuals in the region together around the democratic principles it is based upon. In that sense, especially the Kurds of Rojava (Syrian Kurdistan) seem to appear as the equivalents of the "good Europeans" in Nietzsche. Nevertheless, the personality cult built around their leader Öcalan, the hierarchical organization of the movement around one party, and their alleged intolerance toward other political actors in Syrian and Turkish Kurdistan generates plenty of criticism.

Christianity had arguably lost a great deal of influence over individuals and/or societies in the nineteenth century, due to the advance of sciences since the onset of the Enlightenment (Elbe 2009). Islam, on the contrary, has been losing its grip not so much on the "hearts and minds," but mainly on political establishments, due to the predominance and endurance of national-socialist, nationalist, and dictatorial regimes. This explains, to a great degree, the revanchist tendencies of Islamic political parties and their push for Islamic conservative policies when and where they come to power. It also explains the persistence of civil wars due to the harsh oppression of the opposition by the authoritarian regimes in countries where political Islam, self-rule-demanding minorities, and progressive movements are seen as subversive. In this context, the Kurdish movement's model of political community is worth studying and analysing more closely, because it claims to have found a way to connect the Middle East through transnational political communities without appealing to religion or nationalism.

Thus, the project of Democratic Confederalism revives the fourth grand vision of political community in Kurdistan and in the Middle East and builds a new model upon it: stateless self-rule through transnational political communities. The point of departure for the project is the common history and shared heritage of the Middle Eastern societies.[9] For instance, Öcalan's specific reference to the Islamic heritage of Kurds and Turks in his 2013 Newroz statement implies that not only the pre-modern Middle Eastern tradition of *self-rule without the State,* but also the common Islamic heritage in the Middle East, like Christianity in Europe, lies at the foundation of Democratic Confederalism (Çandar 2013). Nevertheless, the project goes beyond acknowledging the values shared by the peoples of Mesopotamia and the Middle East, and takes a step further. Unlike the pre-modern Kurdish political actors who sought self-rule within the empires, the architects, engineers, and executors of Democratic Confederalism defy the established political order in the Middle East. They aspire to install this model of political community in the whole region.

Focusing particularly on the destructive effects of nationalisms, criticising class formations within nation-states and their role in promoting capitalist modernity—which he associates with environmental degradation, ecological destruction and subjugation of individuals, societies, and their freedoms to centralized States—Öcalan is convinced that

> [T]he foundation of a separate Kurdish nation-state does not make sense for the Kurds. Over the last decades the Kurds have not only struggled against repression by the dominant powers and for the recognition of their existence but also for the liberation of their society from the grip of feudalism. Hence it does not make sense to replace the old chains by new ones or even enhance the repression. This is what the foundation of a nation-state would mean in the context of the capitalist modernity. Without opposition against the capitalist modernity there will be no place for the liberation of the peoples. This is why the founding of a Kurdish nation-state is not an option for me. The call for a separate nation-state results from the interests of the ruling class or the interests of the bourgeoisie but does not reflect the interests of the people since another state would only be the creation of additional injustice and would curtail the right to freedom even more. (Öcalan 2011, 19)

What does Democratic Confederalism stand for then? Öcalan suggests that in the Middle East "a system which takes into consideration the religious, ethnic and class differences in society" should be promoted (2005, 1). He makes it explicit on the same page that his system does not make use of the right to self-determination for establishing a Kurdish nation-state in Kurdistan but builds a new model of home-grown democracy that will surpass boundaries. The project suggests that Kurdish activists, politicians, and organizations build grassroots democratic institutions in each part of Kurdistan. These institutions are communes, councils, popular assemblies, regional assemblies, youth, women, economic, and ecological councils.

Öcalan is convinced that political actors in Kurdistan and in the greater Middle East should not wait for the nation-states to accept the demands for democratization and social justice put forward by citizens. They should take the necessary steps for liberating Kurdistan and creating a peaceful Middle East on their own, relying on their agency and power. This is what Mouffe and Holdengraber (1989) and Jongerden (2015) refer to as radical democracy or radicalising democracy: expanding political space beyond legal and formal institutions, forming grassroots forums, councils and assemblies open to universal participation of residents (not only citizens), building coalitions among different sections and sectors of society, and practicing democracy through a culture of solidarity without being authorized by the State.

The project is proposed by the Kurdish political movement originating in Turkish Kurdistan (*Kurdîstana Bakûr*-North Kurdistan), and it had partially been implemented there in some towns and cities through organizing communes, councils, and assemblies (Akkaya and Jongerden 2013; TATORT Kurdistan 2011). The project is in the process of being fully realized in

Syrian Kurdistan (Rojava/Western Kurdistan), through the ongoing experiment/social revolution. Taussig emphasizes that he was "overwhelmed by the strangeness of it all; by the openness of people, their crazy generosity, and the splendour of their cause, a first in the Middle East if not in world history," referring to his impression of the implementation of the model in Rojava (2015, 3). Graeber (2014a) has voiced similar positive remarks about Syrian Kurdistan and the implementation of radical democratic politics there. Prominent academics in Turkey have hailed the revolution in Syrian Kurdistan and named the experiment as "a model for the whole Middle East" (Altan 2014). Miley argues that "the HDP and the Öcalan model of Democratic Confederalism remain the country's [Turkey's], and the region's, greatest hope for peace" (2015, 1). Hence, it seems that Democratic Confederalism, as a new model of political community that challenges the hegemony of political Islam and the nation-state, has already left its mark on politics specifically in Kurdish regions of Turkey and Syria. However, certain concerns regarding the Kurdish movements, Marxist-Leninist strategies, and its reliance on organised violence, as well as the criticisms I mentioned above, are being raised as well.

HOW DOES THE KURDISH PROJECT DIFFER FROM NATIONALIST MODELS OF POLITICAL COMMUNITY? THE ORIGINS AND THE CONTENT OF DEMOCRATIC CONFEDERALISM

In the first section, I contextualised the project of Democratic Confederalism. In this section, I will focus on what makes the project different from nationalism. The objective here is to support my argument that the Kurdish political movement in Turkey, unlike what mainstream scholarship on Kurds suggests, should not be categorised as a typical ethno-nationalist movement. I will do this through a discussion on the transformation of the movement and the content of the project. The main sources under scrutiny here will be Öcalan's two works on Democratic Confederalism, decisions of party congresses, and secondary sources on the project. The argument of this section is that the project of Democratic Confederalism is not designed to found a Kurdish nation-state or to secure minority rights for Kurds, but aims at the transformation of national/nationalist politics altogether. Therefore, it would be a grave misunderstanding to label the Kurdish political movement as an exclusively nationalist one.

For instance, Tezcür (2010, 2016) uses the terms "insurgency," "ethnic insurgent organization," "ethnic rebellion," and "nationalist movement" interchangeably while referring to the Kurdish political movement. This is the rule in scholarship on Kurds, not an exception. Nevertheless, as I pointed out in the introduction to this chapter, the movement abandoned its previous policy of founding a Kurdish nation-state. Also, the movement challenges both practical manifestations of, and theoretical justifications for, the nation-state. In that sense, it claims to strive to "expand political space" (Knott 2014, 209) beyond national boundaries via replacing representative processes, institutions, and mechanisms of political decision-making with local, provincial, and regional ones that are based on direct citizen participation. Thus, their project is meant to undermine the principle of national sovereignty, question the legitimacy of demarcated borders, challenge representative democracy via establishing institutions of direct democracy, and finally, disapprove exclusive citizenship based on cultural, ethnic, national, and religious identities. Hence, the project is in direct confrontation with the current hegemonic political order: the nation-state in Turkey in particular, and the nation-state system in the Middle East in general.

One might argue that this sounds like civic nationalism on a much smaller scale because it applies the same principles in towns and cities. However, there are two nuances here: civic nationalism must refer to a nation and its right to self-determination in a historical homeland, no matter who the citizens are and how their political participation is arranged. The Kurdish project's point of departure is not a claim of the Kurdish nation to national sovereignty in its historical homeland, Kurdistan. The claim to self-rule in Kurdistan and in the Middle East is presented on the ground of freedom as an ethical principle, not as a political right. In other words, the claim to self-rule is *not* a reflection of the right to self-determination of the Kurdish nation embedded in the international law. Self-rule/autonomy is claimed in the name of *peoples* of Kurdistan, regardless of whether they are a small community like the Assyrians or a large nation of tens of millions like the Kurds. The project also rejects the right to self-determination (Öcalan 2011), which is the bread and butter of nationalist movements and the grounds for national claims to sovereignty, regardless of whether they have civic or ethnic characteristics.[10]

The armed forces and the outlawed branches of the movement, too, are organized on the same principles, and they are joined by voluntary fighters or activists from all around the world. Such a broad-based solidarity and synergy could hardly be generated by a nationalist movement, an ethnic insurgency, or a minority rights movement. The popularity of the movement's struggle against the Islamic State in Rojava (Syrian/Western Kurdistan) resembles that of the Spanish revolutionaries during the Spanish Civil War in the 1930s. Certain ethical principles, other than those we find in a nationalist cause, should be in play in order to garner such a universal support—and

Öcalan (2011) emphasizes this ethical aspect of the project. The movements' struggle in Rojava represents "a revolution in values" in the Middle East (Alexander 2006, 386), although its fruits are yet to be reaped.

There are numerous empirical manifestations of this aspect in the Kurdish project. For instance, although the majority of its human composition is made of those who identify themselves as Kurds, the movement managed to form a coalition between liberal, leftist, and moderate/democratic Islamic organizations and individuals who promote the idea of a pluralist democratic political order in Turkey and in the Middle East. The political party that represents the movement in Turkey, the HDP (Halklarin Democratic Partisi-Democratic Peoples' Party), named its 2015 election campaign as "Great Humanity," in which no specific reference was made to Kurdish national claims (HDP 2015; Tekdemir 2015). It is the only political party in Turkey that has ever had Armenian, Assyrian, LGBT, Roma, Muslim, Christian, Atheist, and Yezidi deputies or deputy candidates within its ranks. It is also the only party that implements a 40 percent gender quota and has the highest number of women deputies. All decision-making positions, starting from mayoral offices in towns and cities to the chairmanship of the party, are occupied by a male and a female. This is due to the central role women play in the movement, as well as the priority given to liberation of women by the movement's theory and practice.

The feminist aspect of the Rojava revolution as well, without doubt, is the most important and unique characteristic of the administration of the Federation of Northern and Eastern Syria. According to Öcalan, the symbolic leader of the Kurdish movements in Turkey and Syria, women were the first colonized "nation" and liberation and equality is not possible without their emancipation first. As Knapp et. al. emphasize, creating "a Middle Eastern society with women at its center" is an endeavour of utmost significance: "The region is otherwise universally considered to be patriarchal and regressive, but the resistance in Kobanî in particular has radically transformed the image of Kurdish women." Discussing the feminist aspect of the Kurdish movement is not the focus of this book. However, it should be noted that the politics of the Kurdish movement cannot be fully grasped without paying due attention to their feminist agendas.

Thus, analysing the movement and its project within the limits of nationalism, ethnic insurgency, and minority rights would be confining it within a framework that it does not fit into. I will now delve into the movements' politics in order to lay out the pillars of the project of Democratic Confederalism. The content analysis here is not about comparing the project with other political communities. It is not about evaluating the model against the theory of political community either. What I try to do here is articulate how

Democratic Confederalism is founding a new political community, via dissecting the nation-state and disrupting the system of nation-states, though not necessarily destroying or abolishing them.

The dissection starts, first, with the ideological pillar that targets ideological, political, cultural, symbolic, and social foundations of the established order. For instance, Kurdistan is depicted as a colonized country by four nation-states, not as territories/regions that are separately parts of these states. However, one does not have to wait for the liberation or independence of Kurdistan in order to experience freedom and live the life of a freed woman/man. In a Fanonian fashion, the political and armed struggle against colonialist powers in Kurdistan is presented as liberating and empowering in itself. The movement promises the creation of a new, free person, to replace the "slave-like" being whose political will is "castrated" by the colonialist master.

This discourse is intended to *delegitimise* State institutions, agents, actors, and their "collaborators" in Kurdistan. This is done through invoking the ethical principle that political freedom is compromised if cities, towns, villages, and minority communities are ruled by officers of the government, not by citizen councils and their elected committees. Replacing centrally appointed officers and their institutions with the ones established by the Kurdish movement is the first step in the foundation of Democratic Confederalism in Kurdistan (I use the term foundation because the movement does this against and despite the State, not with the State's permission, authorization, or consent). Second, it proceeds with a claim to physical control of space through the pillar of *the right to self-defence* against the State. This means that citizen councils and assemblies have the right to defend themselves against the assaults of the security forces of the State, because they are the democratic organs of "true" popular sovereignty through which the people exercise political power. That is why hundreds of councilmen and councilwomen were killed by Turkish forces in several towns and cities in Turkish Kurdistan in 2015 and 2016, during the sieges and assaults against the city councils that declared democratic autonomy in 2015 and the neighbourhoods where militants affiliated with the urban youth guerrillas, the YPS (*Yekîneyên Parastina Sivîlan* - Civilian Protection Units), took up arms with the claim to protect autonomy and name councils, councilmen, and councilwomen as true rulers in Kurdistan.[11] Third, the project introduces a formulation of sovereignty that allows each city and town, even each neighbourhood and village, to have ultimate control over their natural resources and over certain public affairs, offices, and services. Here, sovereignty is reconfigured and disseminated throughout towns, cities, regions/federations, and transnational confederations so that the mechanism/principle of national sovereignty does not consolidate political power in one centre. I will dwell on each of these pillars in a separate section.

The Origins of Democratic Confederalism:
The Shift from Revolution in Turkey and a Socialist
State in Kurdistan to Stateless and Transnational
Political Communities in the Middle East

A typical nationalist movement makes use of the claim that it represents a nation and that it has the right to self-determination; i.e., to found a nation-state of its own (Keating 2001b). For instance, Scotland and Catalonia organized referendums for that purpose in 2014 and 2015, and the Kurdistan Regional Government in Iraq organized one in 2017. Indeed, as Keating has noted, the "integrated nation-state has for some 200 years monopolized our understanding of constitutionalism and forced other claims to justify themselves in relation to it; and it has encouraged the identification of self-determination with the constitution of a separate state" (2001a, 6). A nationalist movement is commonly associated with founding a nation-state in an historical homeland, or at least obtaining territorial autonomy if statehood would not be achievable or desirable for some reason (Smith 2001, 2000; Weber 1994). Although Keating observes that not all national claims amount to statehood, and that some nationalist movements are more comfortable than others with being part of plurinational states, he also emphasizes that nationalism typically presents itself with territorial claims (2001b, 16–20).

As Abizadeh (2012) and Scherz (2013) have noted, national movements legitimize the exercise of political power on the ground that the object of power, i.e., the nation, should also be the subject of power. Nationalist elites claim that they represent the nation, and that the exercise of political power in the name of the nation is legitimate. Representative political institutions, by the same token, are considered to channel the will of the nation through electoral processes, civil society activism, and public discussions and deliberations. Thus, a self-referential mechanism of exercising political power is established; i.e., the claim is that, ideally, the nation makes the law that is abided by via electing their representatives. In other words, the claim is that political power is exercised in the name of the sovereign nation by the elected representatives.

The Kurdish movement, too, was pursuing a national agenda until the late 1990s. "We left Ankara [and] became a party, we arrived in the Middle East [and] became an army, we will achieve statehood [by] opening up to the world"[12] stated Öcalan while in Europe, shortly after he was forced to leave his sanctuary in Syria in 1998. In 2003, however, Öcalan was promoting the idea of "politics beyond the state, political organization beyond the party, and political subjectivity beyond the class" (Akkaya and Jongerden 2012b, 2). He dismissed the idea of founding a Kurdish nation-state, arguing that the State is "the 'original sin' of humanity" (Akkaya and Jongerden 2015, 171).

What should one make of this transformation in Öcalan's ideas, which are followed to the letter by the dominant Kurdish political movements in Turkey and Syria? The PKK, no doubt, was founded to liberate Kurdistan from "colonial" domination, although this was considered the first step in a socialist revolution in Turkey as the greater goal. What then, if not a Kurdish nation-state or a new State in Kurdistan, would achieve this? "The only alternative is *Democratic Confederalism*" declared Öcalan with the goal of "the resolution of the problems of the Middle East" (2005).

Clearly, the high costs of pushing for independence (Keating 2001b) in a Kurdistan divided between four nation-states was the main factor behind this transformation. In its fifth congress in 1995, the PKK leadership set the goal of building a national army of sixty thousand men and women strong, in order to achieve a "national democratic popular revolution" in Kurdistan (PKK Congress 1995, 33–54). Neither of the objectives were achieved in the following years. Moreover, its leader was captured in 1999 and was convicted to lifetime imprisonment. However, these two factors do not explain such a radical ideological shift, although Öcalan is known for his pragmatism. As several sources have pointed out, Öcalan's engagement with contemporary political theory from his prison cell seems to be responsible for the radical turn in his politics (Akkaya and Jongerden 2011, 2013; Biehl 2014; Enzinna 2015; Ruyters 2015).

Öcalan seems to have gone through a rigorous re-evaluation of the politics of the Kurdish movement in the light of his reading of political theorists from the Left. He adopted semi-anarchist politics while preparing his defence to be submitted to Turkish, Greek, and European courts between 1999 and 2004 (Akkaya and Jongerden 2011). I describe his politics as *anarchist* because he sees the State as "the fundamental source of oppression in society," as classical anarchism suggests (Newman 2005, 34). "The system of nation states," Öcalan argues, "has become a serious barrier to the development of society and democracy and freedom since the end of the 20th century" (2005, 1). His suggestion is to organize "a concrete, localised, grass-roots struggle engaged in by those directly concerned, but which, importantly, is able at the same time to transcend its position of particularity by inscribing itself on the universal horizon of equality" (Newman 2008, 102). Öcalan's politics are *semi*-anarchist because he does not recommend the immediate destruction of the State, but leaves room for the "peaceful coexistence" of the nation-state with local and regional autonomous political communities run by popular assemblies and city councils, "as long as the nation-state does not interfere with central matters of self-administration" (2011, 32).

Thus, Democratic Confederalism transforms the goal of the Kurdish movement from achieving a "national democratic popular revolution" and building a socialist Kurdistan, to a *democratic revolution.* This is a rejection of the State altogether. Democratic revolution means stateless democracy in the context of Democratic Confederalism because the State is associated with "fascist and militarist" domination (Öcalan 2011, 28). The PKK leadership had emphasized that it seeks to come to power through a popular revolution (PKK Congress 1995). But this agenda of coming to power was abandoned in the seventh, eighth, and ninth congresses held in 2000, 2002, and 2003, following Öcalan's capture in 1999. His unexpected defence before the court in which he stated that all he tried to do was democratize the State, his written defences, and other writings from prison transformed the movements' structure as well as its goals, which culminated in the development of the project of Democratic Confederalism (Akkaya and Jongerden 2011, 2013, 2015). The Project was finalized and proclaimed by Öcalan in 2005 via a declaration (Öcalan 2005).

The First Pillar of Democratic Confederalism: Autonomy against the State; Towns Councils, Popular Assemblies, and Thematic Councils in Kurdistan and Their Function as a Component of the Wider Framework

Democratic Confederalism seeks to make a political community out of every city and town in the four parts of Kurdistan and connect them with one another through a confederal super-structure. This means founding autonomous but interconnected transnational political communities, with grassroots movements in which people make decisions in forums, councils, and assemblies. This is more than reforming the representative institutions and electoral processes of the nation-state or seeking territorial and/or cultural autonomy for a minority within a nation. The project embodies "a new form of politics, involving the creation of autonomous spaces and relations rather than the representation of identities to power" (Newman 2014, 93). It introduces alternative institutions and processes of political decision-making in order to realize radical democracy—"radical in the sense that it tries to develop the concept of democracy beyond nation and state" (Akkaya and Jongerden 2011, 152).

Beyond nation refers to taking politics to grassroots people via new political institutions and decision-making processes. In nation-states, the nation is the only collective political subject, and it exercises political power indirectly via representatives in the parliament. The new institutions established by the Kurdish project introduces citizen forums, neighbourhood assemblies, towns, and city councils that enable citizens to exercise political power directly over certain issues in certain loci, without abolishing unicameral or bicameral parliaments. Thus, not only the nation, but also town and city dwellers as well as villagers become political subjects who exercise political power directly and indirectly in their collective capacities or as individuals. This is radical democracy. "Beyond the State" means allowing transnational alliance, cooperation, and coordination to take place between political actors and institutions of towns, cities, and regions. The objective here is to open up borders to transnational movement of people and goods and take a step toward creating less rigid boundaries between nation-states in the region. This is the cosmopolitan aspect of the project. Political participation and membership in political communities would benefit from this less rigid regime of border control within the region inhabited by friendly political entities.

Even the most democratic regimes impose, arbitrarily, national boundaries and borders, although they have no solid bases in democratic theory to do so (Abizadeh 2012; Scherz 2013). To compensate for this, certain models of integration, accommodation, and power sharing have been designed in theory and practice. It is up to individual states or state systems such as the European Union to adopt a model of their choosing, to develop a model of their own, or to ignore diversity altogether and carry on with assimilationist or integrationist policies that aim at creating or maintaining a homogenous society.

Democratic Confederalism rejects the principles above and the mechanisms they function through. It is presumably based on ethical concerns, not on national ones (Öcalan 2011). Although the idea that the Kurds have the right to establish self-rule in Kurdistan has been persistently promoted, this is not done in a way typical of nationalist movements. We have already established that the leadership of the Kurdish movement often emphasize that they have no intention to found a Kurdish nation-state (Çamlıbel 2015). They have also stressed that Kurdistan does not belong to Kurds only, and that many peoples live side by side with Kurds and have Kurdistan as their homeland. Therefore, their claim is that they try to establish democratic rights and freedoms for all (Aretaios 2015; Karan 2015; Rojava Constitution 2014; TATORT 2014). Moreover, the Kurdish movement also rejects being confined by and within national borders, being marginalized by representative institutions if and when those institutions are the only political mechanism of the exercise of political power, and they disapprove of the principle of national sovereignty.

Instead of invoking the claim to national self-determination, which would mean independence in the form of a Kurdish nation-state, the Kurdish movement is in pursuit of founding a modified form of Aristotelian face-to-face political communities that are meant to undermine political centralization. The ultimate goal is the abolition of the principal and practice of national sovereignty. Named *Democratic Autonomy*, this is "autonomy from below" as opposed to "autonomy from above."

Democratic Autonomy holds that "the competences or practices of people" should determine the arrangement of public affairs and offices (Akkaya and Jongerden 2013, 167). Here, the term *people* does not refer to a specific cultural or political category, or to a political subject as in *the Kurdish people*. It refers to a random aggregate of individuals and communities—residents, to be precise. The idea is that residents of villages, neighbourhoods, towns, and cities have the autonomy to arrange their public affairs and offices without interference from external political entities and authorities. This is the opposite of territorial or cultural autonomy manifested in a legal status recognized or granted by a superior political authority, which is the dominant form of autonomy in contemporary political theory and practice. In that sense and this is the key in the context of this chapter, the Kurdish movement initiates an "act of foundation" (Arendt 1963): it acts as a *constituting power*, as a power that establishes a new political community. In other words, the project imposes an order and arranges public offices and public affairs according to a specific worldview, as all other models of political community do. In Rousseauian terms, this model as well forces *peoples/ citizens* to be free.

Thus, the project aims at founding multiple face-to-face political communities, i.e., making an autonomous political entity out of every community of settlement; but this is only the first tier in a system of three layers. The second layer[13] binds autonomous towns, cities, and regions together under a loose confederation, ultimately as an alternative to or a substitute for the State. This is what is called *Democratic Confederalism*: a political alliance of cities and towns that is meant to transcend nation-states, but live with them if necessary until states eventually wither away or become obsolete. This is clearly stated both in Öcalan's texts and in the Constitution of the Rojava Cantons in Syria (Öcalan 2011, Rojava Constitution 2014). Öcalan is aware that his project undermines the authority of, and is in direct confrontation with, nation-states. However, he is convinced that a balance can be found between the nation-state system and Democratic Confederalism:

> Revolutionary overthrow or the foundation of a new state does not create sustainable change. In the long run, freedom and justice can only be accomplished within a democratic-confederate dynamic process. Neither total rejection nor complete recognition of the state is useful for the democratic efforts of the civil society. Democratic confederations will not be limited to organize themselves within a single particular territory. They will become cross-border confederations when the societies concerned so desire. The overcoming of the state, particularly the nation-state, is a long-term process. The state will be overcome when *Democratic Confederalism* has proved its problem-solving capacities with a view to social issues. (Öcalan 2011, 32–34)

Likewise, Article 12 of the *Charter of the Social Contract* of the Rojava Cantons, the basic legal document that functions as the constitution of the autonomous Kurdish region in Syria, holds that "The Autonomous Regions form an integral part of Syria. It is a model for a future decentralized system of federal governance in Syria" (Rojava Administration 2014). Thus, the movement challenges the authority of nation-states where it can; but it is not engaged in state-making in the modern sense, where national sovereignty is the spirit and territorial integrity is the form of the political community. Here, communal/communitarian self-rule is the spirit, and the village, the town, and the city is the form. This is a more radical path compared to founding a Kurdish nation-state or demanding territorial/cultural autonomy.

The strategy through which autonomy against the state is put to practice is that first, towns and city councils, and regional assemblies proclaim autonomy against the State when they think it is time. They declare that they no longer accept being ruled from the capital of the nation (see Bozarslan 2016 for the proclamations of democratic autonomy in North Kurdistan in 2015). They also declare that they will defend themselves against the assaults coming from the State, if they have armed forces (this strategy worked in Syrian Kurdistan but failed in Turkish Kurdistan). I will dwell on self-defence in the subsection below; but to add the most crucial sentence of this section: councils, assemblies, and forums embody the political power of the people. Therefore, defending them via armed forces or guerrillas, according to the project, is defending the free will and the political freedom of the people embodied by those councils and assemblies. Their function is channelling the political will of the people into existence, by providing it with its *arena* or *agora*.

The Second Pillar of Democratic Confederalism: Self-Defence against the State and the Fragmentation of Territorial Sovereignty

The most crucial aspect of this project is its formulation of self-defence. Monopoly over the use of legitimate violence, as formulated by Weber, is the hallmark of modern states. Referring to this Weberian formulation, Holmes (2015) argues that the claim of the Kurdish armed forces in Syrian Kurdistan to have monopoly over the use of violence is a bid to found a Kurdish state. However, she notes that forty-four out of forty-six members of Women's Defence Units (Yekîneyên Parastina Jinan-YPJ) she interviewed have stated that they are not in favour of founding a Kurdish state. Holmes bases her argument on Article 15 of the *Charter of the Social Contract,* which holds that "The People's Defence Units (YPG) is the sole military force of the three Cantons, with the mandate to protect and defend the security of the Autonomous Regions and its peoples, against both internal and external threats."

Nevertheless, religious and ethnic communities that form minorities within Rojava cantons such as the Assyrians, Armenians, Turcoman, and Arabs are encouraged to have and keep their own armed forces for their self-defence, although they cannot operate outside their community without the approval of the YPG (Yekîneyên Parastina Gel-People's Defence Units). This is in line with Öcalan's formulation of self-defence, which does not draw on the Weberian principle of state-making. For him, self-defence is not a means to monopolize coercive force in Kurdistan via confronting the security apparatuses of the nation-state, but it serves one purpose only: "*Democratic Confederalism* is not at war with any nation-state but it will not stand idly by at assimilation efforts" (Öcalan 2011, 32).

This principle has its roots in Marxist interpretation of history, which suggests that "the state has not always existed," and that it exists only "in societies in which social classes exist" (Althusser 2014, 13). However, it draws more intimately on Bookchin, who modifies the revolutionary strategy of classical Marxism. Classical Marxism dictates "seizing state power" by a proletariat revolution and abolishing "the bourgeois state," while it is assumed that "the remnants of the *proletarian*state [sic] after the socialist revolution" dies away on its own (Lenin 2016, 13). Bookchin's theory of *Communalism*, on the other hand, "seeks to eliminate statist municipal structures and replace them with the institutions of a libertarian polity. It seeks to radically restructure cities' governing institutions into popular democratic assemblies based on neighbourhoods, towns, and villages" (Bookchin 2015, 36). These "virtually autonomous local communities, [. . .] loosely bound in a federation," should then "create a nationwide confederation of cities and towns to replace the republican nation-state," as instantiated by the Paris Commune in 1871 (2015, 34).

The reference to the Paris Commune is very important. Along with the idea of self-rule and autonomy against the nation-state, the notion of self-defence is also at play. This helps us grasp the whole dimension of self-defence in Bookchin's formulation of *libertarian municipalism*—a pillar of his *Communalism*—and the inspiration for Öcalan's *Democratic Autonomy*. Bookchin argues that revolutionaries should not "delude" themselves with the assumption that the ruling classes will idly stand by while revolutionaries disregard the State's sovereignty via proclaiming autonomy and exercising direct democracy in cities and towns (2015, 37). This notion, with a degree of modification, is adopted by Öcalan: "The self-defence of a society is not limited to the military dimension alone. It also presupposes the preservation of its identity, its own political awareness, and a process of democratization. Only then can we talk about self-defence. Against this background Democratic Confederalism can be called a system of self-defence of the society" (2011, 28).

This amounts to fragmenting state sovereignty as we know it, albeit without a plea to any "ready-made model," although both Öcalan and the constitution of Rojava refer to federalism. Federalism, for Öcalan and in the Rojava Constitution, is not the system in which federal states are formed as part of a centralized union. As Petrovic notes, "in a one-nation, ethnically homogenous republican federation, people as a holder of the constitutional power act both through the federal organs and through the organs of the federal units; the result is a high level centralization, which makes those federations similar to the decentralized unitary states, which, in the essence, they are" (2002, 690). However, in the Kurdish formulation, federal states, i.e., fragments, do not derive their power from the constitution of the federation as decentralized units. In Petrovic's words, here "the state is a federation of state fragments"; which means that the holder of the political power is not the union, but the fragments (2002, 690). In other words, the federal authority derives its power from autonomous entities and their separate constitutions, not the other way around. This is an undertaking to (re)install a structure of fragmented sovereignty in which the hierarchically structured, all-powerful central political authority of the nation-state is replaced by a plurality of centres such as towns, cities, and regions.

The most important trait of such a formulation of sovereignty is undoubtedly the fact that "there can be no holder of the constitutional power that could have the right to make decisions on the existence of the state fragment" (Petrovic 2002, 689). Here, sovereignty is no longer an exclusive prerogative of the central authority of the superstructure, i.e., the nation-state. Regional or local political entities become holders of this prerogative in their relative capacity as well.

As noted, villages, towns, cities, and regions become autonomous political entities in such a system. Now, if the fragmentation of sovereignty holds, each of these autonomous units is meant to exercise a gradual level of sovereign authority and autonomy. This means that the ultimate authority within a residential community is the community itself, not a regional or national authority/assembly/parliament. In such a residential community, all political and public affairs that do not necessitate the intervention or cooperation of another political authority—of course, any such intervention or cooperation will be conditioned on the consent of the said community—will be handled by the community itself. The criteria for public affairs and services that are solely handled by local authorities will vary, depending on negotiations and arrangements with other political entities. But ideally, these communities will act unilaterally when they do not have to act or when they do not choose to act with others. Although these criteria will vary, certain authorities and powers are kept within the monopoly of local administrations, such as self-defence, education, and control over natural resources. By the same token, since these communities are merely fragments that might not be able to mobilize necessary power and resources for self-defence against larger and stronger adversaries, i.e., nation-states, they are bound together in a confederation. Confederation serves the purposes of defence, education, healthcare, free movement of people and goods between members of the confederation, and so on. Most importantly, the confederation aims at rendering boundaries so porous that the exclusionary citizenship regimes that are based on national/cultural identities imposed by nation-states over Kurdistan would not hold. The purpose here, of course, is constructing transnational and trans-border connections between the four parts of Kurdistan, as well as creating a Middle Eastern union in order to build peace in the region.

The Third Pillar: Reconfiguring Sovereignty

Introducing communal/communitarian sovereignty in order to allow self-rule for small communities, towns, and cities, without changing the regime to a federation in countries too obsessed with unitary State, is the third pillar of the model. Thus, the model of Democratic Confederalism is also a reconfiguration of state sovereignty. Sovereignty refers to the "*supreme authority within a territory*" (Philpott 2010, 1). The territory referred to here is a national territory, not a regional or a local one. However, in the model of Democratic Confederalism, sovereignty is filtered from bottom to top: even the smallest residential communities such as neighbourhoods exercise political power and authority autonomously when it comes to certain public issues and affairs. Thus, sovereignty is envisaged as devoid of a centre. The smaller the community, the more power it has. This power is filtered up to towns, regions, confederations, and nations via representatives, but representative institutions play a role only when direct democracy has no application. Plural *supreme authorities*, in the form of forums, councils, assemblies, and congresses appear in the model. Each of these authorities has only a small spatial unit as their jurisdiction. How are the issues that interest more than one municipality handled? Here is where the confederation becomes relevant:

> To address problems and issues that transcend the boundaries of a single municipality, in turn, the democratized municipalities should join together to form a broader confederation. These assemblies and confederations, by their very existence, could then challenge the legitimacy of the state and statist forms of power. They could expressly be aimed at replacing state power and statecraft with popular power and a socially rational transformative politics. (Bookchin 2015, 36–37)

The *commune* is the smallest unit in the organization of this society. Communes make politically binding decisions via their forums and councils, which are open to every citizen. Participation is encouraged as a citizenship duty. Communes and neighbourhood councils send representatives to town councils and city assemblies, which handle the issues that are not in the jurisdiction of commune councils. Communes and their councils, neighbourhood and towns assemblies are established without legal affirmation or permission from State authorities. Apart from and along with communes based on residential units, there are also women, youth, judicial, cultural, environmental, ecological, economic, and social councils, which handle specific issues that are pertinent to their realm. When two or more authorities have claims over the same issue, they must take the problem to a higher council or assembly. This is not to be conflated with hierarchical organization: the way this can work as envisaged is only through the principle of arbitration, not of dictation. I tend to see a political principle that gives the role of *primus inter pares* to the higher councils and assemblies here, but this could be misleading an interoperation. Regional and national parliaments are kept intact for this purpose to handle overarching issues and public services and arbitrate between competing claims of local councils and assemblies. There are also councils established for religious and ethnic minorities in order to have them handle their public affairs. Each of these specific councils has veto rights regarding the specific interests they embody. For instance, women councils have veto rights over a law that is proposed regarding marriage or gender issues; as minority councils have veto rights regarding the laws that affect them.[14] "In these popular assemblies, citizens—including the middle classes as well as the working classes—deal with community affairs on a face-to-face basis, making policy decisions in a direct democracy and giving reality to the ideal of a humanistic, rational society" (Bookchin 2015, 36). Here the project steps outside of hegemonic forms of sovereignty that is defined on the ground of national boundaries.

Sovereignty has been a contested concept. Modern formulations of sovereignty usually have their reference in Bodin and Hobbes, "who argued for sovereignty as supreme authority. The concept continues to prevail as the presumption of political rule in states throughout the globe today, including ones where the sovereign body of law institutes limited government and civil rights for individuals" (Philpott 2010, 8). For Bodin and Hobbes, sovereignty is one, indivisible and absolute; and the holder of sovereignty is the monarch. As Philpott notes, sovereignty, defined as supreme authority within a territory, has three components: a holder of sovereignty, the supremacy of her/his/its authority over all authorities under the purview of this holder, and a territory (2010, 2–5).

The issue with modern formulations of sovereignty lies in what Hobbes suggested: "the main point of sovereign majesty and absolute power consists of giving the law to subjects in general without their consent" (Hobbes, cited in Hardt and Negri 2000, 84). In Philpott's (2010) analogy, sovereignty is like the legal prerogatives of a landlord over real estate. While in the middle ages the nobility, along with the monarch, had such prerogatives over a territory within the State, modern formulations of sovereignty take this prerogative away from petit sovereigns and concentrates it within the hands of a single entity, be it the monarch or the people/nation. While pre-modern political power was exercised by a number of authorities or by multiple self-governing political entities, the modern State monopolized sovereignty through the notion of absolute and indivisible sovereignty and concentrated political power at one centre. In other words, monopoly in the legitimate use of violence follows the monopolization of the exercise of political power. Indeed, it is hard to tell if the two are separate at all. State fragments of the pre-modern world disappeared as the nobility lost their inherited or granted prerogatives. The principle of national sovereignty allows self-rule only if the central authority recognizes the existence of a self-ruling entity. As Hardt and Negri have suggested, "Sovereignty can properly be said to exist only in monarchy, because only one can be sovereign. If two or three or many were to rule, there would be no sovereignty, because the sovereign cannot be subject to the rule of others. Democratic, plural, or popular political forms might be declared, but modern sovereignty really has only one political figure: a single transcendent power" (2000, 85).[15]

The problem is that whereas the king has an actual body, the people have not (Kantorowicz 1957). This creates a crisis and a possibility simultaneously. It is a possibility because "when the people take the place of the king the locus of power becomes an 'empty place.' To Lefort, this lack of a clear definition of the people is ultimately what guarantees the continuity of the democratic struggle" (Näsström 2015, 1). The tension arises precisely because of this lack of clarification about who the people are. As Jennings famously said, "The people cannot decide until someone decides who are the people" (1956, 56). This allows democratic competition and keeps the locus of power open to everyone. Nevertheless, it carries a grave risk as well. Näsström refers to this risk as "institutionalized uncertainty," because while the un-decidability of the identity of the people may broaden democratic possibilities, it could also breed authoritarian regimes (Näsström 2015, 3).

This brings us to the second problem: that "The people 'are a sovereign that cannot exercise sovereignty'" (Loughlin and Walker 2007, 1); or that "The 'people' as a corporate body that speaks in one voice is not an empirical reality and never was" (Chambers 2004, 154). Or, as Arato puts it, "no body, no institution, no person should be able to claim to fully embody the sovereign people, whose place must remain 'an empty place'" (2010, 4). In other words, "'the people' is never directly present to itself as a subject of constituent action," and a political action can be attributed to people only by raising a "'representational or attributive claim'" (Lindahl, cited in Oclopcic 2008, 359).

Nevertheless, electoral processes are no guaranties for a fair competition or for reaching a consensus on the identity of the people. Although representation presents us with a solution to this practical difficulty, it creates another problem: that of alienating citizens/common people from politics or excluding them from participating in public affairs except for voting on election days. This was at the centre of Thomas Jefferson's worries.[16] In Hardt and Negri's words, "the representation that functions to legitimate this sovereign power also alienates it completely from the multitude of subjects" (2000, 84).

Representative democracy is a mechanism that keeps inequalities intact while promising equality, because politics mainly remains as the activity of the elite, since the ordinary citizen is either ill equipped or she lacks the resources needed to engage effectively in electoral politics (Näsström 2015; Arendt 1963; Hardt and Negri 2004). Here arises the issue of "the contemporary disillusionment about election as the embodiment of popular will, and the widespread preoccupation in both domestic and global politics with questions of inclusion and exclusion" (Näsström 2015, 4). Political parties are clearly not being able to address this crisis of representation (Hardt and Negri 2004, 240–70). The reason is obvious:

> Politics has become a profession and a career, and the "elite" therefore is being chosen according to standards and criteria which are themselves profoundly unpolitical. It is in the nature of party systems that the authentically political talents can assert themselves only in rare cases, and it is even rarer that the specifically political qualifications survive the petty manoeuvres of party politics with its demands for plain salesmanship. (Arendt 1963, 277–78)

More importantly, Arendt also notes that the right to vote and political representation are not powers themselves, but are merely designed to offer protection against the abuse of power (1963, 143). In Rousseauian spirit, Arendt does not think that representation is equivalent to exercising one's political will; the will lies with representatives, and all that representation can do is limit the excessive power of the government.

It is therefore argued that contemporary *Occupy* movements and the quest for direct forms of democratic participation in decision-making processes is an answer to this disillusionment and frustration with representative democracy (H. Bozarslan 2015; Maeckelbergh 2012; Newman 2014; Oikonomakis and Roos 2013). Furthermore, in the case of Kurdish politics, "the new model of democratic autonomy and *Democratic Confederalism* is based on active citizenship, with people as subjects in their capacity to decide and act, debating problems and enacting solutions by the people and for the people" (Jongerden 2015, 5). Thus, the waves of protests and occupation of public spaces emerged in several countries such as Spain, Greece, the United States, and Turkey were not only about the exercise of the right to assembly recognized in the constitutions of those countries. As in most of these cases, and in the case of protests in Istanbul in the summer of 2013, neighbourhood assemblies were formed in more than thirty locations throughout the city, by which citizens strongly expressed their wish to bypass representative institutions (Özkırımlı 2014). They articulated their disenchantment with electoral processes through demanding and practicing a form of direct decision-making, although for a limited period of time and in relatively small area in the city centres.

Couldry and Fenton call this "rediscovering the general will" (2011, 1), making reference to Rousseau who emphasizes, throughout *The Social Contract,* that political will cannot be represented and that sovereignty cannot be exercised via representative democracy since "the moment a people allows itself to be represented, it is no long free: it no longer exists" (Book III, Chapter 15). For the Kurdish political movement, however, I contend, drawing on Arendt, that this is not about rediscovering the general will, but about recovering "the lost treasures" of modern revolutions: i.e., citizens' councils and peoples' assemblies. In the sixth chapter, *On Revolution* (1963), Arendt notes that what all modern revolutions (the American, the French, the Russian, the Hungarian) have had in common was, first, the mushrooming of councils and assemblies in neighbourhoods, towns, and cities; and second, the failure of subsequent political institutionalization to incorporate those democratic mechanisms in constitutions. Clearly, the leadership of the Kurdish political movements in Turkey and Syria are inspired by these analyses for the most significant element of their model is the recovery of those mechanisms and their institutionalization through founding them in towns and cities in Kurdistan and the Middle East.

For instance, a striking parallel between Öcalan's formulation of exercising political power directly and Arendt's analysis on the lost treasure of revolutions is the analogy or metaphor of a pyramid-like structure. Arendt refers to councils as "elementary republics" and "grassroots political organs," and notes that (emphasis added)

> No doubt this form of government, if fully developed, would have assumed again the *shape of a pyramid*, which, of course, is the shape of an essentially authoritarian government. But while, in all authoritarian government we know

of, authority is filtered down from above, in this case authority would have been generated neither at the top nor at the bottom, but on each of the pyramid's layers; and this obviously could constitute the solution to one of the most serious problems of all modern politics, which is not how to reconcile freedom and equality but how to reconcile equality and authority. (1963, 278)

In his statement titled "the Declaration of Democratic Confederalism" released in 2005, Öcalan argued that (emphasis added) "[T]he only alternative is Democratic Confederalism, which is a *pyramid-like* model of organisation. Here it is the communities who talk, debate and make decisions. From the base to the top the elected delegates would form a kind of loose co-ordinating body" (2005, 1).

The main problem for Öcalan, then, appears to be the democratic deficit in parliamentary democracies, the alienation of citizens from politics, and the monolithic understanding of popular sovereignty that legitimises even oppressive and authoritarian regimes like Turkey and Syria. Therefore, the project he developed involves autonomous communes, neighbourhood and town councils, city and regional assemblies. These are connected under a confederation, which replaces or lives alongside centralized nation-states in the Middle East. According to Öcalan (2011), national parliaments, representative political institutions, and electoral processes lack mechanisms that ensure active participation of all citizens. The alternative is an arrangement in which political power does not flow from the centre toward the periphery, but flows from communes, councils, and assemblies to confederal unions through delegation.

The purpose here is keeping the political will of individual citizens intact: their will is not transferred to a sovereign person or body that represents the nation, like a national parliament. Individual citizens retain their political will and are as active as they can be in local public affairs through participating in community gatherings and councils. Councils, on the other hand, delegate their executive power (not their political will) to higher councils and assemblies, without giving up their autonomous status and the power to make decisions pertaining to local public affairs, including self-defence.

Öcalan, thus draws inspiration from Arendt, Hardt and Negri, and Laclau and Mouffe to address this trilogy of problems: (I) founding new layers of authoritative decision-making mechanisms such as neighbourhood councils, popular assemblies, and cantonal and regional parliaments, in addition to national institutions, in order to help generate authority at different levels and with the purpose of undermining the hegemonic, monolithic understanding of (national) sovereignty (Arendt 1963); (II) forming permanent connections between a multiplicity of actors in order to transform the subject of revolution or the political subject from parties to an alliance of political parties, civil society organizations, and thematic associations such as women and youth organizations, i.e., the *multitude* (Hardt and Negri 2004); and finally, (III) radicalizing democracy via expanding politics beyond national parliaments by involving the grassroots people in the processes of political decision-making (Laclau and Mouffe 1985; Mouffe and Holdengraber 1989).

Öcalan specifically targets the Turkish constitution of 1982, which defines sovereignty as indivisible and absolute. Also, an ethno-culturally defined Turkish nation is the holder of sovereignty, while the supreme authority is the Grand National Assembly; and finally, this supreme authority rules over the whole demarcated territory. The Turkish nation is identified as the sovereign; however, it exercises its sovereignty through its elected representatives. Nevertheless, the same constitution has eternal clauses that do not allow the people to amend certain characteristics of the Turkish state defined in the first three articles. This constraint over popular will means that in the Turkish case, the constituent power that posited the constitution is sovereign, not the people. This is a well-known principle in Turkish constitutional law and it directs debates on sovereignty.

The significance of this formulation of sovereignty, coupled with eternal clauses, is that it leaves no room for minorities such as the Kurds to make any meaningful gain via remaining within constitutional limits. Therefore, the Kurdish political movement confronts this absolutist, monolithic, and transferable (the people transfer their will to their representatives) formulation of sovereignty. The movement has formulated a version of sovereignty which promotes the component of territoriality, in the sense that spatial units become the basis of sovereign power and its agents as well, while it rules out the transfer of political will and the notion of national sovereignty, which allows an ethno-culturally defined body of people to become the source of sovereignty.

The praxis of the Kurdish political movement, thus, draws on both historical experiences of state fragments within the Ottoman Empire and on modern political philosophy. This indicates that the movement does not pursue an exclusively nationalist agenda. Öcalan makes this very clear: "So far, with a view to issues of ethnicity and nationhood like the Kurdish question [. . .] there seemed to be only one viable solution: the creation of a nation-state. We did not believe, however, that any ready-made political blueprints would be able to sustainably improve the situation of the people in the Middle East" (2011, 7–8). Practically, then, Öcalan rejects the idea of founding a Kurdish nation-state because he does not think it will resolve the Kurdish Question. By the same token, a Kurdish state will not help overcome the ongoing crisis in the Middle East either.

First, it would be too costly, violent, and bloody for Kurds and their neighbours, as nation-states, invariably, Öcalan argues, are products of warfare

(2011, 28). Of course, it is not only the aspect of violence that turns Öcalan away, as he himself is the leader of an armed movement that has been at war with the Turkish state and several other forces for more than three decades. As a commander of the guerrilla army in the Qandil Mountains, Cemil Bayık emphasized, they do not think that a decisive victory against four nation-states can be won (Hamsici 2015). Even if such a victory would be possible for any side, Bayık notes, it would be a *pyrrhic victory*. Hence, Bayık maintains that the Kurdish armed forces are necessary and that they will not dismantle them. However, they will exist only for defence purposes: to preserve the gains obtained so far and to defend the unprotected communities and minorities in Kurdistan against the assault of forces like the Islamic State. Bayık states that they have no intention of waging new wars or continuing to fight the current ones if they are not attacked (Hamsici 2015). For the PKK, according to Bayık, armed struggle has accomplished its mission, and no further fighting is desired.

Second, and more importantly, Öcalan suggests that the idea of a State for each nation is itself the problem: "Had it not been nationalism and nation-states which had created so many problems in the Middle East?" (2011, 8). One could argue that "nationality claims are claims for a state and that, where nationalist leaders claim to disavow this, they must cunningly be disguising their long-term objectives; any goal less than statehood indicates that we are dealing with mere regionalism or ethnic assertion," as Keating notes (2001a, 7). Yet, the Kurdish political movement and Öcalan himself, as mentioned above, reject nationalism on all bases. Indeed, Keating also observes that

> Stateless national movements are now making general claims to self-government and autonomous social regulation, rather than specific cultural demands which might be met by policy concessions limited to the cultural sphere; they are making rival claims to be 'global societies' (Langlois 1991*a,b*). They are contesting the state, therefore, in its own physical territory and normative space. A new politics of nationalism has emerged in which territorial societies are re-invented and rediscovered, below, beyond and across the state system (Keating 2001*a*). Claims to self-determination are reformulated and placed in the context of the emerging transnational order. (Keating 2001b, 17)

Likewise, Democratic Confederalism aspires to establish a new model of political community, and that is much more than demanding ethnic, cultural, and national rights for Kurds. The project is not a model of regional autonomy designed to address minority rights, but it aims at founding face-to-face political communities and city-states without necessarily destroying the hegemonic political community, i.e., the nation-state. That said, it would not be too far-fetched a claim to argue that this ends national sovereignty as we know it. The model is a home-grown project developed by the dominant Kurdish political movement in Turkey and adopted by its Syrian affiliates, and thus has more purchase when one thinks of proposals aiming at the resolution of national conflicts in these countries. It also offers a perspective that enables us to think of political communities other than the nation which monopolizes loyalty and limits it with ethno-cultural identities (although the proponents of civic nationalism would argue otherwise). The model compels us to re-evaluate the virtues of national sovereignty and its legitimation through representative democracy, which grants international and domestic legitimacy to oppressive nation-states but fails to prevent the marginalization and assimilation of minorities in most cases. This *status quo* breeds national and sectarian conflicts all over the region, since neither the dominant groups feel safe and secure, nor do the subordinated ones feel free and "equal in dignity and rights," unlike what the Universal Declaration of Human Rights suggests. Therefore, *Democratic Confederalism* is an attempt to lay the ground for political institutions that will ensure more direct political participation on the part of citizens, thus reducing the perception of threat among the majority and empowering the minority, without appealing to cultural identities and suggesting an abrupt break with the established order.

THE KURDISH VISION OF POLITICAL COMMUNITY IN COMPARATIVE PERSPECTIVE: TRANSNATIONAL AND COSMOPOLITAN POLITICAL COMMUNITIES IN KURDISTAN

Kurdish movements try to found an alternative political community in Turkey and Syria without seeking authorization from the Turkish and Syrian nation-states. This might be interpreted as a kind of secession, but my understanding of secession is akin to a claim to independence: "Secession refers to the exit of a territory from a state to make an independent state of its own" (Keating 2015, 1). In the Kurdish model there is no claim to independence, although there is a claim to a highly broad formulation of autonomy within the nation and across the borders within the limits of that autonomy. My argument is that this amounts to an act of foundation. Coined by Arendt, the term refers to "the framing of a constitution" (1963, 234). However, I use the term in a wider context and expand it to designate all substantial political activities that separate one community from others and make it a political community. This means that Kurdish political movements in Turkey and Syria act as constituting powers.

There is hardly anything novel about this: political communities are built by constituting political subjects in other cases as well. The novelty here is that membership is not exclusively based on a particular ethnic/cultural identity (*jus sanguinis*) or on a particular place of birth (*jus soli*); i.e., a cosmopolitan, or rather, residential, vision of citizenship seems to be introduced. Additionally, boundaries are determined by natural elements such as the physical outstretches of a city (although my interpretation is that borders are always demarcated arbitrarily), instead of by setting national boundaries which would suggest the ownership of a particular land by a particular people. Thus, the argument of the section is that the political community designed in Democratic Confederalism differ primarily in their membership criteria and in the non-demarcation of boundaries.

Residential Citizenship versus Universal Citizenship

Universal citizenship, i.e., "a legal status through which an identical set of civil, political and social rights are accorded to all members of the polity" (Leydet 2006, 5), offered or imposed by nation-states has been criticised on two grounds: first, that it is blind to internal diversity (Bauböck 1994, 20; Leydet 2006, 6), and second, that its meaning "has shifted away from universalism and equality to denote a specific position within an unequal and hierarchical order of nation-states" (Castles 2005, 689). Castles also emphasizes that the uneven value of passports citizens of different countries hold creates a hierarchical international order. It goes without saying that such a hierarchy is established between groups within nation-states as well. Although rights and duties might legally be equally assigned to members of groups within nations, state-sponsored (official) languages and (national) cultures inevitably enable and empower members of some groups more than others, via giving them an upper hand in social, political, and economic life. Education, employment, and participation in elections, for instance, are easily accessible to those who speak official languages, while others must learn a second language in order to gain access to any of these. Thus, it is well established that formal/legal equality does not deliver the promise of providing all citizens, regardless of their cultural and social background, with equality of opportunity, equal treatment, and dignity.

Nevertheless, this is only half of the story. The other half is that nation-states have adopted "various 'nation-building' policies aimed at giving citizens a common identity and a shared culture" in order to "ensure that [. . .] the state and nation coincide" (Kymlicka and Straehle 1999, 66–67). For instance, aggressive nation-building policies may impose a ban on a certain language, identity, and cultural symbols of that identity (e.g., the Kurdish language and cultural symbols were banned in Turkey until 1991). Here, the state leaves the realm of *blindness* to diversity and enters the active realm of *aggression* toward it.

Empirically, the gap between the promises of universal citizenship and its achievements provides a fertile ground for minority nationalisms. Some minorities have dealt in the *business* of state-building for the last two centuries in order to escape persecution and become "the masters of their fate" via building their own nation-states. This is paradoxical in some sense, because they emulate the policies that have been the very problem: *nation-building*.

Theoretically, two strong currents have addressed the shortcomings of universal citizenship and its provider, i.e., the nation-state: *multiculturalism* and *cosmopolitanism. Multiculturalism* is comprised of a variety of models designed for recognizing group rights, which draw mainly on the human rights tradition and suggests that nation-states should introduce a regime of *differentiated citizenship* for groups with distinct cultural and national identities within nation-states (Kymlicka 2007; Song 2010; Taylor 1997). This includes cultural and linguistic rights as well as territorial autonomies if those rights would not suffice. *Cosmopolitanism,* on the other hand, takes as its starting point the idea that globalization and transnational interdependence reduces the capacity of nation-states to determine life chances of their citizens and to exercise their political will democratically (Held 1995). Setting up procedures and mechanisms to ensure that individuals have a say in policies carried out by international/transnational actors and players such as States, NGOs and INGOs appear to be crucial in cosmopolitanism. Reaching to a level where a "transnational citizenship" and a "world government" (Bauböck 1994, vii) could be formed is the ultimate goal. For Bauböck, "Transnational citizenship is the liberal democratic response to the question how citizenship in territorially bounded polities can remain equal and inclusive in globalizing societies" (1994, vii). The main concern here is that economic and technological globalisation is not accompanied by political globalization, and that individuals cannot reap the benefits of globalization as long as they are locked into enclosed political communities within borders demarcated by nation-states, and subjected to exclusive membership criteria. Additionally, *Cosmopolitanism* argues for transcending our particularities such as national and cultural identities in order to better embrace and bring about a rational global community in which political participation is freed from cultural attachments (Calhoun, interview in Eliassi 2014). Also, as Benhabib puts it, "cosmopolitan norms enhance the project of popular sovereignty while prying open the black box of state sovereignty. They challenge the prerogative of the state to be the highest authority dispensing justice over all that is living and dead within certain territorial boundaries" (2007, 22). Thus, the quest and advocacy for creating cosmopolitan political communities and developing a regime of citizenship tailored for such communities arises both from the scepticism toward nation-states and from the worry that nation-states are falling prey to forces of economic globalization.

Nevertheless, the nation-state remains the central political community in both schemes mentioned above, with the exception of Benhabib's approach. This brings us to a third line of thought in political theory, an undercurrent that has not yet surfaced quite as strongly as the two mentioned above: that of a multi-layered co-existence of three forms of political communities. For instance, Kymlicka and Straehle (1999, 84–85) stress that a symbiosis should be established between minority nationalism/self-government, nation-states, and transnational/supranational institutions.[17] Alas, they do not offer a comprehensive model. There is also a serious problem with their approach: the centrality and superiority of sovereign nation-states is not challenged. Their perspective presumes that supranational institutions as well as sub-state self-governing entities would be established by nation-states. The reason is twofold.

First, for the cosmopolitan idea that political communities should not be founded on cultural bonds, i.e., *affinity* (Waldron 2011), to make sense, the dominant form of political community, i.e., *the nation,* has to be dismantled because the nation is a cultural community (Arendt 1958, 28; E. F. Isin 2012, 460). Second, and this is the crux of the issue for the purposes of this chapter, a political community must enjoy a degree of sovereignty. This means that it must hold the ultimate authority regarding certain issues and that no other political authority should be able to legally and legitimately abolish it. Thus, as long as sovereign territorial states determine the conditions under which sub-state and supra-state political entities are formed and abolished, there is no room for gradually organized political communities. There would be three levels of administration and regulation, but not three loci of sovereign power. Both sub-state and supra-state levels would derive their authority from the nation-state, which is the current state of affairs. However, this is exactly what needs to be altered. And with the *affinity* option off the table, only *residency* (Benhabib 2007) or *proximity* (Waldron 2011) would be a suitable basis for political community.

Proposing an alternative ground for founding political communities naturally alters the parameters of membership as well. Understandably, this modification should address the shortcomings of universal citizenship and the hegemony of its patrons, i.e., nation-states. In this section, I present the Kurdish model of political community as an empirical example that fits within this framework.

The relevance of Kurdish politics in Turkey and Syria is that although the dominant political movements in these countries emerged as national liberation movements—with left-leaning ideologies rather than a bourgeois style nationalism—their politics have transformed dramatically, to the extent that they make no appeal to nationalism and state-building. On the contrary, they now promote a mode of politics that opposes and aims to subvert the hegemonic order of nation-states. Although they adopt a radically critical stand toward the nation-state, they do not necessarily suggest an immediate abolition of nation-states either. Their model, Democratic Confederalism, envisages the co-existence of plural political communities at local, municipal, provincial, regional, national, and transnational levels. The model aspires to found a multi-layered system of political communities that reflects and even crystallizes residency/proximity as the basis of political communities. Inclusive, cosmopolitan membership in those communities is another trait of the model. The project promotes a world of plural political communities in which, as Bayır quotes from a report, sovereignty is not "understood to be the exclusive prerogative of the central authorities of the state, but, rather, a collection of functions that can best be exercised at different levels of society, depending on the nature of decisions that need to be made and the manner of their most appropriate implementation" (2013, 9). In a nutshell, the project positions itself against territorial sovereignty of the nation-state, popular sovereignty of the parliament that underpins it, and exclusive citizenship based on affinity. It aims at founding political communities that differ from territorial autonomy *granted* to minorities by nation-states.

This creates a theoretical void, and the question this section tries to answer concerns that void: what theoretical tool(s) are available for analysing a national liberation movement that does not appeal to nationalism? Kurdish politics in Turkey and Syria is one of those cases for which we need an alternative theoretical framework in order to provide a genuine analysis on the developments there.

Why Did the Kurdish Movement Develop a New Model of Political Community, Instead of Opting for the Hegemonic One?

I have discussed the reasons why the Kurdish movement is anti-statist. It is because the leaderships consider the State as the "original sin" and a tool of domination. An ideological shift from Marxism to semi-anarchist ideas and projects is at the basis of the movements' change of heart about state-making or seizing State power. Democratic Confederalism, as mentioned before, is not tailored for minority rights or multiculturalism either. The main reason is that minority status "dispossesses," alienates, and marginalizes communities because minorities are, especially in Turkey, conceived as *external* to the nation. They are not seen as part of the national history, and are excluded from national identity. They are often considered a liability to the body politic and treated, at times, as "parasitic" groups within the nation (Tambar 2016). *Multiculturalism*, on the other hand, is another name for minority nationalism and it creates hierarchies within a single polity (Kymlicka and Straehle 1999). Therefore, the Kurdish movement is sceptical about the virtues of having a minority status that would result from pushing for multiculturalist politics in Turkey.

This begs a question: is there a theoretical framework available to us for analysing the politics of Democratic Confederalism? I hold that the tradition of *political community* is a useful theoretical framework for analysing Kurdish politics in Turkey and Syria. Although it is difficult to arrive at a definition of political community that might enjoy a consensus, from the perspective of this section, political community does not have to be an independent polity or a State. It can be a sub-state political entity or a supra-state union. What separates it from an ordinary community is that it emerges once a political authority encircles a piece of land with the people in it and separates it from the rest of the world by walls or/and by laws, in the name of the very people enclosed in that territory.

The Kurdish Model of Political Community

The dominant Kurdish political movements in Turkey and Syria propose a politics that focuses on building autonomous and partially sovereign political communities inspired by Athenian democracy in political decision-making.[18] This translates into establishing pluralist and inclusive political communities in the towns and cities of Kurdistan via the transfer of the authority of making binding decisions from national political institutions to citizen assemblies. This is a radical alternative to the current parliamentary representative, procedural political decision-making that concentrates political power in the parliament at the capital of the nation. As many have pointed out, representative institutions can hardly be considered democratic (Hardt and Negri 2004; Benhabib 2007; Näsström 2015).

This is more so in Turkey, since the representative of the central government assigned to offices in provinces, cities, and towns hold much more political power than elected office holders. Governors of towns and cities in Turkey are basically capable of nullifying or overruling every decision made by municipalities and mayoral assemblies. Kurdish political actors criticize this state of affairs because their elected mayors cannot even change the name of a street without the approval of governors who generally have no connections with local people and no knowledge of their customs or wishes and choices. Their sole purpose is to carry out orders given by the central government. Thus, the project developed by the Kurdish political movement reflects their frustration with the draconian central government and the parliamentary, representative, national political procedures and institutions. It is no wonder that their project is so much in opposition to the Turkish political establishment, which is based on ethnic Turkish nationalism (Cagaptay 2004; Özdoğan 2010; Xypolia 2016) and in denial of collective rights of all minorities.

The Kurdish model of political community grounds itself on a residential citizenship akin to Waldron's *principle of proximity* (2011, 8). The political community of the Kurdish movement differs from Waldron's framework in its focus on self-rule as a universal right, not on the Kantian philosophy that suggests that political communities should be formed by and among those who are in close proximity to each other, for they are more likely to get into conflict. The Kurdish model, on the contrary, suggests that political communities should be formed among those who share a common geography/space/place, by virtue of living together. Being neighbours and sharing the living space together gives the residents a right to arrange their public affairs on their own, and a duty to be concerned about each other's and the community's well-being. This means that communities of settlement should have the ultimate say on their public affairs because they are the ones who live together side by side and share a common space; not because they are more likely to get into conflict. Küçük and Özselçuk formulate this as the "socialization of politics," which refers to "the patient and continual process of decomposing state power and its bureaucratic centralization by way of instituting diverse and discontinuous organizations of self-governance from the bottom up, thus redistributing sovereignty to local formations" (2016, 190).

The key concept here is *autonomy,* i.e., "the acknowledgment that there are multiple and different needs, values, and concerns, that these needs, values, and concerns can only be properly recognized when localization guides the focus of social relations, and that they can only be adequately supported and cultivated through place-based mechanisms of self-governance" (Küçük and Özselçuk 2016, 190). The project builds on the criticism that "the primary activity of nation-states" is "the production of a homogenous social category called 'the people' marked by a particular cultural identity" (Akkaya and Jongerden 2013, 170). Accordingly, the movement has established hundreds of communes in Turkish and Syrian Kurdistan in the last two decades, without demanding support or permission from, and mostly in defiance to, central states (Küçük and Özselçuk 2016).

Institutionally, the Kurdish political movement invokes a framework that can be summarized, in Benhabib's words, as "republican federalism," which amounts to "The constitutionally structured reaggregation of the markers of sovereignty, in a set of interlocking institutions each responsible and accountable to the other. There is, as there must be in any structuring of sovereignty, a moment of finality, in the sense of decisional closure, but not a moment of ultimacy, in the sense of being beyond questioning, challenge and account-ability" (2007, 31). The movement engages this framework with a slight twist to the superstructure, formulating it as *Confederalism*, but not federalism. Although in the quote above Benhabib refers to transnational institutions, she immediately acknowledges that

> This in turn can only happen if popular movements within donor and member countries force the elites who govern these institutions toward democratic ac-countability. Today we are caught not only in the reconfiguration of sovereignty but also in the reconstitutions of citizenship. We are moving away from citizen-ship understood as national membership increasingly toward a citizenship of residency which strengthens the multiple ties to locality, to the region, and to transnational institutions. In this respect defenders of post-national citizenship are correct. (Benhabib 2007, 30)

Thus, the Kurdish movement embeds its project firmly within current norma-tive accounts of cosmopolitan citizenship and direct democracy. Here, several aspects of the hegemonic political community, the nation-state, are altered. Referring to the questions asked by Stack (2019),[19] I would like to shortly enumerate these modifications.

First, it suggests that members/citizens cannot be *represented* by the politi-cal elite through national institutions, but they should be *participants,* directly contributing in political decision-making processes via local councils and as-semblies. This is meant to replace *obligation* with *solidarity*; since the bond that holds the community together is not vertical loyalty to a distant political authority, but a horizontal commitment to fellow citizens (literally, residents of a city).

Second, it is all residents, not only those who belong to a specific ethnic, national, or religious category that are called upon to govern themselves. In the words of a citizen of Kobane who greeted visitors by saying "Welcome! This town is yours! It belongs to humanity" (Taussig 2015, 2): the city be-longs to everyone.

Third, the authority that is being claimed, or indeed *obtained* by the found-ing actors, is limited to self-governance of the city, the town, the village and to the control of/sovereignty on their natural resources. None of these autono-mous entities cease to exist as a sovereign political entity, nor do they project their power and authority over other entities. Sovereignty is thus fragmented and shared by spatial units and sovereign power stems from residence. In this sense, it reminds us of the process of drafting the constitution of the United States of America by thirteen colonies. The principle here is that only "power

arrests power" and that establishing multiple centres of power does not di-
minish power, but generates more (Arendt 1963, 151–52). Additionally, there
is more emphasis on equal participation of genders, proportional participation
of communities, environmental protection, and the promotion of cooperatives
and communes.

Fourth, the agent of this project is the Kurdish political movement, represented in the person of mainly Kurdish political parties and the armed forces.
It is not the Kurdish nation and not the *multitude* or the aggregate of city
dwellers. The political institutions erected by the movement are open to all
residents, but this only justifies the exercise of political power, and does not
tell us anything about the foundation of those institutions (Näsström 2015).
As Taussig emphasizes, "Some degree of command" seems to be "essential,
especially during war, but always subject to and in compliance with the anti-
patriarchal thrust and with the rotation of positions of authority" (2015, 7).

Therefore, while it is crucial to highlight the novelty and uniqueness of
the project as regards its unorthodox approach to sovereignty, membership
in political community, and participation in decision-making processes, the
agent of the project is nevertheless well organized hierarchical political and
military establishments. In this respect, Democratic Confederalism offers
radical changes to at least three pillars of political community, but the fourth
pillar remains the same: *the act of foundation* is carried out by *force*, and not
by *power* alone.[20]

NOTES

1. The PKK was founded as an armed political party in 1978 in North Kurdistan
(Turkish Kurdistan), with the aim of liberating Kurdistan from colonialism, exploita-
tion, and oppression of the Turkish, Iranian, Iraqi and Syrian states. Soon, the party
separated its armed forces under the name Artêşa Rizgariya Gelê Kurdistan (People's
Liberation Army of Kurdistan-ARGK). Over the years, the Kurdish movement in
Turkey has grown into a complex network of political parties and civil society organizations that enjoy great popular support among the Kurds in Turkey. Also, it is the
ideological, spiritual force that drives the Rojava Revolution, the political and social
transformation that has been taking place in Syrian Kurdistan since 2012. Although
its name and organizational structures have changed several times over the years, the
PKK has retained its central role in a network that includes a guerrilla army, a European front, and a constellation of political parties and organizations in all four parts
of Kurdistan and in Europe.

2. The two military superpowers, the United States of America and Russia, and
their allies were involved in the civil war in Syria to further their geopolitical agenda,
via arming and supporting ground forces from opposing sides with varying affilia-
tions. Since 2014, however, it is not an involvement via proxies anymore. The USA

and allies started intervening directly via carrying out air strikes and sending military personnel in 2014; Russia followed suit in 2015.

3. I am aware that this is too generalizing a comparison. Nevertheless, drawing attention to the similarities, however superficial, helps me to draw a clearer overall picture.

4. This does not mean, though, that the union is an ideal one, either for the West or for "the Rest"; especially now that the union is shaken by economic crisis in several member states, and that it is facing harsh criticisms for its passive stand vis-à-vis and indifference to humanitarian disasters elsewhere.

5. The essay was published in the newspaper *Turk* in Cairo, because Akçura was a member of a secret military organization involved in conspiracies against the Ottoman Sultan. He left the country in order to avoid prosecution. He lived in France until 1903 and studied politics there, and then settled in Egypt under the British rule. He returned to Istanbul after the restoration of constitutional monarchy in 1908. He served the Turkish nationalist elite who seized power through a *coup d'état* in 1913 as a prominent ideologue of German-style organic nationalism and was highly revered by the Turkish political establishment until his death in 1935.

6. Ahmet Davutoglu is a former Turkish Prime Minister and Minister of Foreign Affairs, and the architect of Turkish foreign policy from 2002 to 2016.

7. It is interesting to witness that while the strongest parties that promoted Political Islam used to utter the slogan "Sovereignty belongs to God" in the 1990s, the ruling party has decorated streets with the slogan "Sovereignty belongs to the Nation."

8. Abdullah Öcalan was "the Chairman" of the PKK until his capture by the United States in 1999, after which he gained an impersonal title of "the Leadership," elevating him to the status of an everlasting symbolic figure of the movement. Öcalan then became the ideological guru to and acquired the spiritual leadership of the dominant Kurdish political movements in Turkey and Syria. Although he has no direct control over the PKK's guerrilla forces stationed in Iraqi, Syrian, Iranian and Turkish Kurdistan, he exerts a great deal of power and influence over political developments in all the four parts of Kurdistan.

9. Although Öcalan and prominent Kurdish political figures have repeatedly acknowledged the role of Kurds in the genocides of non-Muslims, issued apologies, and urged governments to make necessary reparations, this aspect of the discourse raises concerns. The Armenian genocide and massacres and pogroms committed against non-Muslims in the last 200 years carry the stamp of a unifying spirit embedded in Islam and the shared values that exclude non-Muslims. The fact that a PKK commander has made some controversial statements about a Greek and Armenian conspiracy exacerbated these concerns (*News.am*, 9 January 2014).

10. The aim here is circumventing international norms and practices that require communities, nations, and peoples to come forward via presenting themselves as political actors with agency. This necessitates recognition from the outside world, especially from the UN. Groups get this recognition through their representatives and institutions. The problem is, this requirement/routine limits the right to self-determination to communities whose agency/representation is not "taken seriously" and "recognized" by international actors such as the UN or a superpower. This is the

routine in acquiring autonomy via the principle of national self-determination. In this routine, many minorities and communities go unnoticed, persecuted, annihilated, or assimilated, because they have not manged to display an ample agency via generating modern political institutions and representative mechanisms that is supposed to make their agency present and visible in domestic and/or international politics. Here, self-rule is not ethical, but political: it is acquired through political processes. Öcalan (2011) criticises this order of business, which he calls the UN System, and presents an idea of collective/communitarian autonomy as a pre-political concept.

11. See the International Crisis Group report (Mandıracı 2016) for the toll of civilian casualties, the majority of whom were these councilmen and councilwomen who refused to leave their neighborhoods.

12. "Ankara'dan çıktık partileştik, Ortadoğu'ya çıktık ordulaştık, dünyaya açılarak devletleşeceğiz." Öcalan was a student at Ankara University when he decided, together with like-minded students, to leave Ankara for Kurdistan and start a revolutionary national liberation movement from there. They founded the party in 1978 in Turkish Kurdistan and left Kurdistan for Lebanon to train in guerrilla warfare. They formed a guerrilla army there, and started the guerrilla war against Turkey in 1984. "Opening up to the world" refers to the forced exile of Öcalan to Europe in 1998.

13. The third layer is *Democratic Republic*, which refers to universal citizenship and equal rights for every individual within national borders of existing nation-states.

14. Gendered veto mechanism is a "women only" practice, as patriarchy is the main concern here. Critics should point to the need for the same mechanism for the LGBT against the heterosexual bias.

15. Arendt takes the criticism a step forward when she argues that "in the realm of human affairs sovereignty and tyranny are the same" (1963, 153).

16. "If once [our people] become inattentive to the public affairs, you and I, and Congress and Assemblies, Judges and Governors, shall all become wolves" (Thomas Jefferson, quoted in Arendt 1963, 238).

17. "Each level of political community/agency can help to ensure the legitimacy of the other. As we've seen, nation-states can no longer protect the interests of their citizens on their own, and this is leading people to question the legitimacy of the state. Establishing well-functioning transnational institutions, capable of resolving the problems which transcend nation-states, should not necessarily be seen as weakening nation-states, but rather as restoring legitimacy to them, by enabling them to focus on those goals which they can successfully pursue. Similarly, self-government for national minorities need not be seen as a threat to states, but rather as a precondition for the long-term stability of states" (Kymlicka and Straehle 1999, 85).

18. The first draft of the Charter of the Rojava Cantons had a direct reference to Athenian democracy, but it did not appear in the later text. This is due to the fact that the main inspiration for the project of *Democratic Confederalism* has been Murray Bookchin, who based his political philosophy on Athenian democracy rather than the Roman republic.

19. "Who (if anyone) claims or is called upon to govern in the name or person of the "people" (broadly conceived) and to what effect? What kind and scope of author-

ity is being claimed, and to what effect? Who is held to be part of the "people," and to what effect? What kind of "people" is held to be able or worthy of "self-governing" in the first place, and to what effect?"

20. "Power can spring up as if from nowhere when people begin to 'act in concert'" (Arendt 1958, xiii).

Chapter Five

Conclusion

This book investigated a distinctive feature of Kurdish politics in Turkey: its orientation toward self-rule and its detachment from state-building. Studying Kurdish politics with a focus on this aspect is important, because this resilient characteristic has been understudied in academia and overlooked by the framers of Turkish constitutions. I started my investigation by highlighting historical manifestations of this aspect of Kurdish politics and ended it with an examination of the pillars of the current project of stateless self-rule in Turkish and Syrian Kurdistan. Along the way, I emphasized that neither academia nor the Turkish political elite pay attention to this aspect of Kurdish politics. This, I noted, condemns Kurdish politics to "ethno-nationalism" as well as "separatism" at best, and "terrorism" at worst, both in academia and in Turkish politics. However, as I have argued, Kurdish politics brings the revival of a tradition of self-rule that leads to the foundation of a new model of political community under the name *Democratic Confederalism*. I laid down the pillars of this model and highlighted the aspects that make it different from existing hegemonic political community.

In chapter 2 I argued that exercising self-rule within larger polities, rather than building a Kurdish state, surfaces as the *modus operandi* of the Kurdish political elite since the incorporation of Kurdistan into the Ottoman Empire in the sixteenth century. I highlighted that the statelessness of the Kurds should also be attributed to the choices made by their political elite. The "failure" of the Kurdish political elite to found a Kurdish state, I argued, is a state-centric and Eurocentric explanation of the statelessness of the Kurds. I emphasized that the Turkish political elite have been too state-centric in their discourse and praxis, and therefore perceive the Kurdish quest for self-government as a challenge to the authority of the State, ever since the Ottoman polity was restructured on the basis of the Westphalian/territorial state in the early nineteenth century. Later, the establishment of a republic on the basis of the national sovereignty of the *Turkish nation*—as an absolute sovereign that replaced the former absolute, the Sultan—exacerbated the political exclusion of the *Kurds* and *Kurdistan*; the former as a self-ruling people and the latter as their country. Thus, self-rule in Kurdistan was eventually transformed from being a privilege that strengthened the alliance between Kurdish and Turkish rulers into a perceived threat to the integrity of the "Turkish state" and "the unity of the nation with its state." Thus, I concluded, the coexistence of multiple political communities in a large polity is what Kurdish political elite have in mind, while Turkish rulers impose a political order based on oneness: one state, one language, one nation, one flag. I noted that the imposition of a single political community with rigid definitions of nationhood and citizenship based on Turkishness clashes head on with the quest for self-rule in Kurdistan in the form of coexisting and multiple political communities in Turkey. Thus, I implied, the phenomenon known as the Kurdish conflict/issue/question in Turkey is also a matter of clashing visions of political community, as much as it is a matter of competing nationalisms.

In chapter 3 I analysed draft constitutions of major political parties in Turkey with a focus on their approach to Kurdish political demands. I pointed out that the over-generalizations and misunderstandings about Kurdish politics I discussed in chapter 2 have been reflected in Turkish constitutional drafts. I argued that there is a correlation between labelling/perceiving the quest for self-rule in Kurdistan as ethno-nationalism, separatism, and terrorism and the exclusion of Kurdish political demands in the draft constitutions. I noted that Turkish framers have mainly preserved the *status quo* in their constitutional drafts and have chosen not to accommodate Kurdish political demands. The drafts maintain a single political community in Turkey, and no reference for self-rule of any kind in Kurdistan can be found in them. I also noted that the pro-Kurdish party's draft was more promising in addressing Kurdish political demands; however, they too do not specifically introduce a form of self-rule in Kurdistan and do not go beyond the multiculturalist framework. I emphasized that the pro-Kurdish party's constitutional draft does not reflect what the Kurdish movement designed for self-rule in Kurdistan, because it campaigned for Turkish as well as Kurdish votes. Therefore, their draft could not answer the question of whether or not the Kurdish movement envisages a political community other than the nation-state, a question I addressed in chapter 4.

I also argued that the Turkish framers' dismissive stance vis-à-vis Kurdish political demands were mainly shaped by the conceptualizations and preferences of the constituent power that founded the Republic of Turkey. The founding fathers had set the terms of debate regarding fundamental political issues such as diversity, citizenship, minority rights, sovereignty, and national will. The founding fathers—or rather the "constituent will" that founded the republic as conceptualized in Turkey—were the first framers who excluded the Kurds in the constitution of 1924. What they "willed" regarding the exclusion of the Kurds, I emphasized, has been serving as a barrier to Kurdish political demands in constitutional drafts ever since. This is because the originalist interpretation of the constitution excludes non-Turks and the eternity clauses perpetuate the initial exclusion.

In chapter 4, I dwelled on the project of Democratic Confederalism, a model of self-rule designed by the Kurdish national movement to answer the question of whether their project remained within the confines of nationalism or not. My analyses of the general historical background in the Middle East and my interpretation of the project of Democratic Confederalism led me to argue that indeed the project introduced a model of political community other than the hegemonic ones: the nation-state and the Islamic Ummah. I argued that the model was a revival of self-rule-oriented Kurdish politics with flavours of cosmopolitan citizenship and Athenian democracy. The Kurdish project, I emphasized, goes beyond *multiculturalism* as a model of self-rule and minority rights, in the sense that it recognizes self-defence and control over natural resources for every community of settlement and identity. This amounts to a fragmentation of national/absolute sovereignty as we know it and the introduction of a gradual diffusion of authority and power throughout space and spatial communities such as villages, neighbourhoods, towns, cities, regions, and nations. Thus, power flows from the periphery to the centre(s), not vice versa, for two reasons: first, local assemblies and authorities/rulers take their power from the community, not from the political authority at the capital. Second, more than one capital is created within the national borders. Therefore, the project reflects the desire of the Kurdish movement to end the tight control of Ankara and other capitals over Kurdish towns and cities and revive Kurdistan as a distinct political entity, as it used to be. This is why I described Öcalan's notion of democratic autonomy as the fragmentation of territorial sovereignty. Autonomy here is not granted from top to bottom, but built from below by autonomous units; or, in fact, by the political subject that builds these units. Thus, it is important to add that since the Kurdish project rejects national sovereignty, it also abstains from paving the way for a Kurdish nation-state. Political and military institutions in the Kurdish project are designed to give each spatial community the utmost autonomy they can enjoy. Regional and national institutions are involved or invoked in matters that do not fall within the jurisdiction of local authorities or those that exceed their economic and defensive abilities. Confederation is created to handle the issues that cannot be expected to be addressed or solved by the concerned local administrations only, or by a few municipalities.

The crucial aspect of the model, I highlighted, is that it is tailored not solely for liberating Kurdistan from foreign or "colonial" domination, although this is the core objective. The project could be seen as another grand vision of political community in the Middle East along with nationalism, Ottomanism, and Islamism. The ultimate goal of the Kuridsh project is ending the ongoing state of war in the Middle East and establishing a political structure that will lead to peaceful cohabitation of a myriad of communities and their autonomous yet interdependent political entities in the region. Thus, the project claims to have designed a form of self-rule for all communities in the Middle East via installing transnational and trans-border political communities, with no specific reference to nationhood. I concluded that the project reflects the themes we see in *Occupy* movements: i.e., challenging the nation-state as the hegemonic form of political community; frustration with representative institutions of political decision-making; demanding or establishing a more direct procedure of political decision-making and participation in public affairs; and altering the exclusive forms and definitions of citizenship based on cultural or civic identity in order to allow transnational/cosmopolitan ideas and practices of citizenship to take root.

IMPLICATIONS

The Kurdish movement has developed a model of self-rule that differs greatly from "ready-made" and existing models (Öcalan 2011). The lion's share of the novelty in the project goes to the dissolution of national sovereignty. Indeed, not even once did Öcalan, the architect of the project, refer to the concept of *sovereignty* in the two primary sources I focused on in the fourth chapter (which are also the main documents of the project of Democratic Confederalism). This reflects the conscious omission of the concept from the main texts of the project. Following Arendt (1958, 54), Öcalan regards political organization on the basis of an abstract concept such as national sovereignty as domination in the name of the nation (2011, 8–13). He chooses his words carefully in order to salvage his project from being labelled as separatist, because any claim to national sovereignty in the name of the Kurdish nation would mean a Kurdish nation-state and thus imply a nationalist separatism.

Although Öcalan's project does not present and promote any claim to national sovereignty as such, the content of his project dismantles and fragments *national sovereignty*. Öcalan circumvents the concept in his project to show that he does not envisage a nation-state for the Kurds. Nevertheless, he challenges the internal and external sovereignty of nation-states with his formulation of self-defence, democratic autonomy, and Democratic Confederalism. This makes the project's engagement with the nation-state and sovereignty confusing, and even a bit chaotic. On the one hand, we see a harsh criticism of the Hobbesian absolute, indivisible, and representative sovereignty. On the other hand, claims to *ultimate authority within certain territories*, which is the very definition of sovereignty, are made in the project via the elements of self-defence, democratic autonomy, and trans-border cooperation of political entities. This claim is formulated as the right of the peoples of Kurdistan and of the Middle East to rule themselves in their homeland, via local and regional political institutions. Moreover, Selahattin Demirtas, the co-chair of the pro-Kurdish political party, the HDP (Halklarin Demokratik Partisi-Peoples' Democratic Party), clearly emphasizes the right to self-rule and sovereignty of the Kurds in Kurdistan, with reference to the bond between the Kurds and their homeland.[1] By the same token, the right to self-rule of other communities are also acknowledged. It is emphasized that not only Kurds inhabit Kurdistan, but that communities other than the Kurds in Kurdistan should also enjoy the collective right to self-rule and even self-defence (Öcalan 2011, 28–33). There is one important implication of this conundrum on sovereignty: that the Kurdish movement envisages two forms of sovereignty, the one that translates into domination and the other without any form of domination attached.

Kurdish Model Claims Home-Rule Without an Appeal to the Principle of National Self-Determination in International Law

Commonly, internationally recognized claims to sovereignty have been presented under the banner of *the right to self-determination.* This has been the dominant pattern in post-World War II political mobilization for self-rule or independence. Nevertheless, only previously independent or autonomous peoples or territories are considered entitled to this claim, as in the case of colonized peoples or countries (Kymlicka 2007). The right to self-determination, thus, works only for certain groups with claims to sovereignty, but does not lend itself to others, such as national minorities and indigenous peoples. During the Cold War period and more increasingly after it, however, these latter groups emerged with stronger claims to self-rule, thanks to the human rights discourse and its evolution into multiculturalism as a system of group-differentiated rights. In the Kurdish case, however, claims to self-rule carry within them a sense of assault upon the classical and modern formulations of sovereignty that is known as indivisible, centralized, absolute, alienable, and representable.

Local as well as regional identities emerge once again, to the expense of national identities, and nation-states start sharing their sovereignty with local and regional sub/supra state political entities (Albo 1993). Dispersed, localized, bottom-up forms of sovereignty and more direct exercise of political power have become increasingly articulated and promoted by political movements. Thus, the sovereignty of a single entity/authority and top-down flow of political power are understood as more and more limiting, constraining, and subjugating.

The distinctive mark that this trend left on the notion of sovereignty is that it made possible, for national liberation and indigenous movements around the world, to envisage a form of sovereignty without the State, as it is not possible for all peoples and nations to have a state of their own. Sovereignty here is envisaged as a relationship *not between* a supreme authority on the one hand, a body of citizens and a territory on the other; but as *a relationship of a community with the piece of land it lives upon*. This approach has empowering and emancipating potential for numerically small/local communities such as indigenous peoples as well as for larger ones such as national minorities. Thus, neither a supreme authority such as the Prince nor a supposedly culturally homogenous group such as the nation can claim sovereignty over a vast territory without violating the right or contesting the claim of distinct and diverse communities living there. Consequently, in this line of thought, sovereignty appears as *a relationship* between village folks and their village; between towns people and their town; between the city dwellers and their city. This becomes a powerful normative principle that empowers certain groups in their quest to demand more direct access to the exercise of political power. That is how the Kurdish movement reconciles the rejection of singular, absolute, indivisible forms of national sovereignty on the one hand, while making claims to communal, communitarian, localized, fragmented, dispersed forms of sovereignty on the other, on the basis of their relationship with Kurdistan as home to Kurds and other communities. More precisely, the Kurdish political movement promotes a notion of sovereignty that is based on their relationship with their homeland, but as residents of settlements and members of *spatial communities* such as villages, neighbourhoods, towns, and cities, not as a homogenous national community that claims supreme authority within the territory known as Kurdistan. Of course, the question of whether these communities are just as homogenizing as imagined or cultural ones is well justified. Ideally, in this model, multiple heterogeneous political communities exercise a fragmented, layered, and dispersed form of sovereignty throughout large body politics such as nation-states, federations, and confederations.

There Are Two Faces of Sovereignty in the Discourse of Kurdish Movement

The formulation of self-rule without a Kurdish state, or more precisely, the claim to political autonomy without invoking the principle of national self-determination for the Kurds, implies that the notion of sovereignty has two faces in the Kurdish model: it can be subjugating or emancipative.

National Sovereignty as Domination

The modern understanding of sovereignty relegates it to the territorial State: the supreme authority in a demarcated geography/space (Philpott 2010). Within this concept, a supreme authority within a marked space maintains a political order in a top-down manner. This form of sovereignty comes with a promoted national identity, culture, language, history, and common good. These supposedly shared or common traits are meant to instil a sense of solidarity, to create ties between citizens in order to bind them together. They also create bonds between citizens and their government. In modern states, a variety of nation-building policies have been implemented to instil both the sense of solidarity between citizens and to legitimize the State. However, the promotion of a culture, language, a political identity, and so on may entail exclusion, assimilation, erasure, and even subjugation of certain cultures, languages, and identities.

Therefore, the sovereignty of the territorial state or the nation-state, according to the architect(s) of the Kurdish model, eventually end up in the domination of the minority. On the one hand, this is a form of domination between citizens; or to be more precise, between the holder of sovereignty, i.e., the dominant ethnic, national, or religious group (e.g., Turkish nation, French nation, etc.) and those that are not part of, or are excluded from, that group (e.g., Kurds, Corsicans, the Roma, etc.). On the other hand, it is a relationship of ownership, as Philpott emphasizes: "International relations theorists have indeed pointed out the similarity between sovereignty and another institution in which lines demarcate land—private property. Indeed, the two prominently rose together in the thought of Thomas Hobbes" (2010, 3). This aspect of sovereignty can arguably give a group of people a supposedly unchallenged legal title over a territory, like the one we see in the concept of national sovereignty. As sovereignty is also relegated to the exercise of political power, institutions or groups may claim an exclusive right to performing collective decision-making in the name of the nation that holds the title to the demarcated land. This is another form of domination that the Kurdish movement points at in their own case.

The Kurdish model equates national sovereignty with domination because:

1. The state promotes a specific culture, language and identity, and thus builds a hierarchy between cultural groups within the territory of the nation-state.
2. It gives the wrong message that the territory belongs to a specific nation as a whole, while there are always more than one group that can make competing claims to the same territory.

Political Liberty as Communal and Communitarian Sovereignty

Ironically, the liberating, emancipative,[2] or empowering aspect of sovereignty that the Kurdish model seems to appeal to is not that far from territorial sovereignty. Indeed, Öcalan does not use the concept of sovereignty in his works where he declares and elaborates on Democratic Confederalism. But his formulation of autonomy and self-defence, based on a relationship of control between resident communities and their settlements (territories with natural resources), is territorial sovereignty on a microcosm.

In Öcalan's formulation, territorial sovereignty on national scale is broken down into bits and pieces, or into a myriad of pockets of sovereignty, in order to allow the smallest community of settlement to exercise a degree of control over the physical space, its natural resources, and public and political intuitions within the community. Here, control over space and its resources is physical as well as economic and political. Decision-making institutions and processes are designed to work, ideally, without the interference of regional and/or national authorities. Issues and public affairs of autonomous units must be handled locally if we are to speak of democratic autonomy, unless the issue necessitates the involvement of regional or national entities or the collaboration with neighbouring municipalities. The community of settlement, i.e., the political community of the Kurdish model, thus functions as a whole before it ever becomes a unit within regional, federal, confederal, and national political entities. The important takeaway here is that the nation-state is bypassed by the communal sovereignty envisaged in the Kurdish model, and thus the model invokes a form of territorial sovereignty on a micro-scale.

Nevertheless, the sovereign subject and the political agents that exercise political power, as well the institutions and processes of collective decision-making differ in the Kurdish model. The community of settlement, rather than a community of identity, e.g., the nation or the people, appears as the sovereign subject (Leezenberg 2016). Finally, not only parliaments, but a variety of city and towns councils and neighbourhood assemblies, as well as village and communal forums appear as political institutions involved in collective decision-making.

According to Öcalan's model, this communal or fragmented sovereignty, which he names as *democratic autonomy*, is not domination, but liberation (Noureddine 2016). Öcalan frames it thusly because the relationship of control between the community and their *natural* habitat here is constituted on the basis of residence, not on the basis of cultural identity or virtual appropriation of a territory as in the case of nation-states. National sovereignty, in the Kurdish movement's discourse, is constituted on the basis of a relationship between a particular cultural group, an imagined community and a contested, *virtual* homeland. Since nations are imagined communities, the argument goes, the object of their claim to sovereignty, i.e., the vast territory claimed as homeland, can only be a virtual reality, demarcated arbitrarily by force and enclosed within artificial borders. The nation, in that sense, has no clear boundaries and no actual connection with the national territory under the control of the nation-state. But a local community has a direct connection, and even a direct bond, with its immediate physical environment, its habitat. The place where a community lives, in the Kurdish model, is its *natural home*. Thus, the community that proclaims democratic autonomy is referred to as a "natural community"—actual physical communities such as a towns and cities with their residents. The assumption here is that every community lives in a physical space, in a habitat. It follows that communities should have control over their habitat if they are to flourish, free of domination and intervention from outside. Therefore, they have the right to rule themselves, and to build self-defence mechanisms against aggression from outside.

This is reminiscent of the Aristotelian idea that "the state is a creation of nature" and that "When several villages are united in a single community, perfect and large enough to be nearly or quite self-sufficing, the state comes into existence" (Aristotle, *Politics* [1999]: Book I, Chapter 2, 1252b-8). In the Kurdish project as well—due to the application of Ancient Greek political thought on Bookchin's theory of *Communalism* that is the source of inspiration for Öcalan—villages, towns, neighbourhoods, and cities are political communities by virtue of being "natural communities." In other words, the autonomous unit is also a "natural community" in the Kurdish model, in the sense that it is not a community of identity, but a community of settlement and its residents. Therefore, every community of settlement (e.g., villages, neighbourhoods, towns, and cities) constitutes a political community in the Kurdish model, without mention of a specific criterion for self-sufficiency. Consequently, the Kurdish model endorses sovereignty when it is a relationship between residents and their settlements, not when it is a relationship between humans and communities.

The question here is, of course, can we speak of pre-political communities and their physical boundaries? For example, do villages, neighbourhoods, towns, and cities have pre-political boundaries? The answer would be no. This is one of the numerous problems with Öcalan's model.

An Unresolved Issue: What Happens to the Nation-State in the Kurdish Model?

> We, the Şırnak People's Assembly, *do not completely disregard the state* but must clarify that we cannot possibly continue with the state institutions as such, thus say it once again that all state institutions in the city have lost legitimacy. No appointed governor shall rule us in this way. From now on, we will take hold of the principle of self-governance, build up our lives in democratic basis. Moreover, from now on, facing any attacks, we will be reverting to self-defence mechanisms. We will be governing ourselves from now, not let anyone rule over us [emphasis added].

The statement above is from the declaration of democratic autonomy proclaimed on 10 August 2015, in Şırnak, a Kurdish majority city in Southeast Turkey (North Kurdistan). This was followed by fifteen similar declarations in other Kurdish towns and cities in the same region during August and September 2015 (Bozarslan 2016).[3] These declarations and the others proclaimed by the Democratic Society Congress (the DTK-Demokratik Toplum Kongresi)[4] since June 2011 present a clear challenge from the Kurdish model to the nation-state as a political system in Kurdistan and its administrative institutions, e.g., the parliament, the central government, and local governorates in provinces and towns. Nevertheless, no immediate abolition of the nation-state as a whole is suggested (note the implication of coexistence in the emphasized part).

What I deduce from the Kurdish model regarding sovereignty is that it "resides in the people," although no specific discussion was allocated to the concept in the texts I used as my primary sources. However, what is meant by *the people* is not a particular cultural or national category, or a supposedly unified, ideally homogenous political subject like *the nation.* The sovereign, in the Kurdish model, is formed of the residents of each autonomous political entity, i.e., communities of settlement. For instance, Kurdish political parties are using the plural form, *peoples,* in their names, statutes, addresses and programs, in order to deliver the message that no single ethnic or civic category is either the source or the agent of political power exclusively.

Communities of settlement are *face-to-face communities* in the Aristotelian sense such as villages, communes (around 200–300 households), and neighbourhoods, as well as "community of communities" (Maunier 2008)—i.e., towns, townships, and cities. This fragmentation of national/nation-state sovereignty is reinforced and complemented by a form of direct democracy. Residents of these communities exercise political power by participating directly in collective decision-making processes and institutions that are open to all residents, such as forums, councils, assemblies, and conventions. These communities of settlement exist as autonomous political communities that have full control over municipal public affairs and natural resources, and organize their self-defence. No (higher) authority can have a claim to rule over the people as a whole, nor can any individual or group claim to represent the will of the people as a unified entity. Also, representative mechanisms of exercising political power are designed for communities larger than "face-to-face" communities. This indicates that regional and national institutions principally remain intact, albeit with a dramatic decline in their authority and their exercise of power over municipalities and smaller administrative units.

The objective, according to Öcalan, is to transform the hegemonic order of centralized nation-states into (direct-)democratic, cosmopolitan, transnational, and open societies. Sovereignty is dispersed and diffused horizontally and vertically, throughout nested and autonomous communities of settlement and their alliances. Öcalan emphasizes that his project is "open for compromises concerning state or governmental traditions. It allows for equal coexistence" (2011, 22). His vision of the system is purposely designed to accommodate for the "contradictory composition of the society [that] necessitates political groups with both vertical and horizontal formations. Central, regional and local groups need to be balanced in this way" (22). Thus, the project principally does not do away with national political, social, or economic institutions of nation-states, as far as they are compatible with Democratic Confederalism. Central authority may coexist with local ones only if it accepts the limits of the project on its own power.

However, it is unrealistic, as both Bookchin and Öcalan put it, to assume that the established nation-state order or individual nation-states will not intervene while all these reconfigurations are made to political institutions and when all power relations are radically altered. More importantly, the principle of self-defence installs another political subject capable of making the claim to "the monopoly on legitimate use of violence" in autonomous towns and cities. Besides, the whole project of Democratic Confederalism is about ultimately overcoming centralized nation-states and eliminating political establishments based on a single sovereign agent that claims to represent a unified nation. The central argument of the project is that the nation-state is the vessel of capitalist modernity with all inequalities and political domination (Öcalan 2011, 13–20), and that Democratic Confederalism should replace them with autonomous municipalities and alliances in the form of federations and confederations.

This inevitably invites a conflict with the State. Although the project does not preach the immediate destruction of the nation-state by force, it nevertheless leads to this outcome, because the nation-state is no longer a nation-state after the project is implemented for the necessary fragmentation of national sovereignty, the principle of self-defence, and the establishment of democratic autonomy. Consequently, the nation-state is discarded as a system, its institutions are stripped off their authority and power, and it no longer has a monopoly over the "legitimate" use of violence. Nevertheless, one can sense that all these effects are open to negotiations, especially for Öcalan, in case nation-state authorities are willing to negotiate with the Kurdish movement.

Two fundamental worries should be underlined here: first, direct democracy functions on the basis of majoritarian premise, and second, collective/communal decision-making processes and institutions tend to generate or reinforce communitarian bias. The former can lead to suppressing minorities, silencing their voices, and ignoring their vote. The latter can lead to undermining individual liberties for notions of common good. These worries are justified and well established in political theory. Both of these principles appear to be dominant in the Kurdish project. This is a matter of concern for the opposition and for human rights activists, although the pillar of *democratic republic* in the project is designed to ensure equality of citizens and guarantee the protection of individual liberties (Jong 2015). Universal human rights for all is a dominant theme both in the project and in the Rojava Constitution (2014) in Syrian Kurdistan, however poor the implementation might be (which is not that good, according to Human Rights Watch [2016] and Amnesty International [2016]). Öcalan emphasizes that his project is best implemented in a constitution that guarantees universal human rights for all, enacted through consensus between all political forces and with national implementation. Thus, ethically, "universal human rights" appear to enjoy a higher authority than democratic principles promoted by the project. Nevertheless, after all is said and done, the nation-state would not survive the project.

PROBLEMS AND CHALLENGES

The Kurdish model adopts a distinct political taxonomy and lexicon, which makes it attractive and threating at the same time, depending on where the interested party stands on the political spectrum. For instance, *autonomy* replaces the notion of *sovereignty*, *coexistence* replaces *independence,* and *pluralism* replaces *national unity* in the model. National categories and institutions are mostly replaced or accompanied by local, municipal, and regional ones. These might be considered as merits of the model, because they will help preserve indigenous communities and empower national minorities, by allowing them to make their own laws. This is a far better deal for these groups compared to what they are entitled to within the framework of indigenous and minority rights regimes in international law, as Kymlicka (2007) has noted. The model prioritizes the choices of grassroots political actors, which has been a trend in liberal democracies and regional organizations such as European Union. Nevertheless, it also weakens the claim of nation-states to a Hobbesian sovereignty and its global order, which is the bread and butter of the current inter-state relations.

The model also promotes a political order and an administrative system of horizontally organized and connected—but autonomous—political communities. These political communities are chiefly municipalities that resemble city-states. Nevertheless, vertically organized political entities such as nation-states, federations, and confederations do have a place in the order installed by the model. In the envisioned order within the project, the coexistence of, and cooperation between, horizontal and vertical political entities and organizations is ideal. This vision is meant to be alternative to the hierarchically organized, centralized, patriarchal, and culturally exclusive nation-states. The main purpose is to avoid battles and bloodshed for founding a State for each nation. Therefore, *coexistence* is repeatedly emphasized in Öcalan's texts.[5]

Problems

However, the model is not without flaws. It manifests problems that have their origins in democratic and political theory, such as downplaying the arbitrariness of boundaries, the inevitability of exclusion/inclusion while setting an administration, and the limits to the power/authority of each level of administration. For instance, the project risks falling into essentialism in two areas: first, it promotes the "right to self-defense" for each community of faith, culture, and space, regardless of their size or legal status. Determining which groups are entitled to this right could create constant tensions between groups as well as between municipal and canton administrations and groups. Second, it seems that *community* appears in the model as a pre-given category in the form of spatial communities such as villages, neighbourhoods, towns, and cities that have physical boundaries that separate one from the others. Although referring to physical boundaries of human settlements could render handling the problem of *closure* in democratic theory easier (Abizadeh 2012; Scherz 2013), it would not make other boundaries any less real as Isin (2007) has argued. Additionally, the model tones down the role of political authorities and processes in determining, creating, and demarcating physical, cultural, and symbolic boundaries and space (Gambetti 2008, 2009). This seems to suggest that there are "natural" communities' and artificial ones. This distinction is problematic because there are no "natural," pre-given communities to speak of: every social and political organization exists and is being shaped by socio-political forces and processes (Harvey 2000, 2012). The decision about where the boundaries of both spatial and cultural communities start and where they end is a political decision, not an *a priori* fact (Abizadeh 2012; Scherz 2013).

Other problems are more about the organization and operation of the movement itself, and well accounted for in Akkaya and Jongerden (2012); Casier and Jongerden (2012); Jongerden and Akkaya (2012); and Leezenberg (2016). For instance, the medium and means utilized by the movement to make the ends meet are controversial, and often counterproductive. The organization of the core party, the PKK, and the branches under the umbrella of Kurdistan Communities Union (KCK-*Koma Civakên Kurdistan)* are highly hierarchical. Not to mention the tough discipline practiced by the guerrilla forces of the movement, although anarchist discourse is a dominant discourse in party publications and propaganda. This hierarchical organization leaves little room for democratic processes, criticism, and free speech. The fact that the movement operates through strictly hierarchical institutions and organizations casts shadow on its egalitarian discourse and its claim to prioritizing, promoting, and building horizontal political institutions. The personality cult of "the leadership" is another weakness of the movement that remains from its Marxist-Leninist days. These problems have already been articulated by authors I referred to above. Another important issue is the internal discord in areas controlled by the movement. Kurdish political parties and actors who do not share the worldview of or are not supportive of the political agenda of the dominant political movement continue to be marginalized. Free and equal participation of opposition parties and actors in political life needs further guarantees in order to address criticisms in this regard.

The most important problem of the movement's discourse and project, however, is neither of the problems pointed out above. The problem I would like to underline most is the fact that although the movement's representatives and the architect of the Kurdish model claim that their priority is constituting *liberty* and that the project of Democratic Confederalism departs from *ethical* concerns (Noureddine 2016; Öcalan 2011)*,* the model is presented as a *solution to the Kurdish Question* (Öcalan 2011, 19). This is a rather limiting approach, because national issues are not problems for which a solution can just be found. They evolve out of complex social processes. A myriad of political actors and dynamics are involved. This makes it almost impossible to find a "solution" that would solve the issue "once and for all." As Keating (2001, 3) has also pointed out, national issues are a "form of politics to be negotiated continually, rather than as *a problem to be resolved once and for all*, after which normal politics can resume [emphasis added]." The armed conflict could probably be addressed by a negotiated peace agreement, but even that would not guarantee that some other factions would not pick up the armed struggle from where the previous actor left.

The problem is, when the political exclusion and persecution of Kurds, followed by their political activism for equality or for more power is named as a *question*, one automatically thinks of the origins of the question in order to diagnose what is *wrong* with the Kurds, and come up with a "solution." When one is conditioned to think of the matter as such, one ends up perceiving and/or treating the Kurds themselves as a problem. Indeed, throughout modern Turkish history, many reports have been prepared to distinguish between "trustworthy" and "untrustworthy" tribes—"good" and "bad" Kurds. It is noteworthy that since the foundation of the Republic of Turkey in 1923, twenty-one reports have been compiled either by the agents of the Turkish government in the center or by Inspector(ate)s General/Supergovernor(ate)s of Emergency Rule (*Umûmî Müfettişlik/Olağanüstü Hal Valiliği*)[6] in Kurdistan, or by academics and political actors (*Today's Zaman*, 25 August 2009). The most famous of those reports are the ones compiled by Ismet Inonu (known and referred to as *the National Chief/Millî Şef*, who served as the chief of staff, prime minister and president, and was "the second man" in the whole republic after Mustafa Kemal) in 1935 and Abidin Özmen (the Inspector General) in 1936 (Al 2015; Güvenç 2011). What was common in those reports was the tendency to designate the Kurdish issue as a *disease*, and prescribe military campaigns, population relocations, and language and cultural bans as the best *treatments* or *cures* (Bruinessen 1994). For the "nationalist, patriotic" statesmen and politician this means arriving at the conclusion that the "problem" needs a "solution." It is not a coincidence that the official name of the Dersim (today's Tunceli province in Turkey) Genocide of the Alevi Kurds in 1938 was "Dersim Disciplining and Relocation Operation" (*Dersim Tedip ve Tenkil Harekatı*). As Bruinessen notes in detail, the republican governments behaved like a colonial power in Kurdistan and those reports then led to massacres, genocides and huge population relocations (Al 2015; Bruinessen 1994, 150–54, 2002). Many such punitive campaigns, massacres, massive population relocations and other human rights abuses have been committed by the Turkish, Syrian, Iraqi and Iranian governments for the purpose of "solving" the Kurdish Question via annihilating, "disciplining," intimidating, and relocating the Kurds (Belge 2011; Bruinessen 1994; Mango 1999).

More importantly, we see that the term *Question* has been utilized to isolate a group of people and treat them like an anomaly within the existing order. Take for instance the example of the *Jewish Question*, which referred to a widespread debate on how European nations should treat European Jews. Or the famous *Eastern Question*, which referred to "maintaining the Ottoman Empire as part of an established order against the expansionist ambitions of Austria and Russia in south-eastern Europe. Change in the existing order was of vital concern to the West because it might have upset the balance of power not only in the Middle East but also in Europe" (İnalcık 1996, 22). Or, as Macfie puts it, the term *Eastern Question* also referred to the "efforts of the Great Powers to come to grips with the consequences of Ottoman decline, first made evident in the Russo-Turkish War of 1768–74" (1996, 3–4).

Likewise, Ottoman rulers first isolated Armenians via categorizing them as "a question," and searched for ways, for decades, to "solve the problem." The Ottoman state "figured out" a final solution for the Armenians in 1915 and wiped them from the country. In the republican era, the Kurds have taken their place. Yegen (1999) notes that the *Kurdish Question* emerged out of Turkey's *Eastern Question.* The dominant Turkish republican elite associated Kurdistan, *the East,* with primitiveness, traditionalism, socio-economic back-wardness and political unrest (Zeydanlıoğlu 2008). Then, with the insistence of Kurdish political actors throughout the 1990s, Turkey's *Eastern Question* was transformed into the *Kurdish Question* (Yegen 1999).

Ever since the term *Kurdish Question* was used to refer to the deprivation of Kurds of self-rule, or to define the aggregate of complex social, economic and political issues Kurds face as marginalized subjects (in pre-World War 1 Ottoman and Iranian empires) and citizens (in post-war nation-states of Iran, Iraq, Syria and Turkey), the priority has been given to diagnosing *the problem* and offering solutions to it. Diagnoses and prescriptions vary, but they are mostly modelled on ideals, principles and examples that best suit the interests of the ruling elite.

Consequently, such a perspective demonstrates the sort of hubris and overconfidence that transformed into social engineering projects and the ca-tastrophes that followed them. Naming issues and problems after national or cultural identities makes one think—or it is meant to make one think—that those groups themselves are the problem. The problem is that of founding polities or transforming the established ones into societies where domination and discrimination is minimized, if not eliminated altogether. Therefore, the proposal here is that we should start thinking of and analysing socio-political phenomena in Kurdistan without invoking the term the *Kurdish Question*.

Challenges

There are millions of Kurds living in western Turkey, and only striving for autonomy in Kurdistan would mean ignoring them. Therefore, the HDP is trying to introduce the Kurdish project nationwide, via proposing that 25 autonomous regions should be established in Turkey. The proposal is inspired by the Spanish system of provincial autonomy. The assumption is that these regions will mean greater autonomy for minorities and more liberty for individuals, since central authority will no longer meddle with certain public services such as education and domestic security. This is also meant to assure the Turkish rulers and the public that their fear of Kurdish secession is not substantiated.

Ironically, while the inclination to abandon the idea of founding a nation-state or obtaining regional autonomy for Kurds would, one expects, attract a milder reaction from nation-states in the Middle East, the movement and its project meets harsh counter-measures, especially from the Turkish state. This is because the project proposes an alternative political and social organization that undermines the whole nation-state system. Thus, the project threatens the very foundation of the existing political order in the whole region, and it is not welcome in that sense. It will be a tough task to sell the project to non-Kurds, or even the Kurds that do not sympathize with the PKK and the HDP.

The PKK is a guerrilla organization and the kernel of a massive social movement. But it has been criminalized by Turkey, the EU, and the United States. The movement uses violence as a means to reach its goals, imposes road, street, and neighbourhood blocks, collects tax, establishes judicial mechanisms, and arms youth in the towns and cities in Kurdistan with the aim of achieving a full-fledged popular revolution in Kurdistan. It does not abstain from using neighbourhoods and communities as its base of armed revolution in towns and cities. These activities are cited as main justifications for the criminalization of Kurdish political activism (Sentas 2015). This also damages a hard-won reputation they earned by providing the Kurdish Êzîdî (Yezidi) community with protection against the genocidal onslaught of the Islamic State forces in the summer of 2014. It will be difficult to "legitimize" the movement and its politics in Turkey. Hence the dilemma of the HDP in Turkey: on the one hand, *democratic autonomy* suggests that towns and cities break away from state structures, declare their autonomy and defend this autonomy by force, if necessary. The HDP is active in legal, representative, parliamentary politics nationwide, trying to "democratize the state." Consequently, the Kurdish and leftist constituency, the voting pool of the HDP, are receiving mixed messages.

As mentioned throughout the section, all the councils, assemblies, and other structures are set, founded and put into motion by the PKK and its affiliates. Although securing broad-based participation of grassroots people in decision-making processes is the purpose, the movement has a great deal of hierarchy within its ranks. In other words, the main actor behind the whole endeavour is a centralized, armed, and hierarchical Kurdish organization. In that sense, the practice does not "reconcile authority with equality" (Arendt 1963, 278). Reconciling practice with theory appears to remain the greatest challenge for the Kurdish movement.

Likewise, no nation-state in the Middle East will willingly reconfigure their centralized political establishments in order to adapt to a system of gradually structured political authorities that fragment their sovereignty. This means that the fate of the movement will be determined by the strength of its actors, rather than the power of the project's positive/progressive elements. In other words, just as it happens with the formation and foundation of other forms of political community, ethics, morality, political principles, and popular support will not decide whether the project will be a success or a failure. The force deployed by political actors, *de facto* and *de jure,* against or in favour of the project will decide its fate, and this is the toughest challenge ahead.

NOTES

1. "If a community with their own language, culture, bonded with their homeland and the soil they live upon, with their own history and past, cannot have any right to that soil, or if they do not have any relationship of sovereignty of this or that sort with their homeland, if they cannot enjoy the right to self-rule and cannot participate in ruling themselves, this is a problem." The original statement: "Dili, kültürü olan anavatanıyla, toprağıyla bağı olan, tarihi ve geçmişi olan bir topluluğun o toprak üzerinde bir hakkı yoksa, şu veya bu düzeyde ama ille de bir egemenlik ilişkisi yoksa, kendini yönetme hakkını kullanabilmesi, katabilme ilişkisi yoksa, bu da bir sorundur." (*Cumhuriyet,* 26 June 2016)

2. One can consider emancipation as a revolutionary or momentary phase in the transition period located between the elimination of old forms of domination and the establishment of another subjugating form of sovereignty. Thus, emancipation could be thought an illusion, and history could be seen as the stage of human activities that eliminate one form of domination only to establish another, as Foucault has suggested.

3. Proclamations of democratic autonomy were made by groups of people who named themselves as members of "People's Assembly" in towns and cities. These assemblies have no constitutional or legal status. They are founded or organized by the dominant Kurdish political movement in Turkey and Kurdistan. Members are comprised of participants from predominantly Kurdish civil society organizations, political parties, women and youth councils, and ordinary citizens.

4. An umbrella organization that brings together legal Kurdish political parties, civil society organizations, and thematic councils such women and youth assemblies.

5. It should be noted that the extent to which the project could be implemented in practice would depend on the context and the balance of power between the parties to conflicts in each of the four parts of Kurdistan. Different Kurdish actors would implement varieties of the project in different localities—as displayed in the dis-

agreement over the timing and the manner of the proclamation of the Federation of Northern Syria -Rojava in 2016 (Noureddine 2016). Even the name above is a matter of disagreement: the PKK representative for foreign relations, for instance, finds the word "Rojava" in the name of the administration as biased in favour of the Kurds, and suggests its removal (Noureddine 2016).

6. Super-governors acted under laws that established varying degrees of *the state of exception* in Kurdistan (Gunter 2003). The state of exception or the state of emergency/emergency rule (*Olağanüstü Hal*) has been literally the norm in Kurdistan, because more than fifty years have passed under such exceptional regimes (Akkaya and Jongerden 2015, 152; Gunter 2003, 47). Considering that the "young republic" is only ninety-seven years old, the state of exception becomes *the normal order* in Kurdistan. Both authoritarian Kemalist dictatorship and authoritarian right-wing governments have imposed the state of exception in Kurdistan. In that sense, Kurdistan is one of the most unpleasant confirmations of Agamben's (2005) thesis that the state of exception has become the rule in contemporary democratic or semi-democratic regimes through making their way into the constitutions of those regimes.

References

Abbas, T., and I. H. Yigit. 2014. "Scenes from Gezi Park: Localisation, Nationalism and Globalisation in Turkey." *City: Analysis of Urban Trends, Culture, Theory, Policy, Action*, 1–16. https://doi.org/10.1080/13604813.2014.969070.

Abizadeh, Arash. 2012. "On the Demos and Its Kin: Nationalism, Democracy, and the Boundary Problem." *American Political Science Review* 106 (4): 1–16. https://doi.org/10.1017/S0003055412000421.

Aboona, Hirmis. 2008. *Assyrians, Kurds, and Ottomans: Intercommunal Relations on the Periphery of the Ottoman Empire*. New York: Cambria Press.

Abrams, Philip. 1977. "Notes on the Difficulty of Studying the State." *The Journal of Historical Sociology* 1 (1): 11–42. https://doi.org/10.1002/9781444309706.ch1.

Agamben, Giorgio. 1998. *Homo Sacer: Sovereign Power and Bare Life*. Stanford, CA: Stanford University Press.

———. 2005. *State of Exception*. London: The University of Chicago Press.

Ağaoğulları, Mehmet Ali. 1986. "Halk Ya Da Ulus Egemenligi'nin Kuramsal Temelleri Uzerine Birkac Dusunce." *AUHFD*, 131–52. http://dergipark.ulakbim.gov.tr/ausbf/article/viewFile/5000099532/5000092698.

Ahmedi, Idris. 2016. "The Role of Kurdish Movements in the Middle East." In *The Role of Kurdish Movements in the Middle East*. Stockholm: The Swedish Institute of International Affairs - Utrikespolitiska institutet (UI). https://www.youtube.com/watch?v=xvLE6ZDvFP4&sns=fb.

Akcam, Taner. 2014. "The Anatomy of Religious Cleansing: Non-Muslims in the Ottoman Empire." In *CSI Co-Sponsored Event: Turkish Scholar Modern Turkey's National Struggles Rooted in Genocide Denial*. Boston: Digital Journal. http://www.digitaljournal.com/pr/2345705.

Akçura, Yusuf. 1904. "Uc Tarz-i Siyaset [Three Policies]." Istanbul: Carrie Books. http://vlib.iue.it/carrie/texts/carrie_books/paksoy-2/cam9.html.

Akkaya, Ahmet Hamdi, and Joost Jongerden. 2011. "The PKK in the 2000s: Continuity through Breaks?" In *Nationalisms and Politics in Turkey: Political Islam,*

193

Kemalism and the Kurdish Issue, edited by Marlies Casier and Joost Jongerden, 143–62. London: Routledge.

———. 2012a. "Reassembling the Political: The PKK and the Project of Radical Democracy." *European Journal of Turkish Studies* 14 (April): 1–16. http://ejts. revues.org/4615.

———. 2012b. "The Kurdistan Workers Party and a New Left in Turkey: Analysis of the Revolutionary Movement in Turkey through the PKK's Memorial Text on Haki Karer." *European Journal of Turkish Studies* 14 (April): 1–18. http://ejts. revues.org/4613.

———. 2013. "Confederalism and Autonomy in Turkey: The Kurdistan Workers' Party and the Reinvention of Democracy." In *The Kurdish Question in Turkey: New Perspectives on Violence, Representation and Reconciliation*, edited by Cengiz Gunes and Welat Zeydanlioglu, 186–204. London: Routledge. https://doi. org/10.4324/9780203796450.

———. 2015. "Reassembling the Political: The PKK and the Project of Radical Democracy." In *Stateless Democracy*, edited by R. I. der Maur and J. Staal, New World, 158–91. Amsterdam: New World Summit.

Aktar, Ayhan. 2014. *Varlık Vergisi ve "Türkleştirme" Politikaları*. 12th ed. Istanbul: Iletisim. http://www.iletisim.com.tr/kitap/varlik-vergisi-ve-turkle-stirme-politikalari/7339#.V9X5TpgrK00.

Aktay, Yasin. 2014. "Toplumsal Sözleşme Olarak Anayasa." Yeni Şafak. http://www. yenisafak.com/yazarlar/yasinaktay/toplumsal-sozlesme-olarak-anayasa-23672.

Akyol, Mustafa. 2006. "The Origin of Turkey's Kurdish Question : An Outcome of the Breakdown of the Ottoman Ancien Régime An Abstract of the Thesis of Mustafa Akyol for the Degree." Atatürk Institute for Modern Turkish History.

Al, Serhun. 2015. "An Anatomy of Nationhood and the Question of Assimilation: Debates on Turkishness Revisited." *Studies in Ethnicity and Nationalism* 15 (1): 83–101. https://doi.org/10.1111/sena.12121.

Alam, Anwar. 2014. "The Limits of Political Islam: The New AK Party." *Turkish Review* 4 (1): 58–61. http://search.proquest.com/openview/6e79395ab9c2500e9db a3fdeefa65b32/1?pq-origsite=gscholar.

Albo, Xavier. 1993. "Our Identity Starting from Pluralism in the Base." *Boundary 2* 20 (3): 18–33. http://www.jstor.org/stable/10.2307/303338.

Alexander, Jeffrey C. 2006. *The Civil Sphere*. Oxford: Oxford University Press. http://scans.hebis.de/HEBCGI/show.pl?17975023_toc.pdf.

Altan, Mehmet. 2014. "'Ortadoğu'nun Yeni Modeli: Kürtler.'" Ilke Haber. 2014. http://www.ilkehaber.com/yazi/ortadogunun-yeni-modeli-kurtler-12260.htm.

Althusser, Louis. 2014. *On the Reproduction of Capitalism: Ideology and Ideological State Apparatuses*. London: Verso. https://doi.org/10.1017/ CBO9781107415324.004.

Amnesty International. 2016. "Amnesty International." *Amnesty International Report 2015/2016- the State of the World's Human Rights*. https://doi.org/10.1017/ CBO9781107415324.004.

Anayasa Mahkemesi. 2016. "Anayasa Mahkemesi." Anayasa.Gov.Tr. 2016. http:// www.anayasa.gov.tr/icsayfalar/mahkemehakkinda/kisatarihce/tarihselbilgi.html.

Anderson, M. S. 1996. *The Ascendancy of Europe 1815-1914*. London: Longman.

Arakon, Maya. 2014. "Kurds at the Transistion from the Ottoman Empire to the Turkish Republic." *Turkish Policy Quarterly* 3 (1): 139–48.

Aralik Hareketi, 10. 2010. "20 Soruda Anayasa Degisikligi." Chd.Org.Tr. 2010. http://chd.org.tr/wp-content/uploads/2013/06/20_Soruda_Anayasa_Degisikligi.pdf.

Arato, A. 2010a. "Democratic Constitution-Making and Unfreezing the Turkish Process." *Philosophy & Social Criticism* 36 (3–4): 473–87. https://doi.org/10.1177/0191453709358543.

———. 2010b. "The Constitutional Reform Proposal of the Turkish Government: The Return of Majority Imposition." *Constellations* 17 (2): 345–50. https://doi.org/10.1111/j.1467-8675.2010.00599.x.

Arendt, Hannah. 1954. "What Is Authority?" http://la.utexas.edu/users/hcleaver/330T/350kPEEArendtWhatIsAuthorityTable.pdf.

———. 1958. *The Human Condition*. 1998th ed. London: The University of Chicago Press. https://doi.org/10.2307/2089589.

———. 1963. *On Revolution*. 1990 ed. London: Penguin Books.

Aretaios, Evangelos. 2015. "The Rojava Revolution." OpenDemocracy. 2015. https://www.opendemocracy.net/arab-awakening/evangelos-aretaios/rojava-revolution.

Aristotle. 1999. *Politics*. Kitchener: Botoche Books.

Arınç, Bülent. 2014. "The Future of Democracy in Turkey : Perceptions and Realities." London: Chatham House. https://www.chathamhouse.org/events/view/197335.

Arslan, Murat, and Hişyar Özsoy. 2016. "Kürtlerle Türkiye Cumhuriyeti Arasında Yeni Bir Toplum Sözleşmesine Ihtiyaç Var." Ayrıntı Dergi. http://ayrintidergi.com.tr/kurtlerle-turkiye-cumhuriyeti-arasinda-yeni-bir-toplum-sozlesmesine-ihtiyac-var-hisyar-ozsoy-ile-soylesi/.

Atakan, Arda. 2007. "Milli İrade Kavramı Üzerine Bir İnceleme." *MÜHF-HAD* 13 (3–4): 39–82. http://dosya.marmara.edu.tr/huk/fakültedergisi/2007C.13S.3-4/39-82.pdf.

Atatürk, Mustafa Kemal. 1923. "Adana Esnaflarıyla Konuşma." Atatürk Araştırma Merkezi. http://www.atam.gov.tr/ataturkun-soylev-ve-demecleri/adana-esnaflariyla-konusma.

Ates, Sabri. 2013. *The Ottoman-Iranian Borderlands: Making a Boundary, 1843-1914*. New York: Cambridge University Press.

Aytar, Osman. 2014. "Nameyeke Bi Hesreta 100 Salî Ji Bo Hêja Şêx Ebdulselam Barzanî." Kurdinfo. http://www.kurdinfo.com/gotar.asp?yazid=22&id=1824.

Bacik, Gokhan. 2014. "Informal Institutions in Turkish Politics: The Case of Proxy Leadership." In *Informal Power in the Greater Middle East : Hidden Geographies*, edited by Luca Anceschi, Gennaro Gervasio, and Andrea Teti, 71–84. London: Routledge.

———. 2016. "Demokrasi İstişareden Üstündür." Maviyorum. 2016. http://www.maviyorum.com/demokrasi-istisareden-ustundur/.

Baran, Oktay. 2010. "İsmet İnönü, Kemalizm ve Demokrasi." Sinif Mucadelesinde Marksist Tutum. http://marksist.net/oktay_baran/ismet_inonu_kemalizm_ve_demokrasi.htm.

Bardakci, Murat. 2015. "AK Partili Vekile En Iyi Yanıtı Sabiha Sultan Veriyor." Radikal. http://www.radikal.com.tr/politika/ak_partili_vekile_en_iyi_yaniti_sabiha_sultan_veriyor-1274859.

Baris, Hanifi. 2016. "The Kurds: 'A History of Deliberate and Reactive Statelessnes.'" In *Conflict, Insecurity, and Mobility*, edited by Ibrahim Sirkeci, 89–99. London: Transnational Press.

Barkey, Henri J., and Graham E. Fuller. 1998. *Turkey's Kurdish Question*. New York: Rowman & Littlefield Publishers, Inc.

Bauböck, Rainer. 1994. *Transnational Citizenship: Membership and Rights in International Migration*. Hants: Edward Elgar.

Bauer, Joanne. 2003. "The Challenge to International Human Rights." In *Constructing Human Rights in the Age of Globalization*, edited by Mahmood Monshipouri, Neil Englehart, Andrew J. Nathan, and Kavita Philip, 239–58. London: M.E. Sharper. http://www.carnegiecouncil.org/publications/articles_papers_reports/905.html.

Bayır, Derya. 2013. "Representation of the Kurds by the Turkish Judiciary." *Human Rights Quarterly* 35 (1): 116–42. https://doi.org/10.1353/hrq.2013.0001.

Belge, Ceren. 2011. "State Building and the Limits of Legibility: Kinship Networks and Kurdish Resistance in Turkey." *International Journal of Middle East Studies* 43 (01): 95–114. https://doi.org/10.1017/S0020743810001212.

Bellaigue, Christopher De. 2016. "Welcome to Demokrasi: How Erdogan Got More Popular than Ever." *The Guardian*. https://www.theguardian.com/world/2016/aug/30/welcome-to-demokrasi-how-erdogan-got-more-popular-than-ever?CMP=share_btn_fb.

Bellamy, Richard, and Dario Castiglione. 2013. "Three Models of Democracy, Political Community and Representation in the EU." *JEPP* 20 (2). http://ssrn.com/abstract=2187388.

Benhabib, Seyla. 2007. "Twilight of Sovereignty or the Emergence of Cosmopolitan Norms? Rethinking Citizenship in Volatile Times." *Citizenship Studies* 11 (1): 19–36. https://doi.org/10.1080/13621020601099807.

Berlin, Isaiah. 1969. "Two Concepts of Liberty." In *Four Essays On Liberty*, 1969 ed., 1–32. Oxford: Oxford University Press.

Beşikçi, İsmail. 1990. *Devletlerarası Sömürge Kürdistan*. Paris: Institut Kurde De Paris.

———. 1998. *Hayali Kürdistan'ın Dirilişi*. Istanbul: Aram Yainlari.

Biehl, Janet. 2014. "Impressions of Rojava: A Report from the Revolution." ROAR Magazine. https://roarmag.org/essays/janet-biehl-report-rojava/.

Bilgel, Fırat, and Burhan Can Karahasan. 2017. "The Economic Costs of Separatist Terrorism in Turkey." *Journal of Conflict Resolution* 61 (2): 457–79. https://doi.org/10.1177/0022002715576572.

Bilginer, Haluk. 2014. "Bilginer: Babalarımızı Öldüremedik, 91 Yıldır Atatürk'e Tapınmaktan Vazgeçemedik." T24. http://t24.com.tr/haber/bilginer-babalarimizi-olduremedik-91-yildir-ataturke-tapinmaktan-vazgecemedik,261244.

Bookchin, Murray. 1994. *Murray Bookchin Reader: Anarchy Is Order*. London: Black Rose Books.

———. 1995. *From Urbanization to Cities toward a New Politics of Citizenship.* London: Cassell.

———. 2015. *The Next Revolution: Popular Assemblies and the Promise of Direct Democracy.* London: Verso.

Boucher, David, and Paul Kelly. 1994. *The Social Contract from Hobbes to Rawls.* London: Routledge.

Bourdieu, Pierre. 1999. "Rethinking the State: Genesis and Structure of the Bureaucratic Field." In *State/Culture: State Formation After the Cultural Turn,* edited by George Steinmetz, 53–75. Ithaca, NY: Cornell University Press.

Bourdieu, Pierre, Loic J.D. Wacquant, and Samar Parage. 1994. "Rethinking the State: Genesis and Structure of the Bureaucratic Field." *Sociological Theory* 12 (1): 1–18. http://links.jstor.org/sici ?sici=0735-2751 (199403)12:1 %3C 1:RTSGAS%3E2.0.C0;2-J.

Bozarslan, Hamit. 2015. "HDP, Kürdistan'ın Türkiye'ye Son Daveti." Agos. http://www.agos.com.tr/tr/yazi/13485/hamit-bozarslan-hdp-kurdistanin-turkiyeye-son-daveti.

Bozarslan, Mahmut. 2016. "Regional Kurdish Party in AKP'S Crosshairs." Al-Monitor. http://www.al-monitor.com/pulse/originals/2016/06/turkey-kurds-democratic-region-party-government-crosshair.html.

Bozkurt, Goksel. 2013. "New Constitution and BDP's Red Lines." *Hurriyet Daily News.* http://www.hurriyetdailynews.com/new-constitution-and-bdps-red-lines.aspx?pageID=238&nID=45816&NewsCatID=342.

Brubaker, Rogers. 2013. "Language, Religion and the Politics of Difference." *Nations and Nationalism* 19 (1): 1–20. https://doi.org/10.1111/j.1469-8129.2012.00562.x.

Bruinessen, Martin Van. 1980. "The Naqshbandi Order in Seventeenth-Century Kurdistan." *Islam Zeitschrift Für Geschichte Und Kultur Des Islamischen Orients,* 89–103.

———. 1992. *Agha, Shaykh and State: The Social and Political Structures of Kurdistan.* London: Zed Books.

———. 1994. "Genocide in Kurdistan? The Suppression of the Dersim Rebellion in Turkey (1937–38) and the Chemical War against the Iraqi Kurds (1988)." In *Conceptual and Historical Dimensions of Genocide,* edited by George J. Andreopoulos, 141–70. Pennsylvania: University of Pennsylvania. http://www.mendeley.com/research/genocide-kurdistan-suppression-dersim-rebellion-turkey-193738-chemical-war-against-iraqi-kurds-1988/?utm_source=desktop&utm_medium=1.12.3&utm_campaign=open_catalog&userDocumentId=%7B76 64b167-4d3d-4d88-baec-1004c4496164%7D.

———. 1998a. "The Kurds and Islam." *Les Annales de l'Autre Islam* 5 (Islam des Kurdes): 13–35.

———. 1998b. "The Kurds as Objects and Subjects of Their History: Between Turkish Official Historiography, Orientalist Constructions, and Kurdish Nationalists' Reappropriation of Their History." In *Between Imagination and Denial: Kurds as Subjects and Objects of Political and Social Processes, Organized by the Kurdology Working Group at the Free University, Berlin, May 19-31, 1998.* Berlin.

———. 1999. "The Kurds in Movement : Migrations, Mobilisations, Communications and the Globalisation of the Kurdish Question." Islamic Area Studies Project. Tokyo. dspace.library.uu.nl/bitstream/handle/.../bruinessen_00_kurds_in_movement. pdf?...3.

———. 2002. "Kurds, States and Tribes." In *Tribes and Power: Nationalism and Ethnicity in the Middle East*, edited by Faleh A. Jabar and Hosham Dawod, 165–83. London: Saqi. http://www.hum.uu.nl/medewerkers/m.vanbruinessen/publications/ Bruinessen_Kurds_States_and_Tribes.pdf.

———. 2004. "The Kurdish Question : Whose Question , Whose Answers ?" In *Wadie Jwaideh Memorial Lecture in Arabic and Islamic Studies, Department of Near Eastern Languages and Cultures & Middle Eastern and Islamic Studies Program, Indiana University, Bloomington, 19 November 2004.* Bloomington, Indiana: Indiana University.

———. 2006. "Kurdish Paths to Nation." In *The Kurds: Nationalism and Politics*, edited by Faleh A. Jabar and Hosham Dawod, 21–48. London: Saqi.

Cagaptay, Soner. 2004. "Race, Assimilation and Kemalism: Turkish Nationalism and the Minorities in the 1930s." *Middle Eastern Studies* 40 (3): 86–101. https://doi.or g/10.1080/0026320042000213474.

Çamlıbel, Cansu. 2015. "PKK Not a Separatist or Nationalist Group: Senior Member." *Hurriyet Daily News*. http://www.hurriyetdailynews.com/pkk-not-a-separatist-or-nationalist-group-senior-member.aspx?pageID=238&nID=80328&NewsCa tID=338.

Çandar, Cengiz. 2013. "Ocalan's Message Is Much More Than a Cease-Fire." Al Monitor. http://www.al-monitor.com/pulse/originals/2013/03/ocalan-ceasefire-newroz-speech-farewell-to-arms.html.

———. 2016. "The Role of Kurdish Movements in the Middle East." In *The Role of Kurdish Movements in the Middle East*. Stockholm: The Swedish Institute of International Affairs. https://www.youtube.com/watch?v=xvLE6ZDvFP4&sns=fb.

Carter, Ian. 2008. "Positive and Negative Liberty." *Stanford Encyclopedia of Philosophy* 363 (9410): 1–12. https://doi.org/10.1016/S0140-6736(04)15657-2.

Casier, Marlies, and Joost Jongerden. 2012. "Understanding Today's Kurdish Movement: Leftist Heritage, Martyrdom, Democracy and Gender." *European Journal of Turkish Studies* 14 (April): 1–18.

Castiglione, Dario. 1994. "History, Reason and Experience: Hume's Arguments against Contract Theories." In *The Social Contract from Hobbes to Rawls*, edited by David Boucher and Paul Kelly, 2005 ed., 97–116. London: Routledge.

Castles, Stephen. 2005. "Hierarchical Citizenship in a World of Unequal Nation-States." *PS: Political Science & Politics* 38 (4): 689–92. https://doi.org/10.1017/ S1049096505050353.

Chambers, Simone. 2004. "Democracy, Popular Sovereignty, and Constitutional Legitimacy." *Constellations* 11 (2): 153–73.

Ciwan, Murad. 2014. "I. Selim'in Çaldıran Seferi'nde ve Osmanlılar'ın Darü'l-İslam'a Açılmasında Bitlis Beyliği'nin Başını Çektiği Kürtler'in Rolü." In *I. ULUSLARARASI BİTLİS SEMPOZYUMU*. Bitlis: https://www.facebook.com/notes/murad-ciwan/i-selimin-%C3%A7ald%C4%B1ran-seferinde-ve-osmanl%C4%B1lar%C4%B1ndar%C3%BCl-islama-a%C3%A7%C4%B1lmas%C4%B1nda-bitlis-bey/10202959360957311?pnref=story.

Colón-Ríos, Joel. 2010. "Legitimacy of the Juridical: Constituent Power, Democracy, and the Limits of Constitutional Reform, The." *Osgoode Hall Law Journal* 48: 199–245.

Couldry, Nick, and Natalie Fenton. 2011. "Occupy: Rediscovering the General Will in Hard Times." Possible Futures. http://www.possible-futures.org/2011/12/22/rediscovering-the-general-will/.

Cox, Robert W., and Timothy J. Sinclair. 1996. *Approaches to World Order*. Cambridge: Cambridge University Press.

Coyne, Christopher. 2010. "Review of James C. Scott, The Art of Not Being Governed: An Anarchist History of Upland Southeast Asia." Www.Coyne.Com. 2010. http://www.ccoyne.com/Review_of_James_Scott.pdf.

Cudd, Ann. 2000. "Contractarianism." *Stanford Encyclopedia of Philosophy*. Stanford University. http://plato.stanford.edu/entries/contractarianism/.

D'Agostino, Fred, Gerald Gaus, and John Thrasher. 1996. "Contemporary Approaches to the Social Contract." *Stanford Encyclopedia of Philosophy*. Stanford University. http://plato.stanford.edu/entries/contractarianism-contemporary/.

Daily Sabah. 2016. "HDP Deputy Yıldırım: Party Not Representative of Muslim Kurds." *Daily Sabah*. 7 Jan. http://www.dailysabah.com/politics/2016/07/01/hdp-deputy-yildirim-party-not-representative-of-muslim-kurds.

Danforth, Nick. 2013. "Rebellious Tribes of Eastern Anatolia." The Afternoon Map: A Cartography Blog, Brought to You by Ottoman History Podcast. http://www.midafternoonmap.com/2013/10/rebellious-tribes-of-eastern-anatolia.html.

Derince, Mehmet Serif. 2013. "In between Oppression and Resilience: Sociolinguistic Situation of Kurds in Turkey." In *4th International Language and Education Conference Bangkok, 6-8 November, 2013*. http://www.lc.mahidol.ac.th/mle-conf2013/PPTnNotes/Mehmet Serif_Derince - PPT - Final.pdf.

Deringil, Selim. 2003. "'They Live in a State of Nomadism and Savagery': The Late Ottoman Empire and the Post-Colonial Debate." *Comparative Studies in Society and History* 45 (2): 311–42. https://doi.org/10.1017/S001041750300015X.

Diken, Şeyhmus. 2013. "Kürdistan Mir'i Bedirxan'ın Sürgün Yılları!" Bianet. http://www.bianet.org/biamag/toplum/145815-kurdistan-mir-i-bedirxan-in-surgun-yil-lari.

Dirlik, Arif. 1996. "Chinese History and the Question of Orientalism." *History and Theory* 35 (4): 96–118.

Dworkin, Ronald. 1996. *Freedom's Law*. Oxford: Oxford University Press.

Earle, Edward Mead. 1925. "The New Constitution of Turkey." *Political Science Quarterly* 40 (1): 73–100. https://doi.org/10.1017/CBO9781107415324.004.

Easton, David. 1959. "Political Anthropology." *Biennial Review of Anthropology* 1 (1959): 210–62. http://www.jstor.org/stable/2949205.

Ebenstein, William, and Alan Ebenstein. 2000. *Great Political Thinkers: Plato to the Present*. Boston: Wadsworth Cengage Learning.

Elbe, Stefan. 2009. "What Future for the European Political Community? Nietzsche, Nationalism and the Idea of the 'Good Europeans.'" In *The Future of*

Political Community, edited by Jens Bartelson and Gideon Baker, 72–89. London: Rotuledge.

Eliassi, Barzoo. 2014. "Nationalism, Cosmopolitanism and Statelessness: An Interview with Craig Calhoun." *Kurdish Studies* 2 (1): 61–74.

Elster, Jon. 1995. "Forces and Mechanisms in the Constitution-Making Process." *Duke Law Journal* 45 (2): 364–96. https://doi.org/10.2307/1372906.

Enzinna, Wes. 2015. "A Dream of Secular Utopia in ISIS' Backyard." *The New York Times Magazine*, November 2015. http://www.nytimes.com/2015/11/29/magazine/a-dream-of-utopia-in-hell.html?emc=edit_tnt_20151124&nlid=56257975&tntemail0=y&_r=1.

Evans, Tony. 1996. *US Hegemony and the Project of Universal Human Rights*. London: Palgrave Macmillan UK. https://doi.org/10.1057/9780230380103.

Fernandes, Desmond. 2015. "Surveillance, Targeting and the Criminalisation of Kurds." Kurdish Question. http://kurdishquestion.com/index.php/insight-research/the-threat-posed-by-unsc-resolution-2178-to-the-pkk-kurdish-diaspora-peace-process-and-civil-liberties.html.

Foucault, Michel. 1980. *Power/Knowledge: Selected Interviews and Other Writings 1972–1977*. Edited by Colin Gordon. 1980 ed. Vol. 23. New York: Pantheon Books.

———. 1990. *The History of Sexuality: An Introduction*. London: Penguin Books.

———. 2003. *Society Must Be Defended. Lectures at the College de France 1975-76*. New York: Picador.

———. 2008. *Birth of Biopolitics (Michel Foucault: Lectures at the College De France)*. Edited by Arnold I. Davidson. London: Palgrave Macmillan. https://doi.org/10.1080/10286630902971637.

———. 2009. *Security , Territory , Population: Lectures Ad The College De France, 1977–78*. Edited by Michel Senellart. London: Palgrave Macmillan.

Galbreath, David J., and Joanne McEvoy. 2012. *The European Minority Rights Regime Towards a Theory of Regime Effectiveness*. London: Palgrave Macmillan. https://doi.org/10.1057/9780230359222.

Gambetti, Zeynep. 2008. "Decolonizing Diyarbakir: Culture, Identity and the Struggle to Appropriate Urban Space." *Re-Exploring The Urban: Comparative Citiscapes in the Middle East and South Asia*.

———. 2009. "The Spatial Dynamics of the Kurdish and Zapatista Movements." *New Perspectives on Turkey: Politics of Place/Space*, no. 41: 43–87.

Gaub, Florence, and Patryk Pawlak. 2013. "Sykes-Picot and Syria." *European Union Institute for Security Studies* 34 (1): 1–2. http://www.iss.europa.eu/uploads/media/Alert_34-Sykes-Picot_and_Syria.pdf.

Gellner, Ernest. 1983. *Nations and Nationalism*. Ithaca, NY: Cornell University Press.

Genc, Ibrahim. 2013. "Millet Nedir, Ulus Kimdir?" *Radikal*, February 2013. http://blog.radikal.com.tr/turkiye-gundemi/millet-nedir-ulus-kimdir-13856.

Gökalp, Deniz. 2007. "Beyond Ethnopolitical Contention : The State, Citizenship and Violence in The 'New' Kurdish Question in Turkey." Unpublished dissertation, The University of Texas at Austin.

Gordon, Andrew, and Trevor Stack. 2007. "Citizenship Beyond the State: Thinking with Early Modern Citizenship in the Contemporary World." *Citizenship Studies* 11 (2): 117–33. https://doi.org/10.1080/13621020701262438.

Graeber, David. 2014a. "Rojava'dan on Yaş Genç Döndüm (Interview in Turkish)." Evrensel. https://www.evrensel.net/haber/100431/david-graeber-rojavadan-on-yas-genc-dondum.

———. 2014b. "Why Is the World Ignoring the Revolutionary Kurds in Syria?" *The Guardian*. 8 Oct. https://www.theguardian.com/commentisfree/2014/oct/08/why-world-ignoring-revolutionary-kurds-syria-isis.

Guida, Michelangelo. 2014. "Feudal Control of Politics in Peripheral Turkey: The Example of the Sanliurfa Province." In *Informal Power in the Greater Middle East: Hidden Geographies*, edited by Luca Anceschi, Gennaro Gervasio, and Andrea Teti, 175–90. London: Routledge. https://doi.org/10.4324/9781315818306.

Gunes, Cengiz. 2012a. "Explaining the PKK's Mobilization of the Kurds in Turkey: Hegemony, Myth and Violence." *Ethnopolitics* 12 (3): 247–67. https://doi.org/10.1080/17449057.2012.707422.

———. 2012b. *The Kurdish National Movement in Turkey: From Protest to Resistance*. London: Routledge.

Gunter, Michael M. 2003. *The A to Z of the Kurds*. Plymouth: Scarecrow Press Inc.

Güvenç, Muna. 2011. "Constructing Narratives of Kurdish Nationalism in the Urban Space of Diyarbakır, Turkey." *Tdsr* XXIII (I): 25–40. http://iaste.berkeley.edu/iaste/wp-content/uploads/2012/07/23.1-Fall-11-Guvenc.pdf.

Haass, Richard N. 2014. "The New Thirty Years' War." Project Syndicate. https://www.project-syndicate.org/commentary/richard-n--haass-argues-that-the-middle-east-is-less-a-problem-to-be-solved-than-a-condition-to-be-managed?barrier=true.

Hamelink, A. W. 2014. *The Sung Home: Narrative, Morality and the Kurdish Nation*. Leiden: Leiden University.

Hamelink, Wendelmoet, and Hanifi Baris. 2014. "Dengbêjs on Borderlands : Borders and the State as Seen through the Eyes of Kurdish Singer-Poets." *Kurdish Studies Journal* 2 (1): 34–60. http://www.tplondon.com/journal/index.php/ks/article/view/350.

Hamsici, Mahmut. 2015. "Bayık: Artık Tek Taraflı Ateşkes Olmayacak." BBC Türkçe. http://www.bbc.com/turkce/haberler/2015/11/151130_bayik_mulakat_1.

Hannah, John. 2016. "How Do You Solve a Problem Like Erdogan?" Foreign Policy. http://foreignpolicy.com/2016/06/15/how-do-you-solve-a-problem-like-erdogan/.

Hardt, Michael, and Antonio Negri. 2000. *Empire*. London: Harvard University Press.

———. 2004. *Multitude: War and Democracy in the Age of Empire*. New York: The Penguin Press.

Harvey, David. 2000. "Possible Urban Worlds. The Fourth Megacities Lecture." The Hague: Twynstra Gudde Management Consultants, Amersfoort, The Netherlands. http://www.kas.de/upload/dokumente/megacities/MegacitiesLectur4Worlds.pdf.

———. 2012. *Rebel Cities. from the Right to the City to the Right to the Urban Revolution*. London: Verso. https://doi.org/10.4067/S0250-71612014000100013.

HDP. 2015. "HDP's Election Manifesto." Istanbul: Kurdish Question. http://kurd-ishquestion.com/oldsite/index.php/kurdistan/hdp-s-election-manifesto/839-hdp-s-election-manifesto.html.

Hegel, G. W. F. 1953. *Reason in History: A General Introduction to the Philosophy of History*. Edited by Robert S. Hartman. 1953 ed. Indianapolis: The Bobbs-Merrill Company, Inc.

Held, David. 1995. *Democracy and the Global Order: From the Modern State to Cosmopolitan Governance*. Cambridge: Polity Press.

Herman, Edward S., and Noam Chomsky. 2002. *Manufacturing Consent: The Political Economy of the Mass Media*. New York: Pantheon Books. https://doi.org/10.2307/2074220.

Hobsbawm, E. J. 1990. *Nations and Nationalism since 1780: Programme, Myth, Reality*. 1992 ed. New York: Cambridge University Press. https://doi.org/http://dx.doi.org/10.1017/CCOL0521439612.

Holmes, Amy Austin. 2015. "What Are the Kurdish Women's Units Fighting for in Syria?" *The Washington Post*. https://www.washingtonpost.com/news/monkey-cage/wp/2015/12/23/what-are-the-kurdish-womens-units-fighting-for-in-syria/.

Hroch, Miroslav. 2010. "Why Did They Begin? On the Transition from Cultural Reflection to Social Activism in European National Movements." www.spinnet.eu.

HSYK. 2016. "Hâkimler ve Savcılar Yüksek Kurulu." http://www.hsyk.gov.tr/Hak-kimizda.aspx.

Hughes, Erin. 2012. "Review of Making Constitutions in Deeply Divided Societies by Hanna Lerner." *Nations and Nationalism* 18 (4): 765–66. https://doi.org/10.1111/j.1469-8129.2012.00560.x.

Human Rights Watch. 2016. "World Report 2016: Syria." *Human Rights Watch World Report*. https://www.hrw.org/world-report/2016/country-chapters/syria#f63c0c.

Hurriyet Daily News. 2015. "Turkish Ruling Party Deputy Says 'the Ottomans Are Back,' but 'Janissaries' Protest AKP." http://www.hurriyetdailynews.com/turkish-ruling-party-deputy-says-the-ottomans-are-back-but-janissaries-protest-akp.aspx?pageID=238&nID=77019&NewsCatID=338.

———. 2017. "President Erdoğan Calls Turkey's Jailed Opposition Co-Chair Demirtaş a 'Terrorist' - POLITICS." http://www.hurriyetdailynews.com/Default.aspx?pageID=238&nID=115289&NewsCatID=338.

İnalcık, Halil. 1996. "The Meaning of Legacy: The Ottoman Case." In *Imperial Legacy: The Ottoman Imprint on the Balkans and the Middle East*, edited by L. Carl Brown, 17–29. New York: Columbia University Press.

Ipek, Aydın. 2008. "Ulus Egemenliği ve Halk Egemenliği Karşılaştırması ve Yeni Anayasa İçin Halk Egemenliği Önerisi." *Dumlupinar Universitesi Sosyal Bilim-ler Dergisi* April (20): 211–36. http://dergipark.ulakbim.gov.tr/dpusbd/article/view/5000126268.

Isin, Engin F. 2007. "City.State: Critique of Scalar Thought." *Citizenship Studies* 11 (2): 211–28. https://doi.org/10.1080/13621020701262644.

———. 2012a. "Citizens without Nations." *Environment and Planning D: Society and Space* 30 (3): 450–67. https://doi.org/10.1068/d19210.

———. 2012b. "Citizens Without Frontiers." *Politics*, no. February: 1–8. https://doi.org/10.1068/d19210.

———. 2013. "Rethinking Citizenship beyond the Nation State. Interview to Engin Isin." Euroalter. 2013. https://euroalter.com/2013/rethinking-citizenship-beyond-the-nation-state-interview-to-engin-isin.

Jalki, Dunkin. 2013. "Colonialism and Its Impact on India: A Critique of Pollock's Hypothesis." *International Journal of Social Sciences and Humanities* 2 (1): 122–29. http://journal.tumkuruniversity.in/.

Jennings, Ivor. 1956. *The Approach to Self-Government*. 1958 ed. Cambridge: Cambridge University Press.

Jong, Alex De. 2015. "Kurdish Autonomy between Dream and Reality." Roar Magazine. https://roarmag.org/essays/kurdish-autonomy-jongerden-interview/.

Jongerden, J., and A. H. Akkaya. 2012. *PKK Uzerine Yazilar*. Istanbul: Vate Yayinlari.

Jongerden, Joost. 2015. "Radicalising Democracy : Power , Politics , People and the PKK." *Research and Policy on Turkey*, no. March: 64–78. http://researchturkey.org/radicalising-democracy-power-politics-people-and-the-pkk/.

Juris, Jeffrey S. 2012. "Reflections on #Occupy Everywhere: Social Media, Public Space, and Emerging Logics of Aggregation." *American Ethnologist* 39 (2): 259–79. https://doi.org/10.1111/j.1548-1425.2012.01362.x.

Kantorowicz, Ernst Hartwig. 1957. *The King's Two Bodies : A Study in Mediaeval Political Theology*. Edited by William Chester Jordan. 1997 ed. Princeton, NJ: Princeton University Press.

Kapani, Münci. 1975. *Politika Bilimine Giriş*. 2001 ed. Istanbul: Bilgi.

Karan, Ceyda. 2015. "'IŞİD Zihniyetiyle Tam 220 Yıldır Savaştayız.'" Cumhuriyet. http://www.cumhuriyet.com.tr/haber/dunya/429881/_ISiD_zihniyetiyle_tam_220_yildir_savastayiz_.html.

Keating, Michael. 1998. *The New Regionalism in Western Europe*. Cheltenham: Edward Elgar.

———. 2001a. *Nations against the State: The New Politics of Nationalism in Quebec, Catalonia and Scotland*. New York: Palgrave Macmillan.

———. 2001b. *Plurinational Democracy: Stateless Nations in a Post-Sovereignty Era*. Oxford: Oxford University Press.

———. 2002. "Plurinational Democracy in a Post-Sovereign Order." In *Queen's Papers on Europeanisation No 1/2002*, 16. Florence. http://heinonline.org/HOL/Page?handle=hein.journals/nilq53&div=35&g_sent=1&collection=journals.

———. 2003. "Sovereignty and Plurinational Democracy: Problems in Political Science." In *Sovereignty in Transition*, edited by N. Walker, 191–208. Oxford: Hart Publishing.

———. 2015. "Negotiated and Consensual Secession." *H-Nationalism*, no. December: 1–11. https://networks.h-net.org/node/3911/discussions/103139/secessionism-and-separatism-monthly-series-"negotiated-and#reply-103402.

Kentel, Ferhat, Levent Köker, and Özge Genç. 2012. "Making of a New Constitution in Turkey Monitoring Report." Istanbul. http://tesev.org.tr/wp-content/

uploads/2015/11/Monitoring_Report_Making_Of_A_New_Constitution_In_Tur-key_October_2011_January_2012.pdf.

Ketsemanian, Varak. 2013. "The Confiscation of Armenian Properties: An Interview with Ümit Kurt." Armenian Weekly. http://armenianweekly.com/2013/09/23/the-confiscation-of-armenian-properties-an-interview-with-umit-kurt/.

Kirişci, Kemal, and Gareth M. Winrow. 1997. *The Kurdish Question and Turkey: An Example of a Trans-State Ethnic Conflict*. London: Frank Cass.

Klein, Janet. 2007. "Kurdish Nationalists and Non-Nationalist Kurdists: Rethink-ing Minority Nationalism and the Dissolution of the Ottoman Empire, 1908-1909." *Nations and Nationalism* 13 (1): 135–53. https://doi.org/10.1111/j.1469-8129.2007.00281.x.

———. 2011. *The Margins of Empire Kurdish Militias in the Ottoman Tribal Zone*. Stanford, CA: Stanford University Press.

Knapp, Michael, Anja Flach, and Ercan Ayboğa. 2016. *Revolution in Rojava: Demo-cratic Autonomy and Women's Liberation in Syrian Kurdistan*. 1st ed. London: Pluto Press.

Knott, Andy. 2014. "Representation and Political Space in Laclau and Hardt and Negri." In *Radical Democracy and Collective Movements Today*, edited by Alex-andros Kioupkiolis and Giorgos Katsambekis, 191–212. London: Routledge.

Küçük, Bülent, and Ceren Özselçuk. 2016. "The Rojava Experience: Possibilities and Challenges of Building a Democratic Life." *The South Atlantic Quarterly* 115 (1): 183–96. https://doi.org/10.1215/00382876-3425013.

Kuehn, Thomas. 2011. *Empire, Islam, and Politics of Difference: Ottoman Rule in Yemen*. Leiden: Brill.

Kurt, Ümit. 2015. "Ankara'nın Çanakkale Manevrası Utanç Verici." Radikal. http://www.radikal.com.tr/politika/ankaranin_canakkale_manevrasi_utanc_verici-1274657?utm_source=sm_tw&utm_medium=free&utm_term=post&utm_content=ankaranin_canakkale_manevrasi_utanc_verici-1274657&utm_campaign=politika&utm_date=18012015.

Kymlicka, Will. 2002. *Contemporary Political Philosophy: An Introduction*. New York: Oxford University Press.

———. 2007. *Multicultural Odysseys: Navigating the New International Politics of Diversity*. Oxford: Oxford University Press.

Kymlicka, Will, and Christine Straehle. 1999. "Cosmopolitanism, Nation-States, and Minority Nationalism: A Critical Review of Recent Literature." *European Journal of Philosophy* 7 (1): 65–88. https://doi.org/Doi 10.1111/1468-0378.00074.

Laclau, Ernesto, and Chantal Mouffe. 1985. *Hegemony and Socialist Strategy: To-wards a Radical Democratic Politics*. London: Verso.

Lawson, Greg R. 2014. "A Thirty Years' War in the Middle East." The National Interest. http://nationalinterest.org/feature/thirty-years-war-the-middle-east-10266.

Leezenberg, Michiel. 2016. "The Ambiguities of Democratic Autonomy: The Kurd-ish Movement in Turkey and Rojava." *Southeast European and Black Sea Studies*, October, 1–20. https://doi.org/10.1080/14683857.2016.1246529.

Lenin, Vladimir I. 2016. "The State and Revolution: Class Society and the State." Marxist.Org. https://www.marxists.org/archive/lenin/works/1917/staterev/ch01.htm.

Lerner, Hanna. 2011. *Making Constitutions in Deeply Divided Societies*. New York: Cambridge University Press.

Lewis, Bernard. 2002. *The Emergence of Modern Turkey*. Third Ed. Oxford: Oxford University Press.

Leydet, Dominique. 2006. "Citizenship." *Stanford Encyclopedia of Philosophy*. http://plato.stanford.edu/archives/spr2014/entries/citizenship/.

Loughlin, Martin, and Neil Walker. 2007. "Introduction." In *The Paradox of Constitutionalism: Constituent Power and Constitutional Form*, edited by Martin Loughlin and Neil Walker, 1–8. Oxford: Oxford University Press. https://doi.org/10.1093/acprof:oso/9780199552207.001.0001.

Lovett, Frank. 2014. "Republicanism." *The Stanford Encyclopedia of Philosophy* (Winter 2014 Edition). https://doi.org/10.1111/1467-9973.00225.

Macfie, A. L. 1996. *The Eastern Question 1774-1923*. London: Longman.

MacMillan, Steven. 2015. "The 'New Thirty Years War' in the Middle East: A Western Policy of Chaos?" Global Research - Centre for Research on Globalization. http://www.globalresearch.ca/the-new-thirty-years-war-in-the-middle-east-a-western-policy-of-chaos/5469351.

Maeckelbergh, Marianne. 2012. "Horizontal Democracy Now: From Alterglobalization to Occupation." *Interface: A Journal for and about Social Movements* 4 (1): 207–34. http://www.interfacejournal.net/wordpress/wp-content/uploads/2012/05/Interface-4-1-Maeckelbergh.pdf.

Mahajan, Gurpreet. 2017. "The Making of a Political Community in a Culturally Diverse Society: Reflections on the Indian Experience." In *Forthcoming*, edited by Trevor Stack.

Majtényi, Balázs. 2017. "From Political to Ethnic Community: The New National Identity of Hungary." In *Forthcoming*, edited by Trevor Stack.

Mandıracı, Berkay. 2016. "Turkey's PKK Conflict Veers onto a More Violent Path." International Crisis Group. https://www.crisisgroup.org/europe-central-asia/western-europemediterranean/turkey/turkeys-pkk-conflict-veers-more-violent-path.

Mango, Andrew. 1999. "Ataturk and the Kurds." *Middle Eastern Studies* 35 (4): 1–25.

Matin, Kamran. 2014a. "Kobanê Democratic Experience Has a Strong Potential for Being Model in Region." Diclehaber. http://www.diclehaber.com/en/news/content/view/426456?from=3534286294.

———. 2014b. "Kobani: What's in a Name?" The Disorder Of Things. https://thedisorderofthings.com/2014/10/15/kobani-whats-in-a-name/.

———. 2015. "Why Is Turkey Bombing the Kurds?" OpenDemocracy. https://www.opendemocracy.net/arab-awakening/kamran-matin/why-is-turkey-bombing-kurds.

Matossian, M. 1994. "Ideologies of Delayed Development." In *Nationalism*, edited by J. Hutchinson and A.D. Smith, 218–25. Oxford: Oxford University Press.

Maunier, Rene. 2008. "The Definition of the City." In *The City: Critical Essays in Human Geography*, edited by Jacques Levy, 11–24. Hampshire: Ashgate.

McCulloch, Allison. 2014. *Power-Sharing and Political Stability in Deeply Divided Societies*. London: Routledge.

McGarry, John, Brendan O'Leary, and Richard Simeon. 2008. "Integration or Accommodation? The Enduring Debate in Conflict Regulation." In *Constitutional Design for Divided Societies: Integration or Accommodation?*, edited by Sujit Choudhry, 41–88. Oxford: Oxford University Press.

Mckeever, David. 2005. "The Social Contract and Refugee Protection: A Comparative Study of Turkey and Germany in the 1990s." 79. TIGER Working Paper Series. Warsaw. http://www.tiger.edu.pl/publikacje/TWPNo79.pdf.

MERIP, The Editors. 2015. "On ISIS." *Middle East Research and Information Project*, no. 276. http://www.merip.org/mer/mer276/isis.

Miley, Thomas Jeffrey. 2015. "The Kurdish Question: Prospects for Peace and Justice in Turkey and the Middle East." The Thots. http://thethots.com/2015/10/05/the-kurdish-question-prospects-for-peace-and-justice-in-turkey-the-middle-east/.

Mishra, Pankaj. 2016. "Welcome to the Age of Anger." *The Guardian*, December 8. https://www.theguardian.com/politics/2016/dec/08/welcome-age-anger-brexit-trump.

Mitchell, Timothy. 1991. "The Limits of the State: Beyond Statist Approaches and Their Critics." *American Political Science Review* 85 (1): 77–96. https://doi.org/10.2307/1962879.

Mouffe, Chantal. 1992. "Democratic Citizenship and the Political Community." In *Dimensions of Radical Democracy: Pluralism, Citizenship, Community*, edited by Chantal Mouffe, 225–39. London: Verso.

Mouffe, Chantal, and Paul Holdengraber. 1989. "Radical Democracy: Modern or Postmodern?" *Social Text*, no. 21: 31. https://doi.org/10.2307/827807.

Mumcu, Ahmet. 2013. "1924 Anayasasi." *Atam*, no. 5. http://www.atam.gov.tr/dergi/sayi-05/1924-anayasasi.

Münkler, Herfried. 2016. "The Year of the Autocrat." Handelsblatt Global. https://global.handelsblatt.com/opinion/the-year-of-the-autocrat-662813.

Näsström, Sofia. 2015. "Democratic Representation beyond Election." *Constellations* 22 (1): 1–12. https://doi.org/10.1111/1467-8675.12123.

Newman, Saul. 2005. *Power and Politics in Poststructuralism: New Theories of the Political*. London: Rotuledge.

———. 2008. "Editorial: Postanarchism." *Anarchist Studies* 16 (2): 101–5. https://www.yumpu.com/en/document/view/34153391/anarchist-studies-16-2pdf-zine-library.

———. 2014. "Occupy and Autonomous Political Life." In *Radical Democracy and Collective Movements Today*, edited by A. Kioupkiolis and G. Katsambekis, 93–108. London: Rotuledge.

Noureddine, Mohamed. 2016. "PKK Foreign Relations Head Speaks Out." Al-Monitor. http://www.al-monitor.com/pulse/politics/2016/07/turkey-coup-pkk-kurds-rojava-us-intervention.html.

Öcalan, Abdullah. 2005. "The Declaration of Democratic Confederalism." Kurdmedia. http://www.kurdmedia.com/article.aspx?id=10174.

———. 2011. *Democratic Confederalism*. London: Transmedia Publishing Ltd.

———. 2015. *Demokratik Kurtuluş ve Özgür Yaşamı İnşa: İmralı Notları*. Neuss: Weşanên Mezopotamya.

Oclopcic, Zoran. 2008. "Review of Martin Loughlin and Neil Walker, Eds., The Paradox of Constitutionalism: Constituent Power and Constitutional Form." *I•CON* 6 (2): 358–70. https://doi.org/10.1093/acprof:oso/9780199552207.001.0001.

Oikonomakis, Leonidas, and Jérôme E. Roos. 2013. "'Que No Nos Representan': The Crisis of Representation and the Resonance of the Real Democracy Movement from the Indignados to Occupy." In *Conference on Street Politics in the Age of Austerity: From the Indignados to Occupy.* Montreal: University of Montreal.

Orhan, Özgüç. 2014. "Türkiye'de Rousseau Algisina Eleştirel Bir Bakiş: Atatürk Rousseau'dan Etkilenmiş Miydi?" *Felsefe ve Sosyal Bilimler Dergisi,* no. 17: 215–35. www.flsfdergisi.com.

Oskay, Çınar. 2015. "Dücane Cündioğlu: İslam Dünyası 'Ey İnsanlar' Deme Yeteneğini Yitirdi." Radikal. http://www.radikal.com.tr/hayat/ducane-cundioglu-islam-dunyasi-ey-insanlar-deme-yetenegini-yitirdi-1491460/.

Özbudun, Ergun. 2014. "AKP at the Crossroads: Erdoğan's Majoritarian Drift." *South European Society and Politics* 19 (2): 155–67. https://doi.org/10.1080/1360 8746.2014.920571.

Özbudun, Ergun, and Ömer F Gençkaya. 2009. *Democratization and the Politics of Constitution-Making in Turkey.* New York: Central European University Press.

Özdoğan, Günay Göksu. 2010. "Turkish Nationalism Reconsidered: The 'Heaviness' of Statist Patriotism in Nation-Building." In *Nationalism in the Troubled Triangle: Cyprus, Greece Amd Turkey,* edited by Ayhan Aktar, Niyazi Kizilyurek, and Umut Ozkirimli, 1–20. London: Palgrave Macmillan.

Ozkan, Behlul. 2014. "Early Writings Reveal the Real Davutoglu." Al-Monitor. http://www.al-monitor.com/pulse/originals/2014/08/zaman-davutoglu-ideologue-behlul-ozkan-academic-akp-islamic.html.

Ozkirimli, Umut. 2013. "Vigilance and Apprehension: Multiculturalism, Democracy, and the 'Kurdish Question' in Turkey." *Middle East Critique* 22 (1): 25–43. https://doi.org/10.1080/19436149.2012.748136.

Özkırımlı, Umut, and Umut Ozkirimli. 2014. *The Making of a Protest Movement in Turkey: #occupygezi.* New York: Palgrave Macmillan.

Özoğlu, Hakan. 2004. *Kurdish Notables and the Ottoman State.* Albany, NY: State University of New York Press. http://scholar.google.com/scholar?hl=en&btnG=Se arch&q=intitle:Kurdish+Notables+and+the+Ottoman+State#1.

Ozturk, Ahmet Erdi, and İştar Gözaydin. 2016. "Turkey's Draft Constitutional Amendments: Harking Back to 1876?" OpenDemocracy. https://www.opendemocracy.net/ahmet-erdi-ozturk-tar-g-zayd-n/turkey-s-draft-constitutional-amendments-harking-back-to-1876.

Öztürk, Emrullah. 2015. "Cumhurbaşkanliği Forsu Ve 16 Türk Devleti Tartişmasi." *Ankara Üniversitesi Türk İnkılâp Tarihi Enstitüsü Atatürk Yolu Dergisi* 57 (2): 79–100. http://dergiler.ankara.edu.tr/dergiler/45/2065/21432.pdf.

Paker, Evren Balta, and Ismet Akca. 2013. "Askerler, Köylüler ve Paramiliter Güçler: Turkiye'de Koy Koruculugu Sistemi." *Toplum ve Bilim,* no. 126: 7–34.

Patton, Alan. 2008. "Beyond the Dichotomy of Universalism and Difference." In *Constitutional Design for Divided Societies: Integration or Accommodation?,* edited by Sujit Choudhry, 92–110. Oxford: Oxford University Press.

Payaslian, Simon. 2007. *The History of Armenia*. New York: Palgrave Macmillan.

Peters, Kim, Michelle Ryan, S. Alexander Haslam, and Helen Fernandes. 2012. "To Belong or Not to Belong." *Journal of Personnel Psychology* 11 (3): 148–58. https://doi.org/10.1027/1866-5888/a000067.

Petrovic, Milan. 2002. "Regions (Forms of Territorial Autonomy) in the Theory of Law and History of Law." *Law and Politics* 1 (6): 683–710.

Pettit, Philip. 2003. "Republicanism." *Stanford Encyclopedia of Philosophy*. http://plato.stanford.edu/archives/spr2003/entries/republicanism/.

Philpott, Dan. 2010. "Sovereignty." *Stanford Encyclopedia of Philosophy*. https://doi.org/10.1111/1467-9973.00225.

PKK Congress. 1995. "PKK 5. Kongre Kararlari." Qandil: Weşanên Serxwebûn. http://www.kurdipedia.org/books/115411.PDF.

Poulton, Hugh. 2001. "Top Hat, Grey Wolf and Crescent: Turkish Nationalism and the Turkish Republic." *New Perspectives on Turkey* 24: 165–68.

Rabinovich, Itamar. 2014. "The End of Sykes-Picot? Reflections on the Prospects of the Arab Satet System." *Middle East Memo*. https://www.brookings.edu/research/the-end-of-sykes-picot-reflections-on-the-prospects-of-the-arab-state-system/.

Radikal. 2015. "LGBT: Altan Tan Bayraklarımızı Gördükten Sonra Yüzünü Bize Dönmedi." Radikal. http://www.radikal.com.tr/turkiye/lgbt-altan-tan-bayraklar-imizi-gordukten-sonra-yuzunu-bize-donmedi-1321354/.

Republic of Turkey. 1982. "Constitution of the Republic of Turkey." Ankara: Turkish Grand National Assembly. https://global.tbmm.gov.tr/docs/constitution_en.pdf.

Reynolds, Susan. 2007. "Secular Power and Authority in the Middle Ages." In *Power and Identity in the Middle Ages: Essays in Memory of Rees Davies*, edited by Huw Pryce and John Watts. Oxford University Press. https://doi.org/10.1093/acprof:oso/9780199285464.001.0001.

Rhys Bajalan, Djene. 2016. "Princes, Pashas and Patriots: The Kurdish Intelligentsia, the Ottoman Empire and the National Question (1908–1914)." *British Journal of Middle Eastern Studies* 194 (January): 1–18. https://doi.org/10.1080/13530194.2016.1138639.

Robins, Philip. 2007. "Turkish Foreign Policy since 2002: Between a 'Post-Islamist' Government and a Kemalist State." *International Affairs* 83 (1): 289–304. http://www.sbu.yildiz.edu.tr/~faksu/Fuatyayinlar/TDPIIdocs/24367788.pdf.

Rojava Administration. 2014. "Charter of the Social Contract in Rojava (Syria)." Qamishlo: Kurdish Institute of Brussels. http://www.kurdishinstitute.be/charter-of-the-social-contract/.

Rousseau, Jean Jacques. 1762. *The Social Contract*. 1979 ed. Edited by Maurice Cranston. London: Penguin Books.

Ruyters, Domeniek. 2015. "Democracy without the State Jonas Staal Builds Parliament in Northern-Syria." Metropolis M. http://www.metropolism.com/en/features/23958_democracy_without_the_state.

Sadan, Mandy. 2010. "Review of The Art of Not Being Governed: An Anarchist History of Upland Southeast Asia." History. http://www.history.ac.uk/reviews/review/903.

Scalbert-Yücel, Clémence, and Marie Le Ray. 2006. "Knowledge, Ideology and Power. Deconstructing Kurdish Studies." *European Journal of Turkish Studies* 5 (April): 1–18.

Schendel, Willem van. 2002. "Geographies of Knowing, Geographies of Ignorance: Jumping Scale in Southeast Asia." *Environment and Planning D: Society and Space* 20: 647–68. https://doi.org/10.1068/d16s.

Scherz, Antoinette. 2013. "The Legitimacy of the Demos: Who Should Be Included in the Demos and on What Grounds?" *Living Reviews in Democracy*, 1–14. http://www.livingreviews.org/lrd-2013-1.

Scott, James C. 2009. *The Art of Not Being Governed: An Anarchist History of Upland Southeast Asia*. London: Yale University Press. https://doi.org/10.1080/0013 9157.2010.493126.

Sentas, Vicki. 2015. "Policing the Diaspora: Kurdish Londoners, MI5 and the Proscription of Terrorist Organizations in the United Kingdom." *British Journal of Criminology* 56: 898–918. https://doi.org/10.1093/bjc/azv094.

Shringarpure, Bhakti. 2014. "Fanon Documentary Confronts Fallacies about Anti-Colonial Philosopher." *The Guardian*. https://www.theguardian.com/world/2014/jul/21/-sp-frantz-fanon-documentary-concerning-violence.

Simhony, Avital. 1993. "Beyond Negative and Positive Freedom: T . H . Green's View of Freedom." *Political Theory* 21 (1): 28–54. http://www.jstor.org/stable/191851.

Simmons, A. John. 1979. *Moral Principles and Political Obligations*. New Jersey: Princeton University Press.

Smith, Anthony D. 2000. *The Nation in History*. Cambridge: Polity Press.

———. 2001. *Nationalism*. 2010 ed. Cambridge: Polity Press.

Smith, David J. 2013. "Non-Territorial Autonomy and Political Community in Contemporary Central and Eastern Europe." *Journal on Ethnopolitics and Minority Issues in Europe* 12 (1): 27–55.

Smith, Thomas W. 2005. "Civic Nationalism and Ethnocultural Justice in Turkey." *Human Rights Quarterly* 27 (2): 436–70. https://doi.org/10.1353/hrq.2005.0027.

Somers, Margaret R. 2008. *Genealogies of Citizenship: Markets, Statelessness, and the Right to Have Rights*. Cambridge: Cambridge University Press.

Song, Sarah. 2010. "Multiculturalism." *Stanford Encyclopedia of Philosophy*. Stanford University. http://plato.stanford.edu/entries/multiculturalism/.

Stack, Trevor. 2013. "Spoken Like a State : Language and Religion as Categories of Liberal Thought." *Studies in Ethnicity and Nationalism* 13 (1): 97–100. https://doi.org/10.1111/sena.12016.

———. 2019. "Wedging Open Established Civil Spheres: A Comparative Approach to Their Emancipatory Potential." In *Forthcoming*, edited by Trevor Stack.

Stansfield, Gareth. 2013. "The Unravelling of the Post-First World War State System? The Kurdistan Region of Iraq and the Transformation of the Middle East." *International Affairs* 89 (2): 259–82. http://www.bu.edu/iis/files/2013/04/INTA89_2_02_Stansfield.pdf.

Subrahmanyam, Sanjay. 2011. "Review of The Art of Not Being Governed: An Anarchist History of Upland South-East Asia by James C. Scott." *London Review of Books* 32 (23): 25–26. https://www.lrb.co.uk/v32/n23/sanjay-subrahmanyam/the-view-from-the-top.

Tambar, Kabir. 2016. "Brotherhood in Dispossession: State Violence and the Ethics of Expectation in Turkey." *Cultural Anthropology* 31 (1): 30–55. https://doi.org/10.14506/ca31.1.03.

Tankersley, Jim. 2015. "This Might Be the Most Controversial Theory for What's behind the Rise of ISIS." *Washington Post.* https://www.washingtonpost.com/news/wonk/wp/2015/11/30/why-inequality-is-to-blame-for-the-rise-of-the-islamic-state/.

Tas, Latif. 2014. "The Myth of the Ottoman Millet System: Its Treatment of Kurds and a Discussion of Territorial and Non-Territorial Autonomy." *International Journal on Minority and Group Rights* 21 (4): 497–526. https://doi.org/10.1163/15718115-02104003.

TATORT Kurdistan. 2011. *Democratic Autonomy in North Kurdistan.* Porsgrunn: New Compass.

———. 2014. "Democratic Autonomy in Rojava." New Compass. http://new-compass.net/articles/revolution-rojava.

Taussig, Michael. 2015. "The Mastery of Non-Mastery." Public Seminar. http://www.publicseminar.org/2015/08/the-mastery-of-non-mastery/#.V-xn5vArK01.

Taylor, Charles. 1997. "The Politics of Recognition." *New Contexts of Canadian Criticism*, 25–73. https://doi.org/10.1037/a0020654.

Tekdemir, Ömer. 2015. "Agonistic Imagination of Podemos in Andalusia and HDP in Anatolia: The Radical Citizenship Project for the European and the Middle-Eastern Demos." *Research Turkey Centre for Policy and Research on Turkey,* IV (7): 6–18. http://researchturkey.org/agonistic-imagination-of-podemos-in-andalusia-and-hdp-in-anatolia-the-radical-citizenship-project-for-the-european-and-the-middle-eastern-demos/.

Temo, Selim. 2013. "Roboskî'ye Gidecekler İçin." Radikal. http://www.radikal.com.tr/yazarlar/selim_temo/roboskiye_gidecekler_icin-1158196.

Tezcur, G. M. 2010. "When Democratization Radicalizes: The Kurdish Nationalist Movement in Turkey." *Journal of Peace Research* 47 (6): 775–89. https://doi.org/10.1177/0022343310386156.

———. 2016. "Ordinary People, Extraordinary Risks: Participation in an Ethnic Rebellion." *American Political Science Review* 110 (2): 1–18. https://doi.org/10.1017/S0003055416000150.

Tilly, Charles. 1985. "War Making and State Making as Organized Crime." In *Bringing the State Back In*, edited by Peter B. Evans, Dietrich Rueschemeyer, and Theda Skocpol, 169–87. Cambridge: Cambridge University Press. http://www.homeworkmarket.com/sites/default/files/q3/28/02/reading_response_4_2.pdf.

Todorova, Antonia. 2015. "Turkish Security Discourses and Policies: The Kurdish Question." *Information & Security: An International Journal* 33 (2): 108–21. https://doi.org/http://dx.doi.org/10.11610/isij.3305.

Tuğal, Cihan. 2016. *The Fall of the Turkish Model : How the Arab Uprisings Brought down Islamic Liberalism*. London: Verso.

Ulgen, Sinan. 2014. "Sleepless in Ankara: The Post-Erdogan Government's Big Challenges." National Interest. http://nationalinterest.org/feature/sleepless-ankara-the-post-erdogan-governments-big-challenges-11005?page=4.

Ulrichsen, Kristian Coates. 2014. *The First World War in the Middle East*. London: Hurst and Co. Ltd.

Ünlü, Barış. 2012. "İsmail Beşikçi as a Discomforting Intellectual." *Borderlands* 11 (2): 1–21. www.borderlands.net.au.

Uzer, Umut. 2013. "The Kurdish Identity of Turkish Nationalist Thinkers: Ziya Gökalp and Ahmet Arvasi between Turkish Identity and Kurdish Ethnicity." *Turkish Studies* 14 (2): 394–409. https://doi.org/10.1080/14683849.2013.802900.

Waldron, Jeremy. 2011. "The Principle of Proximity." *New York University Public Law and Lega Theory Working Papers*, 1–26. http://lsr.nellco.org/nyu_plltwp/255.

Watts, Nicole F. 2009. "Re-Considering State-Society Dynamics in Turkey's Kurdish Southeast." *European Journal of Turkish Studies* 10 (April): 1–16.

Weber, Max. 1994. "The Nation." In *Nationalism*, edited by J. Hutchinson and Anthony D. Smith, 21–25. Oxford: Oxford University Press.

Xypolia, Ilia. 2016. "Racist Aspects of Modern Turkish Nationalism." *Journal of Balkan and Near Eastern Studies* 8953 (February): 1–14. https://doi.org/10.1080/19448953.2016.1141580.

Yamalak, Mahmut. 2013. "Demokratik Çözüm İçin Yeni Bir Toplumsal Sözleşme." *Demokratik Modernite*, September. http://www.demokratikmodernite.com/mahmutyamalak.html.

Yarkin, Güllistan. 2015. "The Ideological Transformation of the PKK Regarding the Political Economy of the Kurdish Region in Turkey." *Kurdish Studies*, May: 26–46.

Yavuz, M. Hakan. 1999. "Search for a New Social Contract in Turkey: Fethullah Gulen, the Virtue Party and the Kurds." *SAIS Review* 19 (1): 114–43. http://muse.jhu.edu/article/30430.

———. 2001. "Five Stages of the Construction of Kurdish Nationalism in Turkey." *Nationalism and Ethnic Politics* 7 (3): 1–24. https://doi.org/10.1080/13537110108428635.

Yegen, Mesut. 1999. "The Kurdish Question in Turkish State Discourse." *Journal of Contemporary History* 34 (4): 555–68. https://doi.org/10.2307/261251.

———. 2016. "Armed Struggle to Peace Negotiations: Independent Kurdistan to Democratic Autonomy, or the PKK in Context." *Middle East Critique*, August, 1–19. https://doi.org/10.1080/19436149.2016.1218162.

Yeğen, Mesut. 1996. "The Turkish State Discourse and the Exclusion of Kurdish Identity." *Middle Eastern Studies* 32 (2): 216–29. https://doi.org/10.1080/00263209608701112.

———. 2007. "Turkish Nationalism and the Kurdish Question." *Ethnic and Racial Studies* 30 (1): 119–51. https://doi.org/10.1080/01419870601006603.

Yeğen, Mesut, Uğraş Ulaş Tol, and Mehmet Ali Çalışkan. 2016. *Kürtler Ne İstiyor?* Istanbul: | İletişim Yayınları. http://www.iletisim.com.tr/kitap/kurtler-ne-istiyor/9308#.V8JTJ5grK00.

Yetkin, Murat. 2014. "Erdoğan May Wait until after Election for a New Constitution." *Hurriyet Daily News*. http://www.hurriyetdailynews.com/erdogan-may-wait-until-after-election-for-a-new-constitution.aspx?pageID=449&nID=72190&NewsCatID=409.

Yinanç, Barçın. 2013. "Unusual Political Figure Now Plays Key Role in PKK Talks." *Hurriyet Daily News*. http://www.hurriyetdailynews.com/unusual-political-figure-now-plays-key-role-in-pkk-talks.aspx?pageID=238&nID=45828&NewsCatID=338.

Zagrosi, Aso. 2016. "Şeyh Ubeydullah Nehri, Bağımsız ve Birleşik Kürdistan Fikri." Zagrosname. http://zagrosname.com/blog/2016/05/26/seyh-ubeydullah-nehri-bagimsiz-ve-birlesik-kuerdistan-fikri/.

Zaman, Amberin. 2016. "Is Washington Enabling Despotism in Turkey?" Al-Monitor. Istanbul. May. http://www.al-monitor.com/pulse/originals/2016/05/turkey-united-states-washington-enabling-despotism.html#.

Zeydanlıoğlu, Welat. 2008. "'The White Turkish Man's Burden': Orientalism, Kemalism and the Kurds in Turkey." In *Neo-Colonial Mentalities in Contemporary Europe? Language and Discourse in the Construction of Identities*, edited by Guido Rings and Anne Ife, 155–74. Newcastle upon Tyne: Cambridge Scholars Publishing.

Zürcher, Eric J. 2004. *Turkey, a Modern History*. London: I.B.Tauris.

———. 2010. *The Young Turk Legacy and the Nation Building: Form Ottoman Empire to Atatürk's Turkey*. London: I.B. Tauris.

Index

About the Author

Hanifi Baris was born to a family of twelve in 1978 in a village near the city of Batman, in Southeast Turkey (otherwise known as North/Turkish Kurdistan). He completed his primary education in the village and was sent to a boarding religious school in the city of Diyarbakir, 70 miles to the west. He completed his secondary school and high school education there. He won a scholarship to study law for his undergraduate degree at Başkent University in Ankara, Turkey, in 1998. Dr. Baris practiced law as a private attorney from 2004 until 2009 in the city of Istanbul. He studied sociology and politics for his graduate degree from 2009 to 2011, at Master of Arts in Inter-Asia NGO Studies (MAINS) at Sungkonghoe University in Seoul, South Korea. After another two years of law practice in Istanbul, he returned to academia in 2012 to study constitutional law and political theory. He obtained his PhD degree in 2018 from Centre for Citizenship, Civil Society and Rule of Law (CISRUL) at the University of Aberdeen in Scotland, UK. He has published journal articles, a book chapter, and conference proceedings, including the award-winning article "Dengbêjs on borderlands: Borders and the state as seen through the eyes of Kurdish singer-poets" co-authored with Dr Wendy Hamelink. Dr Baris also worked at the Grand National Assembly of Turkey as a legislative consultant before taking up his current post as the Leverhulme Research Fellow at CISRUL, University of Aberdeen. An outspoken supporter of human rights and liberties in Turkey, Dr Baris has also been a board member at the prestigious non-governmental organization Toplum ve Hukuk Araştırmaları Vakfı (Foundation for Society and Legal Studies) in Istanbul since late 2018.